D0196169

50 years of *Dissent*

edited by nicolaus mills and michael walzer

with an introduction by mitchell cohen

5 0   y e a r s   o f

DISSENT

yale university press new haven and london

Designed by Sonia Shannon
Set in Garamond type with Scala display
by Keystone Typesetting, Inc.
Printed in the United States of America.

Library of Congress Cataloging-in-Publication Data
50 years of Dissent / edited by Nicolaus Mills and
Michael Walzer ; with an introduction by
Mitchell Cohen.
p.   cm.
Includes index.
ISBN 0-300-10369-7 (pbk : alk. paper)
1. Socialism. 2. Social problems. 3. United States—
Social conditions. 4. Social movements—United
States. 5. Right and left (Political science) I. Title:
Fifty years of Dissent. II. Mills, Nicolaus.
III. Walzer, Michael. IV. Dissent.
HX15.A14 2004
335—dc22
2004040725

A catalogue record for this book is
available from the British Library.

The paper in this book meets the
guidelines for permanence and durability
of the Committee on Production
Guidelines for Book Longevity of the
Council on Library Resources.

10 9 8 7 6 5 4 3 2 1

To the men and women who founded *Dissent*.

Irving Howe
Lewis Coser
Travers Clement
Rose Coser
Emanuel Geltman
Harold Orlans
Simone Plastrik
Stanley Plastrik
Bernard Rosenberg
Meyer Schapiro

Contents

introduction

MITCHELL COHEN

Little political magazines try to traffic in big, often unorthodox ideas—the sort of ideas that don't always enjoy mainstream circulation. *Dissent* has been making this effort since 1954. Its founders came out of the left, and they considered the mood back then to be both smug and wanting. "Ikeism," wrote editor Irving Howe in *Dissent*'s third issue, referring to President Dwight Eisenhower's nickname, was really the longing for an "era BC—Before Complexity," a time when all questions were simple and answers easy. *Dissent*'s initiators, who included sociologist Lewis Coser, a refugee from Hitler's Europe, and Meyer Schapiro, the eminent art critic, didn't imagine that their journal would change the world. ("When intellectuals cannot do anything else," Howe would quip, "they start a magazine.") But they did hope to make intellectual life just a bit more complicated for both the right and the left in an era AD, after *Dissent*'s birth, by provoking debates about political ideas and about American and global issues. They believed in the value of disagreement, especially in a society that celebrated consensus. The same hope and belief animates its editors and writers today.

This anthology presents a sampling of *Dissent*'s engagement with American life from the magazine's launch through the turn of the new millennium (when some readers may find Howe's characterization of the 1950s uncomfortably suggestive of our own times). Wending through these articles, drawn from a quarterly publication, you will encounter arguments about the nature of capitalism, socialism, and democracy and on the impact of the Cold War, McCarthyism, and mass culture. You will find appraisals of liberal and conservative politics along with anger at the malevolence of American racism and dismay over the disaster of Vietnam. You will come upon descriptions of political movements and political moments, together with reflections on culture and countercultures, feminism, pluralism, and the meaning(s) of social inequality. You will find authors thinking about the end of communism, the growth of globalization, and the vicissitudes of America's superpower status. Fifty years cover a lot of politics, a lot of contention, a lot of ideas. The editors have subdivided this anthology into *Dissent*'s

1

decades, and a contemporary *Dissent*er offers introductory comments to each to provide some perspective.

Some readers may find it odd that *Dissent* still calls itself a journal of "left" ideas and "left" opinion. The word "left" is hardly in vogue these days. It is even less popular than "liberal," and it wasn't fashionable when *Dissent* first appeared. American conservatives have sought for decades to stigmatize everything "liberal" or "left," and their public success in doing so has been considerable. Their effort has been made easier by the historical fact that the United States—in contrast to much of Western Europe—never had a mass socialist party that distinguished itself sharply from both undemocratic communists and anti-egalitarian conservatives. Say "left" and American conservatives conjure up images of mass-murdering Stalinists with totalitarian aspirations, of imploding nationalized economies, of strutting third world dictators shouting "liberation" while shooting their critics, and of hectoring, self-important postmodern academics who can justify almost anything on behalf of Otherness. The composite is not appealing.

But this picture is airbrushed (perhaps we should say "digitally remastered," in our high-tech age). Not that those Stalinists, those failed economies, those swaggering, often whiskered tyrants, and those too-clever theorists are imaginary. I wish they were; they are not. Still, consider how everything becomes more complex when we think about who is missing from the canvas, and what is not there. Let's include some of the missing left and some of the missing right in order to get a somewhat larger sense of modern politics.

Start with all the missing socialists, including Marxists, who were communism's first foes, and often its first victims. (Some historians remember them, but who else?) Then sketch in Neville Chamberlain, the Conservative British prime minister who made "peace in our time" with Hitler. Add in social democratic and labor movements, which championed universal suffrage and basic democratic rights in nineteenth- and early-twentieth-century Europe, while conservatives insisted that political equality violated the "natural order of things"—an order in which everyone, naturally, belonged in a proper place. Opponents of the civil rights movement used some like-minded notions not long ago in the United States; so, too, contemporary foes of feminism.

Now include in our picture the "leftists" and trade unionists who argued that democracy ought to be economic as well as political, and who pointed out that considerable discrepancies of wealth in a society translated into imbalances of political power and political voice, subverting the promise of common citizenship. Depict the advocates of social citizenship, that is, people committed to the idea that all of us, as members of a common polity, ought to enjoy a range of basic social goods. Like a decent education, for example. (Without it, how can anyone be an effective, democratic citizen?) Or decent health care. (Should sick people be treated according to their illnesses or according to their status on labor markets? as British philosopher L. T. Hobhouse once queried.) Or decent working conditions and decent pensions. Don't leave off the canvas the foes of such ideas, like American conservatives who reviled Social Security and Medicare as slides down the slippery slope from "individualism" to totalitarianism. Then draw in some of the people who today question the role of unmerited advantages in our society derived from social class, race, or gender. These are people who think that it is not always so that "those who have, deserve" or that social suffering (like hunger) is always the fault of those in distress. And they don't have a mystical belief in the all-curing powers of The Market reminiscent of the old communist faith in The State.

Somewhere, maybe in a corner of our widening canvas, we can sketch a twenty-year-old American in uniform. This soldier wonders aloud: "Why can my life be risked abroad on behalf of patriotism, while prosperous patriots at home holler against paying a fair share of taxes for the public's general welfare?"

By now our picture is multidimensional and multifaceted. Perhaps some strokes might be thicker or the paint thinner in this or that place. Some aspects don't fit so comfortably with others. Unlike art, nothing is ever "whole" in politics (except a totalitarian quest). Still, I think our more complex picture reveals how most of the left's history comprised struggles for democracy, and hopes that social imagination might undo social inequities. Yes, part of the story is unhappy. And yes, part of the left—call it "the left-that-doesn't-learn"—has always thought that if the world doesn't fit its dogmas, the world is disproved. In its post-9/11 guise, it tries to show that somehow, "in the final analysis," all of American history—not fundamentalist terrorists—was responsible for that awful day. As if Osama bin Laden was protesting the fact that Thomas Jefferson owned slaves.

But consider: Isn't the left's history a bit like America's? Millions of people on both sides of the Atlantic identified with "the left" in the hope that the powerless, the voiceless, and the poor might one day have some control over their own days, that they would be able to speak up and to live decently. The American Revolution promised equality and freedom, and since 1776 millions of people have been liberated in a wide variety of ways by coming to these shores. Yet just as the left has had wretched moments, so America's past cannot be airbrushed of some grim matters, like slavery or the fate of Native Americans or discrimination against women or exploitation of working people. The more you think about "anti-leftism" and "anti-Americanism" together, the more they seem to share an untoward one-sidedness. Anti-leftism and anti-Americanism, much like left-wing ideological blinders and conservative nationalist swagger, also represent the longing for an "era BC—Before Complexity."

You won't find a singular "*Dissent*" answer to all questions in these pages, or the aspiration to formulate one. Instead, you will find, broadly speaking, an underlying ethos that is humanist, inclusive, and "equality-friendly." Political ideas are argued in order to address human dilemmas and not to defend a theory's honor; justifications of social inequality are treated with skepticism, with a presumption that the burden of moral proof ought to rest on an apologist for this or that inequality.

The "*Dissent* left"—I hesitate to use this unifying phrase, and it should not indicate too much unity—was born under the shadow of the Two Josephs (Stalin and McCarthy). It dissented from both of them, and has been animated by a democratic sensibility. The magazine's founders usually called themselves "democratic socialists," and some current contributors still do. Others among them identify as "liberal socialists" or "social democrats" or "social liberals" or "liberal left" or some combination of these words—or they may be averse to any label. Howe, who was *Dissent*'s moving spirit from the magazine's founding until his death in 1993, once said that he wanted the "socialization of concern" rather than the nationalization of the means of production. Michael Walzer, political philosopher and co-editor of *Dissent* since 1975, has long been an eloquent proponent of pluralism in American society and within left-wing thinking. Michael Harrington, America's leading socialist from the 1960s through the 1980s and a longtime member of the *Dissent* editorial board, argued for "the left-wing of the possible."

Some of *Dissent*'s founders—Howe, Emmanuel Geltman, Stanley Plastrik—were once activists in a "Trotskyist" variant of the old left, just before and after World War II. Their education and experience in a small organization inspired by Leon Trotsky, Stalin's rival (and victim), immunized them against Communist parties and totalitarian rationalizations. But, finally, they also rebelled against the stiff mindset of their own "party," deciding to leave Bolshevik furies behind and to seek a politics rooted in American democratic radicalism and in an American idiom. They suspected that sectarianism in language and sectarianism in thought constitute a joint venture. (The same suspicions made many *Dissent*ers leery of "postmodern" theories in the 1980s and 1990s). They moved closer to the old American Socialist party of Eugene V. Debs and Norman Thomas. They intermingled with the world of "New York Intellectuals" and read their small magazines like *Partisan Review* and *Politics*.

They also concluded that efforts to stuff the world into an all-encompassing design (derived from an all-knowing theory) result in disaster. That didn't mean casting away all forms of social vision. In an early *Dissent* article entitled "Images of Socialism," Lewis Coser and Irving Howe insisted on the legitimacy of utopian imagination. The word "utopia," they recalled, means literally "nowhere." Failed radical experiments showed how mistaken it was to try to reach nowhere, that is, to try to impose a "perfect," conflict-free society. At the same time, an image of a better, fairer world could and ought to play the role of a "regulative idea," they proposed. Social imagination could and ought to draw everyday politics beyond "curdled realism" to novel possibilities, to innovation in addressing social and political problems. Utopia warranted two genuine cheers, Howe wrote years later (in an essay reprinted in this anthology), but not three. After all, the world is complex. Still, the point was to pull beyond "the provincialism of the immediate" and to grasp "the democratic utopianism that runs like a bright thread through American intellectual life—call it Emersonianism, call it republicanism, call it whatever you like."

A prominent academic told me a few years ago that he had been in the Weather Underground, the violent break-away from Students for a Democratic Society, and that around 1970 his comrades planned to bomb the *Dissent* office—"but we couldn't find it." Other people told me subsequently that this story was fiction. It was true, however, that the *Dissent* circle and the early SDS, who might have been intergenerational allies, clashed politically and temperamentally in the 1960s. Communism was one source of this bitter quarrel, which took place both in face-to-face arguments and in print. Many new leftists later concluded that Howe and Harrington were indeed right to call for a complete divorce of the left from all forms of authoritarianism, but the *Dissent*ers later rued their own ferocity in the debate, regretting that they had perhaps slipped back into the sectarian style they had long rejected.

The famous "generation gap" of the 1960s also played a role. The *Dissent*ers were children of the 1930s, and the murderous fraudulence of the Moscow Trials was for them a formative experience. Members of the early SDS were children of the 1950s, and McCarthy's witch-hunt was their formative experience, disposing them strongly against anticommunism. The *Dissent*ers had in fact been forcefully anti-McCarthy, and the early SDS advocated participatory democracy, not communism. The 1960s was a decade of great idealism (for example, in the civil rights movement) but also bitter disappointments and acrimony, and a process of generational and intellectual mending on the left could begin only later, in the 1970s and 1980s, when the new left was in shambles and the liberal left in retreat. A number of former activists in the new left began contributing to *Dissent*'s pages then and were soon welcomed onto its editorial board.

If members of the Weather Underground had actually set their sights on the *Dissent* office, there was a reason why they failed to find it. It didn't exist. *Dissent*, for years, had a Fifth Avenue address, but there was only a mail-drop. The magazine always published with modest resources and no institutional base, counting instead on the commitments of editors, writers, an underpaid, part-time staff, and a few friends. In order to bomb the *Dissent* office, the Weather Underground would have had to target the Upper West Side apartment of Simone and Stanley Plastrik. First Stanley, and after his death, Simone, managed *Dissent*'s finances. Simone herself was a veteran of a very different underground, the French Resistance during World War II. Her dining room was *Dissent*'s "office" until her death in 1999, after which the magazine finally rented a studio.

Out of its small space, and run editorially now through the less definable space of e-mail, *Dissent* keeps dissenting and appearing in print every three months. I sometimes wonder what sort of exchange might occur if *Dissent*'s original circle were to be transported by some H. G. Wellesian means from a 1954 editorial discussion to a meeting taking place half a century later. They would probably be dismayed to find that they had left one America longing for an "era BC," only to arrive in another. They would be saddened by the steady weakness of the American left as well as the unions. They would be heartened, I think, by *Dissent*'s resilience (most small magazines have short life spans). At first they'd be a little puzzled to hear today's editors discussing what to circulate on the Web. ("The Web?—it sounds like J. Edgar Hoover's idea of a communist plot!") Once they understood better the communications revolution of the past decade, they would probably want to discuss its democratic potentials and the threats it might pose to individual liberties or private life. They might also wonder about the impact of Internet brevity and speed on intellectual life, on reflective reading and thinking habits and public debate—indeed, on the prospects of small magazines that value extended arguments by intellectuals about what is good and what is bad, what is happening and what ought to be happening.

Today's editors would tell them what *Dissent*'s readers have known for the past decade: if it was difficult to be on the left while communism continued, it also hasn't been so easy to redefine the left in communism's wake. Communism's fall came along with globalization's rise and great transformations in the international economy. Many of the old coordinates dissolved in the 1990s, and then some more disappeared after September 11. Yet the world always seems to get simpler for many conservatives. Recall the applause for Francis Fukuyama's claim that all major intellectual issues were resolved by the victory of liberal democracy over communism. His book proclaiming *The End of History* was a flight manual for intellectuals who wanted to go on automatic pilot after the ideological wars of the twentieth century. But this was a bad way to enter a new era. If you expect a postintellectual, postproblem world, you needn't care much about democracy and you probably won't read *Dissent. Dissent*ers cheered the end of communism, but they also mistrusted all-encompassing explanations, partly because someone or something important always seems to be missing from them.

Better to make the picture more complicated, both for your intellectual foes and for yourself. *Dissent* will try to keep doing so in its sixth decade.

FIFTIES

"God," said Tolstoy, "is the name of my desire." This remarkable sentence could haunt one a lifetime, it reverberates in so many directions. Tolstoy may have intended partial assent to the idea that, life being insupportable without some straining toward "transcendence," a belief in God is a psychological necessity, . . . Without sanctioning the facile identification that is frequently made between religion and socialist politics, we should like to twist Tolstoy's remark to our own ends: *socialism is the name of our desire.* And not merely in the sense that it is a vision which, for many people throughout the world, provides moral sustenance, but also in the sense that it is a vision which objectifies and gives urgency to their criticism of the human condition in our time.

Lewis Coser and Irving Howe, "Images of Socialism," 1954

foreword

MICHAEL WALZER

The founding of *Dissent* in 1954 was an act of intellectual insurrection in what Irving Howe called, that same year, "this age of conformity." Throughout the magazine's first decade, its style was polemical and fierce; its editors, independent socialists and radicals, aimed to stir things up, to get into fights, to make something happen. They had a vision of America that was, I think, only partly right, but the parts they got right were central to the whole story. They saw a country ruled, as C. Wright Mills wrote, by "conservatives without ideas"—and defended by complacent or fearful cold war liberals. They saw an escapist mass culture, where criticism and opposition were treated as amusements and where art and literature, in Dwight Macdonald's telling description, were turned into "middle-brow" entertainment. They saw a necessary anti-Communism appropriated by right-wing demagogues and made into an ideology of repression. They saw the growing power of the American state wielded in cruel opposition to liberation movements that might have been drawn toward democratic engagement—so Howe, who was never naïve about third-world politics, argued in a memorable piece that has not, in fact, been well remembered. In the face of all this, every issue of *Dissent* was conceived and written in anger.

In those early years, the magazine was wonderfully exciting for young readers—and I must have been one of the youngest. Above all, it was exciting because of its critical engagement with what was happening here at home. *Dissent's* first "dissent" was against the America not only of Joe McCarthy but of Dwight Eisenhower too. The bland was as much an enemy as the ugly, perhaps more so, because it served to conceal a world of inequality, fear, and domination. But the magazine was also exciting because its second "dissent" was against the Soviet regime—at a time when Russia was still a substitute homeland for many American leftists and when the defense of Marxist dogma and Stalinist tyranny was widely thought to be a necessary feature of left politics. What a liberation it was to be freed from all that and still able to sustain a critique of American society! This was what *Dissent* meant to me at age eighteen: I was set loose from the grip of the cold war; I could oppose

11

communism without joining the American celebration. A Brandeis undergraduate from Johnstown, Pennsylvania, a kid, I was invited into what seemed to me high society: a free association of freewheeling critics, who could turn East or West, this way or that. No one on either side paid our bills or called our tune.

There was only one essential *Dissent* commitment: that was to democracy. Not "people's democracy" but real democracy: an open political arena, free speech, the right of opposition, knowledgeable and active citizens. The many theoretical pieces that the magazine carried in its early years ranged widely but kept coming back to a single message: in the phrase "democratic socialism," the adjective did not merely qualify the noun, it defined it. No socialism without democracy! But also here at home: no "democracy" without democracy. The argument for decentralized structures and popular participation—the crucial feature of the next decade's "new left" politics—was first worked out in our pages. And since "participatory democracy" is the politics of the young, the only people who have the time for it, *Dissent* in the 1950s was truly young, even if its founders, in their thirties and forties, were political veterans of the "old left."

"Age of conformity" is an accusation, but by the end of the decade it wasn't entirely accurate as a description. Our small band was one sign of a critical refusal to conform. And, far beyond our pages, the critique of mass culture, of organization men and women, and of other-directed personalities was also a feature of American life, much discussed and sometimes underestimated by writers in *Dissent*. There were stirrings in the liberal churches, too, and the beginnings of radical speculation on American campuses: C. Wright Mills, Arnold Kaufman, and Herbert Marcuse published important books (and articles in *Dissent*) in the fifties, and unattached intellectuals like Paul Goodman began to find a student audience. But perhaps the key indication of what was to come was the Montgomery bus boycott of 1954, a critical forerunner of the civil rights movement of the sixties, greeted with enthusiasm by *Dissent*'s editors, who found a comrade in Alabama to write about it.

And on the other side of the cold war, two years later, the Hungarian revolution came to contradict the magazine's determined pessimism—but perhaps also to confirm our deepest belief: that totalitarianism was not a "long dark night," that democracy was a permanent and undefeatable human aspiration. In those days, *Dissent* lived a significant part of its political life in Eastern Europe, and articles on the politics of Russia and its satellites filled our pages. Socialism had to be defended in the face of its cruelest and ugliest distortion. Only after the 1989 collapse did the East become an ordinary part of the world, appearing sometimes, but not very often, in the "Politics Abroad" section of the magazine.

There was also more liveliness (and dissent) in popular culture and even in commercial culture than writers in *Dissent* were ready to admit. Norman Mailer provides a strong example of our critique of the mass media and the corruption of leisure, but if his argument were wholly and unequivocally right, it would be hard to explain how the counter-cultural politics of the next decade developed. For in fact the counter-culture was closely connected to the culture it countered (think, for example, of rock and roll). This was one place, I believe, where the magazine was importantly wrong in the 1950s—which was not a bad thing to be at a time when so many writers aimed, fearfully, for nothing more than to be unimportantly right.

the conservative mood
C. WRIGHT MILLS

In the material prosperity of post-war America, as crackpot realism has triumphed in practical affairs, all sorts of writers, from a rather confused variety of viewpoints, have been groping for a conservative ideology.

They have not found it, and they have not managed to create it. What they have found is an absence of mind in politics, and what they have managed to create is a mood.

The psychological heart of this mood is a feeling of powerlessness— but with the old edge taken off, for it is a mood of acceptance and of a relaxation of the political will.

The intellectual core of the groping for conservatism is a giving up of the central goal of the secular impulse in the West: the control through reason of man's fate. It is this goal that has lent continuity to the human-ist tradition, re-discovered in the Renaissance, and so strong in nine-teenth century American experience. It is this goal that has been the major impulse of classic liberalism and of classic socialism.

The groping for conservative ideas, which signifies the weakening of this impulse, involves the search for tradition rather than reason as guide; the search for some natural aristocracy as an anchor point of tradition and a model of character. Sooner or later, those who would give up this impulse must take up the neo-Burkeian defense of irra-tionality, for that is, in fact, the only possible core of a genuinely conser-vative ideology. And it is not possible, I believe, to establish such an ideology in the United States.

Russell Kirk's "prolonged essay in definition" (*The Conservative Mind*) is the most explicit attempt to translate the conservative mood into conservative ideas. His work, however, does not succeed in the translation it attempts. When we examine it carefully we find that it is largely assertion, without arguable support, and that it seems rather irrelevant to modern realities, and not very useful as a guideline of political conduct and policy:

1:   The conservative, we are told, believes that "divine intent rules society," man being incapable of grasping by his reason the great forces that prevail. Along with this, he believes that change must be slow and that "providence is the proper instrument for change," the test of a statesman being his "cognizance of the real tendency of Providential social forces."

2:    The conservative has an affection for "the variety and mystery of traditional life" perhaps most of all because he believes that "tradition and sound prejudices" check man's presumptuous will and archaic impulse.

3:    "Society," the conservative holds, "longs for leadership," and there are "natural distinctions" among men which form a natural order of classes and powers.

When we hold these points close together, we can understand each of them more clearly: they seem to mean that tradition is sacred, that it is through tradition that the real social tendencies of Providence are displayed, and that therefore tradition must be our guide-line. For whatever is traditional not only represents the accumulated wisdom of the ages but exists by "divine intent."

Naturally we must ask how we are to know which traditions are instruments of Providence? Which prejudices are "sound"? Which of the events and changes all around us are by divine intent? But the third point is an attempted answer: If we do not destroy the natural order of classes and the hierarchy of powers, we shall have superiors and leaders to tell us. If we uphold these natural distinctions, and in fact resuscitate older ones, the leaders for whom we long will decide.

It is pertinent to ask Mr. Kirk at what moment the highly conscious contrivances of the founding fathers became traditional and thus sanctified? And does he believe that society in the U.S.—before the progressive movement and before the New Deal reforms—represented anything akin to what he would call orders and classes based on "natural distinctions"? If not, then what and where is the model he would have us cherish? And does he believe that the campaign conservatives—to use the phrase of John Crowe Ransom—who now man the political institutions of the U.S., do or do not represent the Providential intent which he seeks? How are we to know if they do or do not, or to what extent which of these do?

Insofar as the conservative consistently defends the irrationality of tradition against the powers of human reason, insofar as he denies the legitimacy of man's attempt collectively to build his own world and individually to control his own fate, then he cannot bring in reason again as a means of choosing among traditions, of deciding which changes are providential and which are evil forces. He cannot provide any rational guide in our choice of which leaders grasp Providence and act it out and which are reformers and levelers. In the end, the conservative is left with one single principle: the principle of gratefully accepting the leadership of some set of men whom he considers a received and sanctified elite. If such men were *there* for all to recognize, the conservative could at least be socially clear. But as it is, there is no guide-line within this view to help us decide which contenders for the natural distinction are genuine and which are not.

Conservatism, as Karl Mannheim makes clear, translates the unreflecting reactions of traditionalism into the sphere of conscious reflection. Conservatism is traditionalism become self-conscious and elaborated and forensic. A noble aristocracy, a peasantry, a petty-bourgeoisie with guild inheritance—that is what has been needed for a conservative ideology and that is what Prussia in the early nineteenth century had. It was to the spell of tradition among these surviving elements of a pre-industrial society that conservatism could appeal. The Prussian upper classes lacked the elasticity of the English, and their country lacked an important middle class. Accordingly, they could avoid the English gradualism and the blurring of clear-cut ideologies in parliamentary compromises. In addition, caught between military neighbors, their military set could become a key element in Prussian society. Burke was the stimulus, but it was the German elaboration of his response to the French Revolution that resulted in a fully developed conservatism, sharply polarized against liberalism.

If England already softened conservative thought with liberal elements, in America, liberalism—and the middle classes that bore it as a deep-seated style of thought—has been so paramount as to preclude any flowering of genuinely conservative ideology.

Here, from their beginnings the middle classes have been predominant—in class and in status and in power. There is one consequence of this simple fact that goes far to explain why there can be no genuinely conservative ideology in the United States:

There is simply no stratum or group in the population that is of any political consequence to whose traditions conservatism could appeal. All major sections and strata have taken on, in various degrees and ways, the coloration of a middle-class liberal ethos.

The greatest problem of those American writers who would think out a conservative ideology of any political relevance is simply the need to locate the set of people and to make clear the interests that their ideology would serve. There are those, of course, who deny that politics has to do with a struggle for power, but they are of no direct concern to politics as we know it or can imagine it. There are also those who deny that political philosophies are most readily understood as symbols of legitimation, that they have to do with the defense and the attack of powers-that-be or of would-be powers; but by this denial a writer makes himself rather irrelevant to the intellectual features of the public decisions and debates that confront us.

The yearning for conservative tradition, when taken seriously, is bound to be a yearning for the authority of an aristocracy. For without such a more or less fixed and visible social anchor for tradition and for hierarchy, for models of conduct in private and in public life, that are tangible to the senses, there can be no conservatism worthy of the name. And it is just here—at the central demand of conservatism—that most American publicists of the conservative yen become embarrassed. This embarrassment is in part due to a fear of confronting and going against the all-pervading liberal rhetoric; but it is also due to three facts about the American upper class:

First, American writers have no pre-capitalist elite to draw upon, even in fond remembrance. Mr. Kirk, for example, cannot, as European writers have been able to do, contrast such hold-overs from feudalism, however modified, with the vulgarity of capitalist upper elements. The South, when it displayed an "aristocracy" was a region not a nation, and its "aristocrats," however rural, were as much a part of capitalist society as were the New England upper strata.

Second, the very rich in America are culturally among the very poor,

and are probably growing even more so. The only dimension of experience for which they have been models to which serious conservatives
might point is the material one of money-making and money-keeping.
Material success is their sole basis of authority.

Third, alongside the very rich, and supplanting them as popular
models, are the synthetic celebrities of national glamor who often make
a virtue out of cultural poverty and political illiteracy. By their very
nature they are transient figures of the mass means of distraction rather
than sources of authority and anchors of traditional continuity.

Fourth, it is virtually a condition of coming to the top in the American political economy that one learns to use and use frequently a liberal
rhetoric, for that is the common denominator of all proper and successful spokesmen.

There are, accordingly, no social strata which serious minds with
conservative yens might celebrate as models of excellence and which
stand in contrast to the American confusion the conservatives would
deplore.

The American alternative for those interested in a conservative ideology seems to be (1) to go ahead— as Mallock, for example, in his 1898
argument with Spencer did—and defend the capitalist upper classes, or
(2) to become socially vague and speak generally of a "natural aristocracy" or a "self-selected elite" which has nothing to do with existing
social orders, classes and powers.

The first is no longer so popular among free writers, although every
little tendency or chance to do it is promptly seized upon by conservative publicists and translated into such pages as those of *Fortune* magazine. But, more importantly, if it is useful ideologically it must be a
dynamic notion and hence no fit anchor for tradition. On the contrary,
the capitalist elite is always, in the folklore and sometimes in the reality
of capitalism, composed of self-making men who smash tradition to rise
to the top by strictly personal accomplishments.

The second alternative is now the more popular. In their need for an
aristocracy, the conservative thinkers become grandly vague and very
general. They are slippery about the aristocrat; generalizing the idea,
they make it moral rather than socially firm and specific. In the name of
"genuine democracy" or "liberal conservatism" they stretch the idea of

aristocracy in a quite meaningless way, and so, in the end, all truly democratic citizens become aristocrats. Aristocracy becomes a scatter of morally superior persons rather than a strategically located class. So it is with Ortega y Gasset and so it is with Peter Viereck, who writes that it is not "the Aristocratic class" that is valuable but "the aristocratic spirit"—which, with its decorum and *noblesse oblige,* is "open to all, regardless of class."

This is not satisfactory because it provides no widely accepted criteria for judging who is elite and who is not. Moreover, it does not have to do with the existing facts of power and hence is politically irrelevant. And it involves a mobile situation; the self-selecting elite can be no fixed anchor. Some have tried to find a way to hold onto such a view, as it were secretly, not stating it directly, but holding it as a latest assumption while talking about, not the elite, but "the mass." That, however, is dangerous, for again, it goes so squarely against the liberal rhetoric which requires a continual flattery of the citizens.

Both these alternatives, in fact, end up not with an elite that is anchored in a tradition and hierarchy but with dynamic and ever-changing elite continually struggling to the top in an expanding society. There is simply no socially, much less politically, recognized traditional elite and there is no tradition. Moreover, whatever else it may be, tradition is something you cannot create. You can only uphold it when it exists. And now there is no spell of unbroken tradition upon which modern society is or can be steadily based. Accordingly, the conservative cannot confuse greatness with mere duration, cannot decide the competition of values by a mere endurance contest.

In one of its two major forms, as instanced by Mr. Kirk, the defense of irrationality rests upon pre-capitalist, in fact pre-industrial, bases: it is simply the image of a society in which authority is legitimated by traditionalism and interpreted by a recognized aristocracy.

In its other major form the defense rests upon what is perhaps the key point in classic liberal capitalism: it is the image of a society in which authority is at a minimum because it is guided by the autonomous forces of the magic market. In this view, providence becomes the unseen hand of the market; for in secular guise Providence refers to a faith that the unintended consequences of many wills form a pattern, and that this pattern ought to be allowed to work itself out.

In contrast to classic conservatism, this conservative liberalism, as a call to relax the urge to rational planning, is very deep in the American grain. Not wishing to be disturbed over moral issues of the political economy, Americans cling all the more to the idea that the government is an automatic machine, regulated by a balancing out of competing interests. This image of government is simply carried over from the image of the economy: in both we arrive at equilibrium by the pulling and hauling of each individual or group for their own interests, restrained only by legalistic and amoral interpretation of what the law allows.

George Graham has noted that although Americans think representative government a wonderful thing, they hold that representatives are merely "politicians" who as a class are of a fairly low order; that although they willingly honor the dead statesmen of the past, they dishonor the politicians of the present. Professor Graham infers from this, as well as other facts, that "perhaps what Americans yearn for is a complete mechanization of politics. Not a dictator but a political automat is the subconscious ideal," something that will measure up "to the modern standards of being fully automatic and completely impersonal."

In the United States the economic order has been predominant among institutions, and therefore the types of men and their characteristic traits are best interpreted in terms of the evolving economic system. In turn, the top men, almost regardless of how top is defined, have always included in one way or another those who are at the top of the economic system.

Insofar as one can find a clue to the basic impulse of the Eisenhower administration, it is the attempt to carry out this sacrifice of politics to the free dominance of economic institutions and their key personnel. It is a difficult task, perhaps even one that only crackpot realists would attempt, for now depression and wars, as well as other perils and complications of modern life, have greatly enlarged the federal government and made it an unwieldy instrument.

At the center of their ideology, the capitalist upper circles and their outlying publicists have had and do have only one political idea: it is the idea of an automatic political economy. This is best known to us as simply the practical conservatism of the anti-New Dealers during the Thirties of which the late Senator Robert Taft was perhaps the prime exemplar. It has been given new life by the frightening spectacle of the enlarged, totalitarian states of Germany yesterday and Russia today. And now it has become the only socially anchored conservative rhetoric in the American managerial elite, who now blend with the formal political directorate.

And yet on the practical political level the conservative groping has not been much more than a set of negative reactions to any signs of "liberal" or "progressive" policies or men. Conservatives have protested their individual rights rather than any common duties. Such duties as they have set forth—the trusteeship of big corporations, for example— have been all too transparently cloaks for harder and narrower interests. For a dozen years, the New and Fair Deals carried forth a series of specific personalities and policies and agencies that have been the shifting targets of conservative bile. Yet, for electoral purposes, that bile had to be ejected into the "*progressive*" atmosphere carried forth and sustained by the New Deal.

American conservatives have not set forth any conservative ideology. They are conservative in mood and conservative in practice but they have no conservative ideology. They have had no connection with the fountainheads of modern conservative thought. In becoming aware of their power they have not elaborated that awareness into a conscious ideology. Perhaps it is easiest for people to be conservative when they have no sense of what conservatism means, no sense of the conservative present as being only one alternative to what the future might be. For if one cannot say that conservatism is unconsciousness, certainly conservatives are often happily unconscious.

The poverty of mind in U.S. politics is evidenced in practice by the fact that the campaign liberals have no aim other than to hold to the general course of the New and Fair Deals, and no real ideas about extending these administrative programs. The campaign conservatives, holding firmly to utopian capitalism (with its small, passive government and its automatic economy), have come up against the same facts as the liberals and in facing them have behaved very similarly. They have no real ideas about how to jettison the welfare state and the managed war economy.

In the meantime both use the same liberal rhetoric, largely completed before Lincoln's death, to hold matters in stalemate. Neither party has a political vocabulary—much less political policies—that are up-to-date with the events, problems and structure of modern life. Neither party challenges the other in the realm of ideas, nor offers clear-cut alternatives to the electorate. Neither can learn nor will learn anything from classic conservatism of Mr. Kirk's variety. They are both liberal in rhetoric, traditional in intention, expedient in practice.

You can no more build a coherent conservative outlook and policy on a coalition of big, medium and small business, higher white collar employees and professional people, farmers and a divided South than you could build a racial outlook and policy on a coalition of big city machines, small business men, lower white collar people, a split and timid labor world, farmers and a divided South.

Within each party and between them there is political stalemate. Out of two such melanges, you cannot even sort out consistent sets of interests and issues, much less develop coherent policies, much less organize ideological guidelines for public debate and private reflection.

This means, for one thing, that "politics" goes on only within and between a sort of administrative fumbling. The fumbles are expedient. And the drift that they add up to leads practically all sensitive observers to construct images of the future that are images of horror.

One thinks of the attempt to create a conservative ideology in the United States as a little playful luxury a few writers will toy with for a while, rather than a serious effort to work out a coherent view of the world they live in and the demands they would make of it as political men.

More interesting than the ideas of these would-be conservative writers is the very high ratio of publicity to ideas. This is of course a characteristic of fashions and fads, and there is no doubt that the conservative moods are now fashionable. But I do not think we can explain intellectual fashions, in particular this one, by the dialectic that runs

through intellectual discourse, nor by the ready seizure by vested interests of ideas and moods that promise to justify their power and their
policies.

For one thing, policy makers often do not usually feel the need for
even reading, much less using in public, much less thinking about, the
conservative philosophies. When Robert Taft, before his death, was
asked if he had read Russell Kirk's book, he replied that he did not have
much time for books. Like the radical writers of the previous decade,
conservative writers of the 40's and 50's are not in firm touch with power
elites or policy makers.

Another reason America has no conservative ideology is that it has
no radical opposition. Since there is no radical party, those who benefit
most from such goods and powers of life as are available have felt no
need to elaborate a conservative defense of their positions. For conservatism is not the mere carrying on of traditions or defense of existing
interests: it is a becoming aware of tradition and interests and elaborat-
ing them into an outlook, tall with principle. And this happens usually
only when the tradition and the top position which benefit from it are
really attacked.

Neither a radical ideology nor a conservative ideology but a liberal
rhetoric has provided the terms of all issues and conflicts. In its generic
ambiguities and generality of term this rhetoric has obfuscated hard
issues and made possible a historical development without benefit of
hard conflict of idea. The prevalence of this liberal rhetoric has also
meant that thought in any wide meaning of the term has been largely
irrelevant to such politics as have been visible.

Underneath the immediate groping for conservatism there is, of
course, the prosperity that has dulled any deeper political appetite in
America's post-war period. It is true that this prosperity does not rest
upon an economy solidly on its own feet, and that for many citizens it is
not so pleasant as they had probably imagined. For it is a prosperity that
is underpinned politically by a seemingly permanent war economy, and
socially by combined incomes. Still, no matter how partial or how
phoney, by old fashioned standards the atmosphere is one of prosperity.

It is true, of course, that the radicalism of western humanism did not
and does not depend for its nerve or its muscle upon fluctuations of

material well-being. For those who are of this persuasion are as interested in the level of public sensibility and the quality of everyday life as in the material volume and distribution of commodities. Still, for many, this prosperity, no matter how vulgar, has been an obstacle to any cultural, much less political, protest.

More specific than this general climate of prosperity has been the tiredness of the liberal, living off the worn-out rubble of his rhetoric; and, along with this, the disappointment of the radical, from the turns of Soviet institutions away from their early promise to all the defeats that have followed in the thirty years of crisis and the deflation of radicalism.

The tiredness of the liberal and the deflation of radicalism are in themselves causes of the search for some kind of a more conservative point of view. It is good, many seem to feel, to relax and to accept. To undo the bow and to fondle the bowstring. It is good also, perhaps, because of the generally flush state of the writers and thinkers, for we should not forget that American intellectuals, however we may define them, are also personally involved in the general level of prosperity. To this we must also add the plain and fancy fright of many who once spoke boldly; the attacks upon civil liberties have touched deeply their anxieties and have prodded them to search for new modes of acceptance.

These are sources of the conservative impulse from the standpoint of the old left and liberal centers—to which most of the intellectuals have felt themselves to belong. From the right of center, there have also been impulses—impulses that were always there, perhaps, but which have come out into large print and ample publicity only in the post-war epoch. First of all there are interests which no matter what their prosperity require defending, primarily large business interests, and along with this, there is the need, which is felt by many spokesmen and scholars as great, for cultural prestige abroad. One prime result of the increased travel abroad by scholars, stemming from the anti-American rebuffs they have experienced, is the need to defend in some terms the goodness of American life. And these little episodes have occurred in a large context of power: a context in which the economic and military and political power of the U.S. greatly exceeds her cultural prestige, and is so felt by the more acute politicians and statesmen at home and abroad.

The campaign conservatives will continue to go in for public relations more than for ideology. Just now they do not really feel the need for any ideology; later a conservative ideology of the kinds we have been discussing will appeal to no one. The radical humanist will continue to believe that men collectively can and ought to be their own history-makers and that men individually can to some extent and should try fully to create their own biographies. For those who still retain this minimum definition, the current attempts to create a conservative ideology do not constitute any real problem.

In the meantime, political decisions are occurring, as it were, without benefit of political ideas; mind and reality are two separate realms; America—a conservative country without any conservative ideology—appears before the world a naked and arbitrary power.

—1954

the problem of u.s. power
IRVING HOWE

The uneven development of the world economy has resulted in a disastrous split between the industrialized West and primitive East; but it has
also brought another split, at the moment quite as important, between
the United States and its own allies. Those theoreticians of liberalism
who advance claims for American uniqueness generally do so in a spirit
of eulogy, but if they were to stand back a little from the problem and
see it in some historical perspective, they might make a genuine contribution. For there *is* a sense in which America is becoming unique. Even
as it is inextricably drawn into the historical dilemmas of Europe and
Asia, even as Europe and Asia become "Americanized," there has developed in this country such a concentration of wealth and power, with so
many new attendant values, as to make America increasingly isolated
from the rest of the world.

Far more than good or bad will is at stake. A kind of symbiotic
relationship can be traced: the decline of Europe has proceeded in direct
ratio to the rise of America. The power potential of the country, its
unprecedented emphasis on norms of accumulation and efficiency, its
literal incapacity to understand and irritated refusal to sympathize with
the patterns of thought which dominate Europe and Asia—these are
factors, sometimes the result of bad will but more often of a multiplying
cultural distance, which make America into a lonely power colossus,
alternating between gestures of humiliating generosity and crude intimidation, sincerely convinced that only by the imposition of its will can
the world be saved. But the world resists this will; it cannot, even if it
would, surrender its own modes of response.

Eisenhower's victory rested upon an appeal to the imagination of the
middle class. He was popular not merely because he was a general; it
seems likely that a swashbuckling military man would not have won the
election. Eisenhower was popular because he was a certain kind of
general: unspectacular, old-fashioned, *sound*. His political appeal had
been shrewdly designed to elicit the vision of a pulling-back from the
bewilderments of that highly complex world with which the Truman
administration had, willy-nilly, established occasional commerce. The

middle class voter who put Eisenhower in office recognized in "Ikeism" the same benign indifference to the *idea* of Europe or the *idea* of Asia that he himself felt. "Ikeism" represented a wish to return to the era BC—Before Complexity.

Had there been any possibility for the realization of this wish, all might have gone well. Then, we might have had a little more or less of scandal than under Harding, a little more or less of social mediocrity than under Grant. But no one, except obsolete moralists, would have cared. The whole tragi-comedy of "Ikeism" is that it represents the hunger for normalcy at a time when normalcy is utterly impossible.

1) The Anatomy of "Ikeism"

A few years ago C. Wright Mills suggested a rough but usable distinction between sophisticated and practical conservatives. The first might be represented by the editorial position of *Fortune,* the second by a small town Republican paper. The sophisticated recognized the need for "internationalism," while the practical resisted his recognition of the same need. The sophisticated believed in a measure of Welfare economics while the practical liked to think he didn't.

Now, one way of looking at the Eisenhower victory is as the fruit of a union between these two conservative impulses. The sophisticated conservatives understood that victory was possible for the Republican Party only by appealing to the images of the practical conservatives, which embodied the ostrich yearnings of the American middle class. And the practical conservatives knew they couldn't win without the high-powered manipulations of the sophisticated.

Once the Eisenhower administration took office, the two mentalities worked with surprising smoothness. They struck upon a convenient formula: each acquiesced in the worst features of the other. The coarse psychology of the practicals dominated domestic policy: tideland oil, tax "relief" for corporate business, plundering of national resources, acceptance of a reserve army of four to five million unemployed. The sophisticated conservatives provided the cynical rationale for a continued whittling away at civil liberties, the infamous persecution of scientists, the imprisonment of Communists, etc.; they knew the formula by which an excuse for the exceptional becomes a justification for establishing it as the routine. And in foreign policy the Eisenhower administration charted a dizzying compromise. Talking loudly while carrying a small stick, it turned a face of political schizophrenia to the outer world: now it purred like a slick Machiavellian, now it snarled like a frightened small-town politician.

The most important fact about the Eisenhower administration is the climate it has established: fear, cowardice, suspicion, anti-intellectualism, swagger, distrust, denunciation. The Oppenheimer case represents "Ikeism" at the low political and moral point where it touches upon McCarthyism. But the over-all tendency toward a garrison state—a tendency, happily, that is still far from having reached its goal—has little to do with McCarthyism, for it was already present under Truman. It is all too easy to blame McCarthy for the social and political ills which are the responsibility of his betters.

Now the world's greatest power, the United States and its administration are perplexed by the problem of power. The men in Washington know that they are extremely *powerful*, but the possession of power does not solve the problem of how to use it. The men who rule in Washington sincerely believe that material strength, wealth, money, technology, *know-how* will vanquish all obstacles; that the sum of these constitutes a policy. They demonstrate, thereby, an inadequate sense of reality.

2) McCarthyism as Malaise

Various theories have been suggested to explain the social roots of McCarthyism in America, and we hope to return to them in a later *Dissent*. Here we would suggest a simple but perhaps fundamental explanation for the power of McCarthyism: the deep-seated if frequently suppressed state of *panic,* itself the result of the split between American power and American inability to use its power, which has seized large sections of the American population. Panic restrained or frozen under the mask of homely confidence—that is frequently the content of "Ikeism." Panic released and allowed to luxuriate—that is the syndrome of McCarthyism.

When America faced the Nazi threat, it could react to a new phenomenon with a certain shocked confidence. Once it realized that

Nazism went beyond the bounds of conventional immorality, that Nazism contained an impulse to make terror into the norm of life, the American mind could use this analysis to meet the Nazi danger. And whatever its inadequacies, this view of Nazism did have a genuine relation to reality. Where Stalinism pretends to be the fulfillment of Western humanism, Nazism frankly proclaimed itself the enemy of humanism, which has made the Stalinists harder to cope with.

Stalinism is cold not hot; calculating not irrational; cautious not maniacal. It cannot be understood as the emanation of pure evil; that is all very well for Whittaker Chambers, but not of conspicuous help in the rice paddies of Indochina. It cannot be understood merely as totalitarianism, for the problem is to make the proper discriminations as to what kind of totalitarian movement it is. Nor can it be understood as the legitimate heir of Marxism—though official American ideology, wilfully eager to discredit radicalism by identifying it with totalitarianism, does treat the Stalinist movement in these terms. For the American government to act upon what is peculiar to Stalinism—for the American government to treat it as a blend of reactionary and pseudo-revolutionary appeals, as a movement both anti-capitalist and anti-socialist, as a movement that thrives upon the vacuum created by the collapse of capitalism as a *world* economy—all this would require a political openness inconceivable in the present atmosphere, a willingness to recognize its own social obsolescence, and a readiness to support anti-Stalinist movements in Asia and Europe which, to be politically effective, must also be anti-capitalist in one or another way.

The greater American bewilderment and irritation in failing to stop Stalinism internationally, the greater the success of McCarthyism. The secret of McCarthy's power is to be found in the pervasive and undifferentiated frustration which millions of Americans, and particularly those who bear the burdens of power, feel with regard to the international Communist movement.

Nothing seems to work, nothing seems able to stop them! Contain the Stalinists in Europe, and they thrive in Asia. Bottle them up in Berlin, and they break loose in Guatemala. Something uncanny, something magical seems to attach itself to the Stalinist victories, in a way that did not seem true for the Nazis. War—a full, terrible, releasing war—might be a way out, but our very progress in atomic weapons makes it risky. And besides, the Stalinists seem entirely satisfied with a series of small bleeding wars rather than one grand apocalyptic blowout. So runs a dominant thread of American feeling.

And the result, among many Americans, is frustration, bewilderment, impotence and occasional bursts of anger. If one can't figure one's way out of a labyrinth, one will try in final desperation to barge through it headfirst. And that, we would suggest, is the socio-psychological material from which McCarthyism is made. "Ikeism" too expresses the same frustration, but expresses it through an effort to deny its reality. McCarthyism and "Ikeism" are of course very different, but they are also symmetrical: both are symptoms not merely of the inability of the Republican Party to rule, but more fundamentally of *a loss of social confidence and cohesion in American life.*

It is not to be supposed that this disintegration begins only with the day Eisenhower takes office. Signs of it, and very heavy signs, can already be seen in earlier years. The Oppenheimer scandal points to McCarthyism, to be sure; but it also points back to the Truman policy of promiscuous "loyalty" regulations and promiscuous "subversive lists" which provided a quasi-juridical base for what has happened during the past two years. When America lost China, the process of panic began. Stalinism won the largest country of Asia; the United States "discovered" that the Communist Party was plotting and put Eugene Dennis in jail.

Today McCarthyism functions on several levels: as the personal voice or *charisma* of the creature himself; as his secret apparatus of informers and tipsters who constitute a kind of "parallel center" or "dual power" within and against the legal government; as a political mood which cuts through all layers of American society. And most important of all, it constitutes a paralyzing veto upon American foreign policy, *any* American foreign policy: on the one hand, it is prepared to sabotage as "treason" any policy which takes into account the realities of Stalinist power by making temporary arrangements with it, and on the other hand, it pushes for a policy that can only have meaning in or lead to a major war but without being willing to take responsibility for that war. It is sometimes said that McCarthyism has no foreign policy of its own, but that is not, strictly speaking, true: McCarthyism combines the gesture of extreme war-hawk provocation with the underlying impulses of isolationism.

As yet, McCarthyism is not a full-fledged fascist movement. To become that it would have to have at its disposal a chronic economic crisis and a coherent mass movement. The second of these could perhaps be quickly improvised, but the first is not likely to be available for some time—hence, incidentally, McCarthy's shrewdness in concentrating on the Communist issue, which will be available for a long time.

McCarthy may suffer defeats, but the political mood he personifies will not disappear. So long as America remains on the defensive internationally, so long as we continue to have Indochinas and Guatemalas, trying to stop Communist mass movements with inane "Emperors" and Latin dictators, McCarthyism will survive, ebbing now but rising later. If a prerequisite for fascism is the crumbling of social cohesion, then McCarthy is doing that work, and doing it with the help of the major, respectable forces of the country. Anyone who compares Eisenhower's cowardice toward McCarthy with Hindenburg's toward Hitler is likely to know some chilling moments.

3) The H Bomb as Politics

In the H Bomb, the Eisenhower administration faced its greatest test. When it announced its ability to wipe out cities with one bomb, a shiver of foreboding ran through the world; yet America, the greatest power on earth, could only repeat at this moment of severe moral-political crisis, the empty catchword, Massive Retaliation. This means, and so large sections of the world took it to mean, that the H Bomb is the core of American foreign policy.

A foreign policy geared to nuclear weapons is realistically a disaster and morally a scandal. Immediately, the H Bomb made things harder, not easier, for American foreign policy. If the Bomb seems to remove global atomic war from the realm in which *any* political objectives can be achieved by either combatant, it makes all the more plausible those small localized wars the Stalinists promote. The very magnitude of the new atomic weapons encourages the Stalinists into the not unwarranted belief that they may still be able to chew off a bit here and there. Mao

Tse-tung has shrewdly remarked that China is too backward a nation to be overly worried by atomic weapons, while Secretary of War Wilson, back from a trip to the Far East, reports that the war in Asia is today "90 per cent political." Add these facts together and you see that the idea of Massive Retaliation is both hollow and disastrous.

Not only is the Bomb as Foreign Policy a moral horror, it also makes the task of breaking millions of Europeans and Asians from the Stalinist orbit infinitely more difficult. The image of America as the country of the Bomb throws large sections of the world into political torpor, which in turn makes them easy prey for the Stalinists and the Stalinist-controlled sections of neutralism. It is hopeless to speak of American good will or democracy, to scatter bits of Point Four money here and there, when in the eyes of millions of people we are the nation of the Bomb. And is this merely the result of malicious anti-American propaganda? Let us remember which nation was the first, and thus far the only, one to use atomic weapons.

At the very least, America might have considered with a certain seriousness and courtesy Nehru's proposal for an international conference designed to institute a ban upon further use and manufacture of the Bomb. Instead of hinting darkly that Nehru is soft on communism or even something of a fellow-traveller, America might have responded immediately with a dramatic public gesture to allay the fears of the world and proclaim its eagerness to stop atomic war production. This would not at all have meant to "trust" the Russians. There is no reason to trust the Russians, but *there is every reason to speak to the world.*

The very locale of the H bomb experiments tells us something about American mentality. Implicit in the decision to explode the Bomb in the Pacific is the traditional contempt of the white man for the colored peoples. Marshall Islanders can be shunted from one place to another; a few Japanese fishermen may get burned. . . . And when the Asian press expressed its resentment, U.S. reaction was mainly that these Asians, unduly sensitive as Orientals are known to be, were making too much of a fuss.

For once, considerations of morality and realism come very close to one another. To rely on the H Bomb as the power behind our policy can lead only to the disaster of the cobalt bomb. It may well be, as many people argue, that unilateral atomic disarmament is at present too great a risk. But between the proclaimed extremes of Massive Retaliation and unilateral atomic disarmament lies the real problem: political struggle against Stalinism. By an old twist of history, the very madness of the armament race now makes it likely that we will not have a global war in the near future and that consequently the decisive struggle with Stalinism will be fought in the arena of politics. Precisely, that is, where the West is least prepared.

4) Foreign Policy in an Age of Revolution

It now seems highly probable that Stalinism has achieved a major victory in Indochina. If the West does not intervene militarily, the Viet Minh is almost certain to take complete control of the country; if the West does intervene, there follows the likelihood, not of wresting the country from the Stalinists, but of a long bleeding war. We are paying for decades of imperialist cupidity and obtuseness. As Walter Lippmann has put it with classical brevity: "The French lost the war in Indochina, not because they were not brave, but because they failed to win the confidence and support of the Vietnamese nation. . . ."

In 1946, when a coalition Vietnamese regime was established in the north of the country under the leadership of Ho Chi Minh but not yet under the domination of the Stalinists, political measures of a bold and imaginative kind might have saved the country. But the French, who had collaborated with the Japanese and been restored to power by British bayonets, suddenly withdrew, later in the same year, their recognition from this government in the north. Thereby they drove many nationalist, non-Communist Vietnamese into Ho's arms, and transformed what should have been a domestic political struggle between Vietnamese integrity and Stalinist intervention into a colonial war against a foreign imperialist power. Every political move of the French was incredibly stupid—but stupid not in an individual sense. What was involved was a *class* stupidity, the rigid stiffened reaction of a class losing control. As a consequence, the Stalinists were helped into power, the anti-Stalinists demoralized and atomized. Political measures can defeat Communist guerrillas in Asia, but they have to be taken *in time.* Today things are almost hopeless in Indochina, but the lessons of Indochina need to be drastically applied to Malaya and Indonesia, where crises of a

parallel kind are rapidly maturing. To suppose that an antedeluvian pro-
consul like General Templer, until recently British chief in Malaya, can
defeat, let alone understand, Stalinism, is to suppose we are still living in
the age of Kipling. And for such mistakes we shall pay.

The central fact is that we continue to live in a revolutionary age.
The revolutionary impulse has been contaminated, corrupted, debased,
demoralized; it has been appropriated by the enemies of socialism. All
true. But the social energy behind that revolutionary impulse remains.
Now it bursts out in one part of the world, now in another. It cannot be
suppressed entirely. Everywhere except in the United States, millions of
human beings, certainly the majority of those with any degree of political articulateness, live for some kind of social change. The workers of
Europe are consciously anti-capitalist, the populations of Asia and
South America anti-imperialist. These are the dominant energies of our
time and whoever gains control of them, whether in legitimate or distorted forms, will triumph.

But American foreign policy is enacted in ignorance or contempt of
this central fact. America now has several possible courses. One may
recognize that the basic struggle in the world is political and therefore
try to undercut the hold of Stalinism by a genuine appeal of radical
democracy. Or one may believe that the political appeal is either useless
or unavailable and that only war can end the Communist danger. But if
the political struggle is discarded and if war seems too risky, what then
remains? The necessity for maneuver and some sort of breathing spell.
Here too, however, Dulles's policy proves impossible. Because of the
legalistic-moralistic frame of Dulles's own mind, and more important,
because of the heavy pressures of the McCarthyite wing of the Republican Party, which presses toward a war policy without being ready to face
up to its consequences, the U.S. government is committed to skimping
the usual diplomacy of bargaining which involves a simple recognition
that other forms of national power, like them or not, do exist. Except for
a reliance upon its material strength, the U.S. has today no foreign
policy: neither political nor diplomatic nor adventurist.

For the sake of simplification, let us say that the two major social
problems facing humanity are: the obsolescence of the European
nation-state with its equally obsolescent economy, and the extreme
unevenness of world economy, which dooms Asia, Africa and South

America to poverty and backwardness. The first of these problems might be solved, at least in part, by the creation of a United States of Europe able to achieve a measure of independence from the two great power blocs. The second is even more complex, since it involves the consciousness of millions of people still on the edge of illiteracy, as well as the difficulty of accumulating in Asia a sufficient capital reserve without thereby becoming dependent on the West. Let us assume—though we doubt that, in the absence of a large-scale political activization in Asia, even this would be sufficient—that a tremendous aid program of $30 to $40 billions from the West could raise the economic and cultural level of Asia to a significant degree.

Can we seriously suppose, however, that such a program will or is likely—or can—be instituted by any *status quo* government in the United States, be it conservative or liberal? Consider how different the whole political-social atmosphere in this country would have to be before such a proposal could even be seriously discussed. Consider the taxation, upon the population at large or the corporate interests or both, that would be necessary for such a program. Consider the competitive dangers a vigorous industrialized Asia might then present to American capitalist economy. Consider, in short, the serious political struggles that would inevitably occur in America consequent upon such a program.

It is here that the liberals, who also recognize the need for massive aid to Asia, fail to think through the implications of their ideas. They refuse, or are unable, to weigh the inescapable consequences of such a proposal: namely, serious political and social struggle at home. They fail to see that the battle for the mind of Asia can be successful only if and when Asia is presented with an image of a radically different America, and an image based on reality, not a press agent's phrases. That America has a high standard of living, a high level of productivity, may arouse feelings of envy among the politically articulate Asians; but not admiration. Their behavior is frequently based on other assumptions, neither more nor less "idealistic"—simply different.

America speaks today as if it wants to sell the Asians the final product of a long history of social and economic development; but it does not do anything to let them first engage in those revolutionary and liberating movements through which we have ourselves entered modern history. America may speak in the name of the American revolution, but the policies it proposes and the images it advances are those of an American restoration. For it is not merely stupidity or cussedness that makes U.S. policy favor Syngman Rhee or Chiang Kai-shek—it is our basic inability, which would in large measure be shared by a liberal Democratic regime as well, to come to terms with the future of Asia.

We are not trying to suggest a "program" here. Far more important is an understanding of the root situation. Nor are we saying that "only" a socialist America could help solve the problems of Asia, for that, while perhaps ultimately true, does not impinge upon any immediate possibilities. We are merely trying to suggest the direction, the trend in which America would have to go—toward a radical democracy, toward a profound and humble effort to grasp the outlook of peoples different from itself, toward a willingness to share its unprecedented wealth in order to revive the health of the whole world, toward a sense of community and equality.

Whether such an America could be created short of socialism is perhaps an academic question—we doubt that it could be created *very* short of socialism. On the other hand, much could yet be done, in terms of concrete short-range measures, to undercut the roots of Stalinism in Asia. There is nothing inherent in capitalist society which produces the extreme inanity of the Dulles policy: something must be left to accident. There is nothing inherent in capitalist society which requires the American Secretary of State to ask the European nations permission to search their ships for possible arms to Guatemala (shades of 1812)—a proposal which is not merely insanely stupid but reeks of the imperialist psychology.

If America, at the very least, were to present itself not as a "savior" of Asia, but simply as a power that will do all it can to allow the Asian peoples to work out their own destinies, that too would be helpful. We have no illusions whatever about the possibilities of reaching permanent agreements with the Russians; but certainly temporary agreements might be possible in order to give Asia, and the whole human race, *a little more time.* With the equalization of atomic power, there may be a possibility of reaching highly limited arrangements of the sort that were reached with regard to poison gas—and which were observed by the totalitarian powers during the Second World War for reasons, of course, not founded in humanitarian sentiments. For if we cannot hope for a fundamental solution to the problem of Stalinism from the bourgeois world, we can at least hope for temporary balances of power which will allow us more time to live, to grope for solutions. This, however, is what the politics of panic which characterizes the Eisenhower administration is least calculated to give us.

Meanwhile, the tragedy of American power becomes more terrible and terrifying each day. The very resources that could lift mankind to new levels of well-being serve only to increase the distance between America and the rest of the world. The very resources that should help in the triumph of democracy seem, by an almost devilish process of bewilderment, to work in behalf of relatively impoverished totalitarian nations. Between America and the remainder of the world communication becomes increasingly uncertain, sporadic, bitter. American power multiplies—but the power to dispose of it creatively, with human warmth and intelligence, has never seemed smaller than today.

—1954

america! america!

DWIGHT MACDONALD

When I came back to New York last fall, just in time for the Sputnik, after a year in London and two months in Tuscany, I felt I had crossed a boundary much wider than the Atlantic. We are an unhappy people (I felt), a people without style, without a sense of what is humanly satisfying. Our values are not anchored securely, not in the past (tradition) and not in the present (community). There is a terrible *shapelessness* about American life. These prosperous Americans look more tense and joyless than the people in the poorest quarters of Florence. Even the English seem to have more *joie de vivre*.

No nation in history has been richer or has had a more equal distribution of wealth, and since 1940 there has been a fantastic increase in the wealth and a considerable decrease in economic differences. If Socialism be the equal sharing of plenty, then we are far along the road. We have more of everything a human being can conceivably, and inconceivably, want than Fourier, Proudhon, or Marx could have imagined possible. According to *Fortune* (June, 1954), we spend over $30 billion a year on pleasure ("The Great Fun Market"): sports, travel, hunting and fishing, books and magazines, liquor, gardening, home workshops, movies and television, etc. Yet we are, I insist, not happy. Why not? Let me put down a few impressions.

(1) The British and the Italians know how to live together, we don't. Each does it differently, the British with all sorts of formal, moral, legalistic inhibitions against interfering with the "rights" of The Other; the Italians with a vivacious pleasure in the human otherness of The Other; but each people in its own way has very good manners. Our manners are either bad or non-existent, which is perhaps the same thing. (I'm referring to public, not private, manners; Americans are generous, kindly, and hospitable to people they've been introduced to, but their "street manners" are atrocious, as are the manners of those whose jobs bring them into constant contact with strangers—taxi-drivers, bus-conductors, sales clerks, waiters, policemen, porters, etc.). This is not as trivial as it might seem. When manners are defective, ego clashes nakedly against ego, the I collides with The Other, and the results are

distressing and even catastrophic. In our frontier West, as every movie-goer knows, differences of opinion were settled with six-shooters.

(2) I think the lack of manners is connected with the sense of violence one has in this country. The Italians are excitable and passionate, they shout, curse, and gesture broadly; yet one feels far more secure, physically, in Italy than here. In a single recent issue of the *New York Times* there is a report of a twelve-year-old girl being raped in a Brooklyn public school by a fifteen-year-old fellow-student; of a traffic argument terminated by one driver shooting the other and then later killing himself; of two teen-age girls being stabbed in the back at noon outside a subway station by some teen-age boys who had tried to get money from them; of the principal of a city school who killed himself because he was being questioned by a Grand Jury about violent episodes among students (another rape, several assaults on teachers and one on a policeman *inside* the school). It's true I live in New York, where there are many Negroes and Puerto Ricans whose crime rate, for understandable reasons, is exceptionally high. But there are lots of Irish, Italian, and even "good Anglo-Saxon" names in our daily crime reports. Nor is the hinterland exactly pacific. About the same time as the above, the Nebraska National Guard was called out to protect the people of Lincoln, the state capital, against a 19-year-old boy. Young Charles Starkweather killed eleven people in three days, for various reasons: because they disapproved of his "dating" their daughter, because they had cars or other possessions he wanted, or because they happened to be around. "Here was a totally defeated ego which had no satisfactory anchorage in social life," explained Dr. James Reinhardt of the University of Nebraska—no American crime story is complete without the psychologist's report. "Socially he was simply an empty man. The only way he could become important was by killing." Look, mom, I'm famous.

(3) The American landscape is lovely save where American man has touched it, and since by now he has touched it almost everywhere one is likely to go—and torn down the structures of earlier American men who had more sense of fitness—we live in ugliness. There is the great American roadside, lined with motels and diners and hot-dog stands, paved with the best quality concrete (and the worst quality intentions) that writhes through the land like a tapeworm. And there are the cities, vast deserts of the present that sometimes look spectacular

from a distance, like the Grand Canyon—and are as pleasant to live in. By comparison, in London or in Tuscany one lives embedded in the past, a state of being I, personally, like.

(4)   *There:* a community, each person differentiated by status and function but each a part of an orderly social structure. *Here:* everybody "equal" in the sense that nobody respects anybody else unless he has to, by *force majeure;* the national motto should be not "E Pluribus Unum," not "In God We Trust," but: "I got mine and screw you, Jack!" (or better, "Brother"—"friend" and "brother" being used by Americans to express extreme hostility and contempt). *There:* continuity with the past, so that some level is taken for granted; there is a bottom, some things aren't done; the bottom may be broken through—as in the London mass newspapers—but at least there is a sense of something being violated. *Here:* no bottom, no continuity, no level; it's a jungle in which anything can happen without anybody's thinking it out of the ordinary. Each individual makes his own culture, his own morality, and sometimes very well—our individual saints and savants don't compare unfavorably with those abroad—but it's all on his lonesome. The same *tendencies* exist in Europe—the same destruction of the order of the past, physical and social, by the cancerous growth of mass society—but they are much less advanced. When one hears Europeans complaining about the Americanization of Europe, one wishes they could spend a few weeks over here and get a load of the real thing. Or rather a few years— most European tourists, except for Madame de Beauvoir, seem to like America. For them, the customs and the landscape are as strange as if it were Java or Tibet, and they find it all "stimulating" and "fascinating," as I dare say it is if you don't have to live here. The tourist's exotic is the native's poison.

(5)   Our Cult of Youth. Old people bore us, and we send them to nice rest-homes if we can afford it. In London and Tuscany, where the idea of a community persists, the old are a normal part of life; they are considered interesting because they know about the past. But we think of them as has-beens, forgetting that what has been is sometimes better than what is and in any case is the root of what will be. Americans think of the ideal age as somewhere around twenty. In the next two decades, this will become crucial because both Old and Young will increase much faster than the rest of us. The teen-age population will grow fantastically

by some 70 per cent, because of the post-1945 war babies. The over-50 population will grow next fastest. So far, the social workers are worrying about the old folks, but everyone else is fascinated with the teen-agers.

(6)   When we come into contact with other peoples, as our post-1945 imperial rôle has forced us to do—never has a world power taken up the insignia of *imperium* so reluctantly—we don't impress them. The British and the French weren't popular with their wards, but they weren't laughed at. Even the Soviet Russians, for all their ruthlessness, barely covered by the fig of ideology, seem to speak a more common language with other peoples than we do. I think the difference is that Americans appear to other nations to be somehow at once gross and sentimental, immature and tough, uncultivated and hypocritical, shrewd about small things and stupid about big things. In these antinomies fatally appears our lack of style. John Foster Dulles, the pious Artful Dodger, is our perfect prototype in world affairs. I remember what a London journalist, years ago, remarked to me, apropos Henry Luce's organization: "I can deal with gangsters or with Boy Scouts, but I must admit I'm at a loss with Boy Scouts who act like gangsters."

The point was illustrated during Mr. Nixon's recent agony in Latin America. On the one hand, Nixon getting himself chronically mobbed while attempting to spread "goodwill" and let's-talk-it-over-boys reason in those dark regions—"Don't you want to hear *facts?*" he cried desperately to the students of Lima amidst the jeers and stones. On the other hand, Eisenhower's instant explosion of anger when he learned of the violence in Caracas, and his instant reflex: send in the marines! "The President of the United States," spoke the Secretary of State to the Venezuelan ambassador, "expects the authorities in Venezuela to take every possible measure to protect the Vice-President. . . . And if there is any lack of will or capacity to give that, we would like to know about it quickly." Eisenhower expects every Venezuelan to do his duty by Nixon. This was backed up by airmailing four companies of marines and paratroopers to our military bases in the Caribbean, lest the Communists have trouble keeping green the memory of Haiti and Nicaragua. Thus a goodwill tour ended up with the marines. It was all very American. American in the notion that a big smile, a firm handshake, and a sincere willingness to Talk It Over will soothe the most savage breast—our old faith in democratic discussion and our new faith in public relations are combined here—and American in the quick resort to force when this naïve illusion collapses.

Eisenhower's handling of the Little Rock school integration crisis is curiously parallel, and not only because the 101st Airborne Division was involved both times. Racial integration is as explosive an issue in the South as anti Yanquism is in Latin America, and with as deep roots; the Supreme Court since 1954 has been dealing with it admirably, with a combination of firmness and patience; but Eisenhower first tried to "talk it over" with Governor Faubus, a sort of goodwill tour of an intractable issue, and then, when Faubus, a demagogue with a perfect cause, expectably made trouble, at once went to the other extreme and sent in the troops. It has so far cost us over four million dollars to keep eight Negro children in Little Rock High School, nor does the wound show signs of healing. Indeed, the use of troops, objectionable in principle as a violation of states' rights (since other means of enforcing the law had by no means been exhausted), has inflamed and prolonged the infection. There are some issues that yield *neither* to the public-relations smile nor to the paratroopers. Most puzzling.

Since I've been away, the March of Progress has been progressing. Out of every ten American houses, eight (81 per cent) now have television sets, almost nine (87 per cent) have washing machines, and practically all (96 per cent) have electric refrigerators. Everybody but me has a new car. The Negro janitor of my apartment building has a bigger, sleeker one than I have ever been able to afford. I can't say I entirely envy him. The new cars are hideous beyond the imagination of a Dante (or a Steinberg), mobile juke-boxes that violate every principle of taste and functionalism, longer and lower and more insanely powerful than ever, lathered with chrome in fantastic zigs and zags and rhomboids, their behinds elongated and streamlined until one can't tell if they're coming or going, with upswept fins and quadruple tail-lights winking and gleaming like a moon-rocket about to take off. (Anal eroticism? Protecting the rear lest a certain backward country "catch up with and overtake" us in the March of Progress? Or both? A traveller back from New Guinea says the natives sum it up: "This fella Sputnik him bugger-up Uncle Sam.") We are contemptuous of Victorian taste, or used to be until we entered the fluorescent age, but what, oh what will they say about these cars in 2058, assuming there is a 2058? And what will they say, what do *we* say about a phenomenon like Mr. George Walker, vice-president and chief-of-styling at Ford Motors, as reported in *Time* of November 4 last:

> George Walker sits in an office fit for an Eastern potentate: a $50,000 production done in creamy-white and black with raw silk draperies, sumptuous leather couches, a jungle of tropical plants along one end, a bank of hi-fi, TV, refrigerators, and cabinets at the other. On the floor spreads a carpet of inch-thick black lambskin. Reported cost: $30,000. Says Walker happily: "Ain't it sexy!"
>
> There, in command of an $11,500,000 red-brick styling center set in an expanse of playing fountains and shimmering pools, Style Boss Walker works at the head of a staff of 650 artists, draughts-men, modellers, and engineers. Most are young (average age: 31); all have what automen call "gasoline in their veins." Says Walker: "You just got to love cars." . . .
>
> "A stylist," says Walker, "has got to show style in his cars, in his home, his clothes, and his person." He even smells stylish, slather-ing on Faubergé cologne so liberally that it lingers on long after he leaves the room. He owns 40 pairs of shoes (at $60 a pair), 70 suits, once had Saks Fifth Avenue make up four "cocktail suits" (at $250 apiece) in white with blue braid, white with black braid. "I didn't wear them," grins George. "People might think I was eccentric." . . .
>
> Says he, happily recounting what he considers his "finest mo-ment" while on a vacation in Florida: "I was terrific. There I was in my white Continental, and I was wearing a pure-silk, pure-white, embroidered cowboy shirt and black gabardine trousers. Beside me was my jet black Great Dane, imported from Europe, named Dana von Krupp. You just can't do any better than that."

So, Mr. Walker. But the really awful thing is that the American people like what he and his 650 young artists produce.

The march of labor has continued. For a long time now—in America this means about ten years—unionism has been part of the normal

American Way of Life. While this is on the whole good, it also means that another disruptive force in our society—which I think could do with a little more disrupting—has been neutralized. . . . The average worker has now completed twelve years of schooling, that is, he has gone through high school; as recently as 1940, it was only nine years. . . . One Leo Perlis, Director of Community Service Activities for the AFL-CIO (that such a post exists is a sign of labor's maturity, if not, indeed, its senility), has revealed that his department is about to train bar-tenders in social-work techniques. "Bar-tenders," he explained, "see more people with social problems than social workers do. Instead of just listening to a customer with a problem, these trained bar-tenders would be able to refer them to the proper community agency." . . . The Welfare and Retirement Fund of the United Mine Workers announces, for the year ended June 30, 1957, receipts of $157,000,000, of which $138,000,000 was spent on pensions ($100 a month), medical benefits (the UMW now has a string of ultra-modern hospitals and clinics that give its members better medical services than all but the wealthiest non-miners can afford), and payments to widows and orphans. When one remembers Ludlow, Harlan, and other mine-workers' battles in this century, one is again impressed by the phenomenon of John L. Lewis, the Winston Churchill of our labor movement, a leader of large, courageous, and retrograde views who in 1946 bullied the mine-owners into financing the Fund. "No pen can write, no tongue can tell, no vocabulary of language is large enough to express the many benefits that will come to the American coal-miner and his family through the establishment of the Welfare and Retirement Fund," Mr. Lewis observed at the time. Like Churchill, he exaggerated, but not much. . . . There has even developed a union of union organizers, the Field Representatives' Federation which for many months has been demanding from the AFL-CIO recognition as the collective-bargaining agent for its 225 organizers, as well as grievance procedures, a better pension plan, and higher dismissal pay. The employer has not only refused to bargain, but also has very nearly fired almost half of its organizers. One report is that the AFL-CIO is planning to initiate a million-dollar publicity campaign, financed in part with what it will save by cutting its organizing staff. The class struggle vaporizes into Public Relations.

I arrived in London in the summer of 1956 just as the reputation of Colin Wilson's *The Outsider* was swelling to its most majestic proportions, and I got back to New York just in time to witness the similar inflation of James Gould Cozzens' *By Love Possessed,* which was unanimously praised by the critics and which was for months at the top of the fiction best-seller lists. Since I have analyzed at some length in the January *Commentary* both the novel and the nonsense written about it, I won't re-hash it all here. But it may be interesting to compare the two episodes.

In each case, a bad book not only became a best-seller—there's no news in *that,* after all— but became one because it was extravagantly praised by critics and journals that normally (or so one thought) were more discriminating. Furthermore, both books are ambitious efforts, not pot-boilers for the mass market but the work of serious writers laboring at their very highest bent. In fact, I think it was their seriousness, indeed their portentousness, that sold them; Max Beerbohm, for example, a far more original and vigorous thinker than either Mr. Wilson or Mr. Cozzens (not to dwell on his considerably greater talent as a writer) never had the kind of sales they have been enjoying. The reviewers have become so disoriented through constant exposure to potboilers that they assume almost automatically that any book which is clearly *not* written for the market is to be taken seriously. This, of course, is not the case. It is perhaps the critic's most important job to discriminate between the true-good and the false-good, since the humbler practitioners of best-sellerdom are so easily distinguished that they don't threaten our standards. It is when you have a sincere and ambitious attempt (to create a new philosophy or to write a "big" novel) that the temptation to be a good fellow and applaud is strongest—and most dangerous. The critics and the mob find a common ground: both feel they are doing their duty by Culture.

But there are differences. A minor one, possibly of sociological interest, is that the English reviewers overpraised *The Outsider* because its author was young (24) and so deserving of encouragement of his first book (I would say our age is much too permissive with the young) while their American colleagues overpraised *By Love Possessed* because its author was aging (54) and so deserving of encouragement of his twelfth book, especially since none of its predecessors had been a great *succès d'estime.* (The Devil has never lacked arguments.) The major difference, certainly of cultural interest, was that while there were three hostile reviews of *The Outsider* in important places (*The Times Literary Supplement, Spectator, Encounter*), over here the only hostile reviews of *By Love Possessed* were in two distinctly minor periodicals (*National Review, Yale Review*). Not a good showing. Especially when two of our serious quarterlies, the *American Scholar* and the *Hudson Review,* have printed respectful notices. However, *By Love Possessed* did fail to get either the important National Book Award or the Pulitzer Prize; if the voting had been last fall, it probably would have. But this kind of mania seems to be cyclic and we are now recovering our wits.

One of the hardest things for an ex-patriate to get used to is our advertising. Not only that it's blatant and vulgar; it's that too but not so much as Europeans think, and often it's more sophisticated then their advertising. After all, we've been at it longer. In fact, judging by its ads, American capitalism is mature to the point of decadence. For several generations, our economy has been organized around consumption rather than production. The consumer has manfully, doggedly done his best. (*Life* once reported that the average American family has accumulated in its closets and on its shelves about 10,000 separate possessions; these constitute "a major problem of family life"—our national symbol is not the overflowing cornucopia but rather the overflowing wastebasket.) But by now the poor fellow is just picking at his plate. His appetite must be stimulated by outré refinements:

A left-handed check-book. An underwater scooter that motorizes lazy skin-divers ($350). The Executone, an inter-office communication system with "built-in courtesy"—about the only kind you get around an American office—that announces calls by "soft chime and signal light." A fountain pen that fills itself by capillary attraction. A toothpaste that is shot out by compressed air at the touch of a button (no more of that laborious squeezing), and another that comes out in red and white stripes. Parallel-O-Plate, a new window-glass that "keeps buildings from looking wrinkled." A beer-foaming machine that sends "a silent sound wave" (?) of "21,000 cycles a second" (??) through newly-filled bottles of beer and thus speeds up capping ($1,570). A heart-shaped electrical anti-snoring device called "Turn Over, Darling" that buzzes under the pillow of the party of the first part when the party of the second part presses a button ($10). A new girdle with the perhaps unfortunate name, "Open Sesame." An Esso lubricant that makes pop bottles shiny: "Oil research adds a bright note to your moments of pleasure. Take the clean, glistening bottle that lets the sparkle of a soft drink shine through. . . . " Etc., etc., etc.

In the balmy pre-Goldfine days, Sherman Adams, the "Assistant President," revealed that the actual President had asked "some able people" to work up "a world-wide cultural conference" on ways and means of Using Scientific Progress for Peace not War. (This is presumably a supplement to the guided missile program.) "Who is there who can say," asked Mr. Adams in one of the longest rhetorical questions since Demosthenes, "Who is there who can say that a convocation in this country of scholars, historians, artisans [sic], theologians, educators, sociologists, philosophers, artists, and musicians—representatives of the cultural pursuits of all the human race—meeting each other in their respective groups, could not suggest new and better ways for human beings to exist peaceably together and to reap the greatest rewards from man's scientific discoveries?" Well, I am one who can say they could not. And I can also tell the Research Society for Creative Altruism (founded by Professor Pitirim A. Sorokin of Harvard in 1949) which lately convened at the Massachusetts Institute of Technology to work out "a scientific approach to man's moral problems," that its efforts will come to naught. Unfortunately, space doesn't permit giving the reasons for these predictions, but of their accuracy there is, also unfortunately, no doubt whatsoever.

Last fall the New York Board of Education removed *Huckleberry Finn* from its approved text-book list for public schools because Negro groups had objected to its use of the term "nigger," as in "Miss Watson's big nigger named Jim." That the book is (in part) a protest against the indignity of slavery, that Jim is its moral hero—these trivia didn't weigh in the scale against "nigger." Doubtless Mark Twain should have had his backwoodsmen refer to "Miss Watson's big Negro named Jim." After this *putsch* against *Huckleberry Finn,* another news item appeared. In 1942, the National Association for the Advancement of Colored People met with the Motion Picture Producers Association to protest against "the stereotyped representation in films of Negroes as bumbling, comical characters." The protest was effective and fewer "undignified" roles were offered to Negro actors. In fact, fewer roles of any kind were offered to them: between 1945 and 1957 the number of Negro movie performers declined from 500 to 125. Last fall, the NAACP was therefore constrained to hold a second conference with the MPPA. "At the meeting," reports the *N.Y. Times,* "Mr. Wilkins, executive secretary of the NAACP, said 'misconceptions' had arisen [and] disavowed any intention on the part of the Association to act as a 'censor.' . . . He said there was no objection to Negro actors playing 'menial' characters, such as maids, butlers, or janitors, or being cast in comedy roles. He stressed that the Association wanted to dispel the notion that it insisted on a 'one-for-one policy,' whereby if a Negro were shown in a menial role there must also be a dignified representation of another Negro." In short, Mr. Wilkins climbed down. The arts are a chancey field for pressure groups, even ones with aims as admirable as those of the NAACP. Censorship has what our ad-writers would call a Built-In, Automatic Kick Back.

The *New Yorker* for October 26, 1957 contained some extremely important (and extremely disturbing) data on the American Way of Life: a lengthy article by Eugene Kinkead summarizing the findings of a team of Army experts, mostly psychiatrists, who have completed a man-by-man study of the 4,428 American soldiers who came back from Communist prison camps after the Korean war. The Army made the study to find out what lay behind two shocking statistics: (1) "roughly one out of every three American prisoners in Korea was guilty of some sort of collaboration with the enemy," and (2) over one-third of our war prisoners—2,730 out of 7,190—died in captivity. It was not starvation or hardship that caused the high American death rate—the Army report shows the Communists fed their prisoners fairly well.

"It is a sad fact, but it is a fact [said Major Anderson] that the men who were captured in large groups early in the war often became unmanageable. They refused to obey orders, and they cursed and sometimes struck officers who tried to enforce orders.

Naturally, the chaos was encouraged by the Communists, who told the captives . . . rank no longer existed [and] they were all equal as simple prisoners of war released from capitalist bondage. At first, the badly wounded suffered most. On the marches back from the line . . . casualties on litters were often callously abandoned beside the road. Able-bodied prisoners refused to carry them, even when their officers commanded them to do so. If a Communist guard ordered a litter shouldered, our men obeyed; otherwise, the wounded were left to die. . . . The strong regularly took food from the weak. . . . Many men were sick, and these men . . . were ignored, or worse. Dysentery was common in the camps and . . . on winter nights, helpless men with dysentery were rolled outside the huts by their comrades and left to die in the cold."

Many of the 2,730 prisoners who died, died because they simply lay down and gave up. It was partly that no one washed them, fed them, kept them on their feet—"I got mine—screw you, Jack!"—but it was also that they had lived too long in the land of plenty:

What struck Major Anderson most forcibly was the almost universal inability of the prisoners to adjust to a primitive situation. "They lacked the old Yankee resourcefulness. This was partly . . . the result of some new failure in the childhood and adolescent training of our young men—a new softness." For months . . . most prisoners displayed signs of shock, remaining within little shells they had created to protect them from reality. There was practically no communication among the men, and . . . very few seemed to be interested even in providing themselves with the basic necessities of food, warmth, and shelter. . . . "An American soldier goes into the field with comforts that the majority of the world's population doesn't have even at home," said Anderson. "The average prisoner seemed lost without a bottle of pills and a toilet that flushed."

So, too, with collaboration. The Army researchers found there had been "a fantastic amount of fraternizing with the enemy." The majority of American prisoners "yielded in some degree to Communist pressure." Quite a large majority--87 per cent, in fact. The basic reason was the same as that which had caused the high death rate, a lack of solidarity:

> Major Segal told me that most of the repatriates came home thinking of themselves not as a part of a group, bound by common loyalties, but as isolated individuals. This emerged in their response to questions about what their service unit had been. Where the Turks proudly gave their regiment and brigade the Americans were likely to respond with the number of their prison camp.

Thus the latest effective authority (as with the Americans obeying their Communist guards but not their own officers) is the one the isolated, rootless American obeys. This is not individualism, it might better be called floating collectivism. The Chinese Communists who ran the camps exploited it. They did not use physical brutality or executions, because these would have defeated their purposes, which were (minor) to control the prisoners with the least difficulty and (major) to affect their way of thinking. In this, they were successful: "Most returned prisoners expressed sincere gratitude for the way the Chinese treated them. . . . When they talked about politics, they often used the term 'Socialism' rather than 'Communism' . . . and many of them said that while Socialism might not work in the United States . . . it was a good thing for China and other less advanced nations [shades of Henry Wallace!]." Who but the Communists, and in fact the Chinese Communists, would have the boldness to use war prisoner camps as propaganda centers, and the subtlety to make it work? Of course, they knew their enemy, in this case, U.S., or us.

—1958

from surplus value to the mass-media
NORMAN MAILER

No one can work his way through *Das Kapital* without etching on his mind forever the knowledge that profit must come from loss—the lost energy of one human being paying for the comfort of another; if the process has become ten times more subtle, complex, and untraceable in the modern economy, and conceivably a hundred times more resistant to the careful analysis of the isolated radical, it is perhaps now necessary that some of us be so brash as to cut a trail of speculation across subjects as vast as the title of this piece.

Let me start with a trivial discrepancy. Today one can buy a can of frozen orange juice sufficient to make a quart for 30 cents. A carton of prepared orange juice, equal in quality, costs 45 cents. The difference in price is certainly not to be found by the value of the container, nor in the additional cost of labor and machinery which is required to squeeze the oranges, since the process which produces frozen orange juice is if any-thing more complex—the oranges must first be squeezed and then frozen. Of course orange juice which comes in quart cartons is more expensive to ship, but it is doubtful if this added cost could account for more than 2 or 3 cents in the price. (The factors are complex, but may reduce themselves as follows: The distributors for cartons of prepared orange juice are generally the milk companies who are saved most of the costs of local distribution by delivering the orange juice on their milk routes. While the cost of shipping whole oranges is greater, because of their bulk, than cans of frozen juice, it must be remembered that the largest expense in freight charges are loading and unloading, and the majority of freshly picked oranges have in any case to be shipped by freight to a freezer plant, converted, and shipped again.)

What is most likely is that the price is arrived at by some kind of developed if more or less unconscious estimation by the entrepreneur of what it is worth to the consumer not to be bothered with opening a can, mixing the frozen muddle with three cans of water, and shaking. It is probable that the additional 12 or 13 cents of unnecessary price rise has been calculated in some such ratio as this: the consumer's private pro-ductive time is worth much more to him than his social working time,

because his private productive time, that is the time necessary to perform his household functions, is time taken away from his leisure. If he
earns $3.00 an hour by his labor, it is probable that he values his leisure
time as worth ideally two or three times as much, let us say arbitrarily
$6.00 an hour, or 10 cents a minute. Since it would take three or four
minutes to turn frozen orange juice into drinkable orange juice, it may
well be that a covert set of values in the consumer equates the saving of 3
or 4 minutes to a saving of thirty or forty *ideal* cents of his pleasure-time.
To pay an extra 12 actual cents in order to save this forty ideal cents
seems fitting to his concept of value. Of course, he has been deprived of
10 actual cents—the extra comfort should have deprived him of no more
than two of his actual cents. So the profit was extracted here from
a disproportionate exploitation of the consumer's need to protect his
pleasure-time rather than from an inadequate repayment to the worker
for his labor. (Such contradictions to this thesis as the spate of Do-It-
Yourself hobbies, or magazine articles about the problem of what to do
with leisure are of too serious a nature to dismiss with a remark—it can
however be suggested that the general hypothesis may not be contradicted: the man who is bored with his leisure time, or so industrious as
to work at handicrafts, can still resent those inroads upon his leisure
which he has not chosen. Indeed it might be argued that the tendency
to be attracted to private labor-saving devices is greatest in the man who
doesn't know what to do with himself when he is at home.)

At any rate, if the hypothesis sketched here should prove to have any
economic validity, the consequences are worth remarking. When the
source of profit is extracted more and more (at one remove or another)
from the consumer's at-home working-time, the consumer is paying a
disproportionate amount for the desire to work a little less in his leisure-
time. Over the economy as a whole, this particular germ of profit may
still be miniscule, but it is not at all trivial once one includes the
expenses of the war economy whose costs are paid by taxation, an
indirect extraction of leisure-time from the general consumer, who then
has noticeably less money in his leisure to pursue the sports, occupations, and amusements which will restore to his body the energy he has
spent in labor. (To take the matter into its real complexity, the con-
flicting anxieties of living in a war-and-pleasure-oriented environment

opens most men and women to a daily spate of psychic havoc whose damages can be repaired only by the adequate exercise of a *personal* leisure appropriate to each, exactly that leisure which the war economy must impoverish.)

By this logic, the root of capitalist exploitation has shifted from the proletariat-at-work to the mass-at-leisure who now may lose so much as four or five *ideal* hours of extra leisure a day. The old exploitation was vertical—the poor supported the rich. To this vertical exploitation must now be added the horizontal exploitation of the mass by the State and by Monopoly, a secondary exploitation which is becoming more essential to a modern capitalist economy than the direct exploitation of the proletariat. If the origin of this secondary exploitation has come out of the proliferation of the machine with its consequent and relative reduction of the size of the proletariat and the amount of surplus value to be accumulated, the exploitation of mass-leisure has been accelerated by the relative contraction of the world market. Through the post-war years, prosperity has been maintained in America by invading the wage-earner in his home. Nineteenth century capitalism could still find its profit in the factory; when the worker was done, his body might be fatigued but his mind could look for a diversion which was relatively free of the industry for which he worked. So soon, however, as the surplus labor of the proletariat comes to be replaced by the leisure-value given up by the consumer, the real expropriator of the wage-earner has to become the mass-media; for if the domination of leisure-time is more significant to the health of the economy than the exploitation of the working-time, the stability of the economy derives more from manipulating the psychic character of leisure than forcibly subjecting the working class to its productive role. It is likely that the survival of capitalism is no longer possible without the creation in the consumer of a series of psychically disruptive needs which circle about such wants and emotions as the desire for excessive security, the alleviation of guilt, the lust for comfort and new commodity, and a consequent allegiance to the vast lie about the essential health of the State and the economy, an elaborated fiction whose bewildering interplay of real and false detail must devil the mass into a progressively more imperfect apperception of reality and thus drive them closer to apathy, violence, and psychosis. Nineteenth century capitalism exhausted the life of millions of workers;

twentieth century capitalism can well end by destroying the mind of civilized man.

If there is a future for the radical spirit, which often enough one can doubt, it can come only from a *new* revolutionary vision of society and its sicknesses, its strengths, its conflicts, contradictions and radiations, its self-created incapacity to solve its evasions of human justice. There is the root of the social problem. An injustice half-corrected results in no more than a new sense of injustice and suppressed violence in both parties, which is why revolutionary situations are meaningful and liberal situations are not, for liberal solutions end by compromising a society in the nausea of its past and so bog the mass-mind further into the institutionalization of social habits and methods for which no one has faith, and from which one cannot extract the psychic marrow of culture upon which everyone in a civilization must depend. If this revolutionary vision is to be captured by any of us in a work of works, can one guess that this time it will explore not nearly so far into that jungle of political economy which Marx charted and so opened to rapid development, but rather will engage the empty skies, dead spaces, and sentimental cancers of that mass-media whose internal contradictions twist and quarter us between the lust of the economy (which radiates a greed-to-consume into us, with sex as the invisible salesman) and the guilt of the economy which must chill us with authority, charities for incurable disease, and all reminders that the mass consumer is only on drunken furlough from the ordering disciplines of church, F.B.I., and War.

—1959

SIXTIES

The big changes in Harlem are in the people I know who have changed my sympathy to respect and admiration. If you've ever known a junkie for any length of time, you'll understand the struggle he has to go through to get off the poison kick. He can't leave the world entirely, so for him to become master and dispenser of the thing that ruled him for so long and so destructively is a great achievement. Harlem still has a much greater number of the miserable than any place else I know. This is inspiring also. Where else can one find so many people in such pain and so few crying about it?

Claude Brown, "Harlem, My Harlem," 1961

foreword

TODD GITLIN

In the heat of the Sixties—and it sometimes felt as though the Sixties were nothing but heat—moral and political positions went incendiary. The political was personal. Families and friendships broke down; so did organizations, institutions, and movements. As new social forces emerged and old social forces retrenched, arguments easily degenerated into shouting matches. Family life, in other words.

Reading *Dissent* then felt like family life—mine, anyway—and then some. It was often a stirring experience, sometimes a frustrating one. Overall it was a challenge to pieties. Of course how you judged the challenges depended on whether the pieties were your own. Early on in the decade, reading the magazine as a college student, I rejoiced in *Dissent*'s seriousness. It dwelled on political fundamentals. It followed no party line. It was sober, unillusioned, at times a bit utopian. A lot of its social criticism was deep, unpredictable, trenchant. (I was especially drawn to Paul Goodman's work.) I was pleased to read radicals who criticized the Communist world, and took its dissidents seriously, yet didn't succumb to paranoia. I thought other articles credulous about the beneficence of American foreign policy, especially on Cuba.

Still, I respected *Dissent*'s editors for their openness to wide-ranging debate on foreign policy. So, too, during my year as president of Students for a Democratic Society, 1963–64, and the subsequent year I spent helping to organize the first national demonstration against the Vietnam War. Later in the decade, the journal felt at times retrograde on Vietnam. As the new left veered toward revolutionary fantasy, I, a relative skeptic, left *Dissent* behind. In this unwise judgment I was not alone. True, sometimes *Dissent* was intemperate—as who wasn't? In retrospect, *Dissent*'s skepticism about the new left's hallucinatory self-hypnosis was far more right than wrong.

The four articles at hand exhibit *Dissent* at its best during that period. All explore problems of strategy, the ugly duckling of political life, and do so with a high order of moral and intellectual seriousness. Strategy governs how people try to multiply their strengths and manage their weaknesses, but questions of strategy are hard to approach honestly, because everyone, to some degree is self-serving, welcomes bravado, and gives short shrift to the opposition. In and around movements, people develop passionate attachments to their positions, but too often these attachments take the form of statements and restatements of moral convictions. The quality of the disputes is brought low into a sort of he-said-she-said back-and-forth, where passions substitute for analysis and wishes for sharp appraisals.

But *Dissent,* at its best, practiced heresy with brains, believing that strategic questions were so important that they deserved the highest journalistic and argumentative rigor. So what strikes me about the four articles here is not just the positions they take but the way they go about taking them. They are mainly attentive to reasons why serious people might disagree. They attempt to grasp the social and political setting in which the debates are taking place. They are philosophically sophisticated but at the same time jargon-free. They are all prophetic: some of the immediate questions have faded—like the draft and war-tax refusal— but the larger contours of these debates still matter, even urgently.

Michael Walzer's 1960 report on the North Carolina sit-ins is wonderfully observant. This is fresh though modest journalism about the fresh activity that launched the other movements of the decade and transformed the tenor of American life. Unfancily, Walzer captures the moral quality of the protest, the activists' spirit and mood, the significance of their nonviolence and the religious sensibility that marked what he called "the new temper." He suggests the moral force and tensile strength of the civil rights movement which, in turn, kindled all the other movements that made the sixties a turning point in the history of human freedom.

Irving Howe's fierce polemic on radical style, highly controversial when it appeared in 1965, prefigures generational and political tensions that would soon prove explosive. At the time, many of us in the new left read him defensively. Here was a challenge to be repelled, even if Howe was at pains to say that he was singling out "a segment or fringe," not a majority of the new radicals. He not only condemned the gestural politics of lefter-than-thou, he was interested in its roots. Within a few years, the fringe had spread, and Howe's article read—and continues to read—prophetically. He was early to recognize the importance of style as a basis for politics—style instead of strategy, style masquerading as strategy. He was, if you will, prematurely anti-stylish.

Bayard Rustin's 1966 critique of Black Power also outlasts its occasion, for it anticipates the recklessness with which a growing critical mass of activists isolated themselves. In this early attempt at a sociology of black scorn toward Jews and cops, Rustin was fearless. You needn't follow his every move to appreciate his no-nonsense vigor and commonsense wisdom at a time when revolutionary political fantasy was rife. Two years later, the catastrophic collision between black nationalists and Jewish teachers was to crack the chances of liberal coalition for a generation.

Vietnam was, of course, the moral morass of the decade, and it is instructive to follow Michael Harrington's 1969 reasoning on questions of conscientious objection and civil disobedience. Again, the point is not that his positions are wholly, irresistibly right, but that he wrote transparently about factors that needed considering, and carefully about the political and moral consequences of direct action. In politics, pure goodness and intense will weren't—aren't—enough.

Thus did *Dissent* hurl itself into the fires looking for light. Sometimes it emerged tempered, sometimes simply hot and smoky. Remarkably often, it found light.

a cup of coffee and a seat
MICHAEL WALZER

Durham, North Carolina is probably a town like many others; I doubt that ordinarily I would have found it unfamiliar. I saw it, however, only at night and carried away only two memories. The first is of a drug store with its lunch counter closed, where I did not get a cup of coffee. The second is of a policeman to whom I showed an address, who did not give me directions. The address was that of a Negro church where Martin Luther King was speaking at 8:00 that evening, February 16. The policeman said he had never heard of the street. Later I learned it was the main street in the Negro section of town.

Two days later I was in Raleigh, a half hour by bus from Durham. Raleigh is a handsome town; its main street, dominated by the state capitol, is wide and spacious; the store fronts are plain, not gaudy. In front of four of those stores some twenty Negro students were picketing. As a Northerner I expected, and felt, the tenseness of the city. The day before there had been a fight on the picket lines and a Negro boy had been hit with a tire chain. What I found there, by talking to Negro students and visiting their colleges, was a spirit and a method of action which made such incidents . . . incidental. Dangerous they were—and are—but they are not the key to the sitdowns. For the Negro students, like the earlier Montgomery bus boycotters, are engaged in a new kind of political activity, at once unconventional and non-violent.

Late in the afternoon of Monday, February 1, four freshmen from the Agricultural and Technical College, an all-Negro school in Greensboro, North Carolina, walked into a downtown Woolworth's, purchased a few small articles and then sat down at the lunch counter. Not one of them had ever sat there before. They each asked for a cup of coffee and were told that they would not be served. This was the customary policy of the store: "We don't serve colored here." Yet the students refused to leave; they remained seated, and ignored, until 5:30 when the store closed. The next morning at 10:30 the freshmen reappeared with sixteen friends and resumed their sitdown. Again they were not served. Again they did not leave until 5:30. During the seven hours they studied or talked quietly. The counter in front of them was not covered with the usual cups and saucers but with books, notebooks, sliderules. Several policemen came in and walked up and down the aisle that ran the length of the lunch counter, staring at the sitdowners. There was no disturbance; nor were the students intimidated.

On the third day the Negroes occupied virtually all the forty seats at the Woolworth's counter. Describing that day one student wrote:

> After attending a mass meeting in Harrison Auditorium, I was . . . inspired to go down to Woolworth's and just sit, hoping to be served. . . . By luck I was able to get a ride with six other fellows. We rode down to the parking lot and there left the car, after which we walked to Woolworth's, read a passage from the Bible and waited for the doors to open. The doors opened and in we went. I almost ran, because I was determined to get a seat and I was very much interested in being the first to sit down. I sat down and there was a waitress standing directly in front of me, so I asked her if I might have a cup of black coffee and two donuts please. She looked at me and moved to another area of the counter.

The number of sitdowners continued to increase, spilling over into other chain stores. A few white sympathizers joined in—an act of considerable bravery in the South. Finally the lunch counter was closed. The students agreed to a two-week "truce"; the manager agreed to negotiate. At this writing, a full month later, the counter remains closed.

Sitdown in the South has a very literal meaning. In the past, the variety and five and dime stores have freely invited Negroes to every counter but the lunch counter. There they were not permitted to sit down on any of the long row of stools, but were served standing up at a far end. Negroes were often hired to cook the food or to wash dishes, hard jobs and especially in restaurants of this sort. But the counter was a color line: on the side with seats only whites sat.

As in the buses, sitting down together at a lunch counter symbolizes a kind of equality which Southern whites have not been prepared to admit. Nor have Southern Negroes, until very recently, been prepared to demand it. Now the sitdowns have made clear the immediate and central issue in the integration battle. "We don't want brotherhood," a Negro student told me when I visited Durham, "we just want a cup of coffee—sitting down." This was a demand for an end to the ordinary, unrecorded, day-to-day indignity of Negro life in the South—an indignity more demoralizing, perhaps, than the terror of lynching or murder has ever been. The A&T students were "tired of humiliation." The method which they found in their "tiredness" was so dramatically effective that in the week following their demonstration, sitdowns were staged in half a dozen North Carolina towns and within two weeks had spread to more than twelve cities in four states: Virginia, Tennessee and the Carolinas. The sitdowns spread unpredictably; it is obvious that there was no central organization. Yet it is not entirely fair to call the movement spontaneous. "*In a way,*" one student said, "*we have been planning it all our lives.*"

Everywhere the pattern was more or less the same. The Negro students, well-dressed and quiet, came into the stores—always the local branches of national chains—and sat down at the lunch counters. They were jeered at more frequently as news of the demonstrations spread, but did not reply. There were occasional fights. The counters were closed or roped off after a day, sometimes after only an hour; signs were posted saying "Closed for repairs," or "Closed in the interest of public safety." At this point in many of the towns a mayor's committee hastened to arrange some sort of negotiations. For a moment the students were confused: they could not continue their sitdowns once the counters were closed, yet they had a deeply ingrained distrust of Southern negotiation. "If we negotiate," the editor of a Negro college paper told me, "my grandchildren will still be worrying about that cup of coffee."

Now, in the last few days of February, action has been resumed; picketing, boycott, mass marches are the new methods of the students. Their activity continues to be orderly, disciplined, non-violent. Yet the number of incidents, usually provoked by white hecklers, has increased; several students have been attacked and beaten up; many more have been arrested. Negro high-school students have imitated their older brothers, but in larger numbers and without the same organization or discipline. And in the meantime, the movement has spread to the deep

South; sitdown demonstrations have taken place in South Carolina and Alabama.

I asked every student I met what the first day of the sitdowns had been like on his campus. The answer was always the same: "It was like a fever. Everyone wanted to go. We were so happy." In Durham students were still pouring into town after the original sitdowners had closed the counters and started home. The two groups met with cheers, many of the students raised two fingers in the air for victory. The news from Greensboro was spread rapidly by the press and radio; more effectively, it spread along the basketball circuit. Most of the schools involved in the early weeks were athletic rivals; basketball games were occasions for the transfer of enthusiasm. A&T played five games in two weeks and students at each of the five schools were shortly involved in sitdowns.

Organization on each new campus was amazingly rapid, accompanied by the usual bickering over leadership positions ("Everyone wanted to be on a committee"), but fundamentally shaped by a keen sense of solidarity. The student council was usually at the center of what was invariably called, with no self-consciousness, the Student Movement. Sometimes command was assumed by the campus NAACP, sometimes by an *ad hoc* committee. Few students talked about anything else; the seemingly endless discussions of tactics among the leaders and within the committees were repeated in the dorms, in the canteen, in the local (illegal) beer hall. Even in the last it seemed to dominate the more usual topics: basketball and girls.

After the counters had been shut in Durham and negotiations begun with a "human relations committee" appointed by the mayor, a sign appeared on the door of the student council office at North Carolina College: "*Please stand by for further instructions concerning movement. (signed) Leaders.*"

The office really looked like a room from which a movement was being run. A bulletin board extended the length of one wall. Newspaper articles about sitdowns throughout the state were posted, along with various notices, instructions and a few recently received CORE pamphlets. Piled high on the desk of one of the council officers were schedules filled out by more than 500 students, listing their free hours so that the sitdowners could be relieved and a minimum of classes missed. The office was almost never empty; students came in to hear the latest news, do a little work, or jubilantly read their clippings.

When I reached the council office at Shaw University in Raleigh it was even busier. The students at Shaw and at nearby St. Augustine's College had been the first to begin picketing once the lunch counters had closed. I visited the office on the sixth day of picketing. Two old desks stood at either end of a rectangular room; chairs lined the longer sides. At one of the desks a girl sat, checking the pickets in and out and arranging transportation into town. The students sat around, waiting for their rides, the boys restless, the girls more quiet.

The placards they would carry stood on a ledge along the wall: "*Do we eat today?*" "*How do we get invited to lunch?*" "*Temporarily closed. Why? Just a cup of coffee. Shame!*" "*Let's be Just for a change. No traditions attached.*" At about ten o'clock the first carload of pickets, four girls and three boys, drove downtown. Before they left they received instructions which I heard repeated many times that day: "Walk in a single file. Don't bunch up. Don't talk. We'll get relief out." It was pouring outside; it rained all day and well into the night.

At the other desk sat a boy from Jamaica, small, smart, a member of the Intelligence Committee which was running things at Shaw. He was there all day. "We say we don't cut classes," a student told me, "our teachers say we don't cut classes; but we cut classes." On the desk in front of the Jamaican boy were a few old textbooks, left there by student pickets. Among them I found a copy of Big Bill Haywood's *Autobiography*, with the bookmark near to the end. The Jamaican boy knew about Haywood, but wouldn't talk to me about him. He spent the day—when he wasn't on the phone—reading an Ibsen play.

Posted on a wall over one of the desks was a giant placard headed "Shaw University-St. Augustine College Student Movement." The placard was covered with a detailed diagram of the movement's organization, which looked as if it had been copied out of a textbook on bureaucracy. At the center was the Intelligence Committee; straight lines pointing downward connected it with the student councils of the two cooperating colleges; lines radiated upwards to various subsidiary committees: transportation, negotiation, etc.

Every night since the sitdowns started, the Intelligence Committee had called mass meetings at both Shaw and St. Augustine's. Together the two schools have about one thousand students; Shaw, slightly larger, is a Baptist school, St. Augustine's Episcopalian. The meetings have been marvelously well attended. But the night I was there the rain was pouring down outside, and only about 200 students assembled in the Shaw auditorium; there were seats for twice as many. The leaders were immediately afraid that student enthusiasm was waning and sent runners to the library and dorms. Meanwhile the meeting began, with a prayer from the floor and the singing of a hymn. The president of the student council called it "our national anthem"; the hymn had as its appropriate refrain: "March on, march on, until victory is won."

There was a leak in the roof of the auditorium and throughout the meeting, during singing and speech making, I could hear the water sloshing about in a giant bucket perched precariously upon two seats about halfway to the back of the room.

In the middle of a report on the size of the picket lines that day, the entire basketball team shuffled sheepishly into the hall; they were dragged along by the captain of one of the picketing groups. He rushed to the front of the auditorium and began denouncing the players for practicing during mass meetings. One of the players, obviously no militant at all, tried to defend the team: "We can't disrupt the whole basketball schedule," he said, "for just one movement." But he was shouted down and the student who had dragged him in took the floor again to display a remarkable talent for oratory. There had not been enough men on the lines that day, he said. (In general the girls were more ardent about picketing than the boys.) Several girls had been pushed, one had been slapped, by white men. That would never have happened had enough male students been walking. There could be no excuses; the girls needed protection, and—after all—the boys might meet their future wives "in the movement."

The students in Greensboro called their demonstration a "passive sitdown demand." What was most impressive about it, however, was the number of students it involved in *activity*. None of the leaders I spoke to were interested in test cases; nor was there any general agreement to stop the sitdowns or the picketing once the question of integration at the lunch counters was taken up by the courts. That the legal work of the NAACP was important, everyone agreed; but this, I was told over and over again, was more important. Everyone seemed to feel a deep need finally to act in the name of all the theories of equality. Once the sitdowns had begun, marching into Woolworth's or picketing outside became obvious, necessary, inevitable activities.

After a week or more of comparative neutrality, the police also began to act, supported by an interpretation of the trespassing law provided by the attorney-general of North Carolina. In that "liberal" state where race relations—so the newspapers but not the Negro students said—were "good," state officials, like the store managers, had at first declined to take the students seriously. They had no real contact with Negro students and were hardly capable of understanding their new temper. During the first week the Greensboro newspaper periodically announced that the sit-downers were losing both numbers and staying power. Someone compared their activity to college panty raids; it was all a prank. But as the movement began to spread, the astonished whites took a harder line. On Thursday of the second week, 43 students were arrested in Raleigh, charged with trespassing on private property. The story of those arrests reveals better than anything I know the nature of the student movement. It was told to me by a boy at Shaw University in a slow deliberate drawl with an undertone of pure joy.

On Wednesday, the Shaw-St. Augustine students had shut down the lunch counters at four stores on Fayetteville Street, a few blocks from the state house. The following day a small group of more ambitious students started out to Cameron Village, a suburban shopping center. There they were told that the entire center, including streets and side-walks, was private property. They telephoned to the council office and someone consulted a Negro lawyer in Raleigh. He told them that the streets and sidewalks were public; he thought the police interpretation of the trespassing law should be tested. Fifteen more students drove out to the center. They were window-shopping when the vice-president of Cameron Village Inc. appeared on the scene with a single policeman. The students were officially notified that they were trespassing and given two minutes to leave. At the end of the two minutes—the vice-president looking at his watch—the policeman arrested one of the students. Apparently he thought that would be sufficient, for it would provide a test case. *But the other students refused to leave; they crowded around the policeman and demanded that they too be arrested.* One by one they were asked to leave and given two minutes. They waited their turns. When five had been arrested the policeman phoned for a paddy wagon. Eighteen students were under arrest when it arrived. Later twenty-five more came out to Cameron Village to "windowshop." When the news of the first arrests reached campus, there had been a rush for cars. "Everyone wanted to be arrested."

Two weeks later when the now famous forty-three came up for trial, so many of their fellow-students jammed into the courtroom, that the judge postponed the case. The fire chief said that the crowd constituted a fire hazard. Perhaps it did. But the remarkable solidarity of the Negroes constituted a far greater danger to white supremacy. In Tennessee where some eighty sitdowners were fined for "disorderly conduct," thousands of Negroes gathered on the courthouse steps singing hymns and the national anthem. Inside, the sitdowners insisted that they would all go to jail rather than pay the fines.

The fact that many of the Negro colleges were state supported has provided an obvious opportunity for North Carolina politicians to bluster and threaten. At first it was only the college presidents who were under attack; later students were threatened with expulsion. The attorney-general of the state—now a candidate for governor—is widely quoted among Negro students as having said, "If these administrators can't control the kids, we'll get administrators who can." The result of such threats has been that students have sometimes had to fight on two fronts: both in the stores and on the campus—and the fight has become both complicated and confusing. When I left Durham negotiations were in progress between a committee appointed by the mayor, which could not speak definitely for the chain store managers, and a committee appointed by the president of North Carolina College, on which the sitdowners were not represented. Having closed the lunch counters downtown, the students returned to campus and began circulating a petition against their president's committee.

At North Carolina College, Durham, three young men led the student movement. They were described to me by the editor of the campus paper as the righteous man, the prudent man and the proud man. The righteous man most fully embodied the spirit of the movement. He was a veteran and had spent two years in Japan. That was the only time in his life, he told me, when he had lived like a free man. When it was time to come home, the white boys were happy and he was afraid. Now he led the younger students with a quiet determination; he was the only one of the leaders I met who clearly possessed charisma. "We won't stop, regardless . . ." And he took the strongest position I heard on the confusing problem of negotiations. "If I have to negotiate for a cup of coffee, I won't pay for it. I won't negotiate across the table and then again across the counter."

The most remarkable thing about these students is their self-confidence. They have grown up in a South which is no longer a terror for them, but still a continual source of insult and indignity. They have been in the army or spent time in the North—summers at church camps, a year working in New York, a visit to relatives. They have developed thin skins; segregation is no longer tolerable to them. They have unlearned, perhaps they never learned, those habits of inferiority which have cursed Negro life in the South for a century. They have felt every insult—as an insult. They could not understand the "complacency" or the "fearfulness" of their parents. Students told me many times that their parents had been "brainwashed." "When the insurance man comes to the door," one boy said, "he asks, 'Is Thomas there?' I tell him my father's name is Mister Brown. But my father answers to Thomas and says yes, sir."

Less than twenty years ago, in the early forties, a Negro soldier was shot and killed by a Durham bus driver when he refused to move to the back of the bus. The bus driver was acquitted by an all white jury. I learned this from a white man, a German refugee who taught philosophy to the Negro students of North Carolina College. Not one of the students mentioned the murder. Instead they told one story after another about more minor but to them terribly important incidents in the buses, in stores, on the job. The stories usually ended with some version of: "I ran out of that store. I almost cried . . ." One student told how he had held a door open for a white woman who refused to come through. "I slammed the door. I stopped being courteous."

The schools I visited had one-third to one-half Northern students, most of them from Pennsylvania, New York and New Jersey. But it was the Southern students who were supplying the fervor which kept the movement going. And among the Southern students it was especially the girls—perhaps because they are less mobile, more likely to stay South. The Northerners were often too blasé or too cynical to play a major part in the fight for integration. The Southerners were more militant (and more religious), committed to a long and gruelling struggle. None of them seemed to expect anything else. It probably is hard to be a Negro in the South and grow up naive. So their every act seems to have something of calculation in it: on the buses in Durham I noticed older Negroes moving as if by habit towards the back, while the Negro college students sat as far front as possible. And this surely was an act of will; one boy told me that after being insulted once, he had not ridden a bus for two years.

At a mass meeting of more than 1500 Negro adults in Durham a young woman from a Methodist church sang a hymn whose refrain (I may not have it exactly) was: "Give me Jesus, you can have all this world." The words did not seem appropriate at a meeting whose purpose was so emphatically to win a place for the Negro *in* this world. Yet it revealed the tone of the meeting almost as surely as did the chant begun by Martin Luther King: We just want to be free. A religion which seizes upon, dramatizes and even explains the suffering of the Negro people is joined here to an essentially political movement to end that suffering. Out of that combination, I believe, comes the stamina, the endurance so necessary for passive, non-violent resistance. The new self-confidence of the young people, however, is as important, and among them I found occasional discontent with "camp-fire religion." One boy told me that for King passive resistance might be a faith, but for him it was only a strategy. Another boy, smiling, said that he expected God to help the student movement, but meanwhile the students "would help the hell out of God." Though the press has played up the role of divinity students in the sitdowns, I discovered that most of the leaders on the campus were sociology, psychology, economics and physics majors. And yet for all of them, religion is a habit whose forms are fortifying and strengthening. Prayers and hymns are normal features of student meetings.

Several students I spoke with had read Gandhi, more had read about him. But I rarely felt Gandhi present among these Negroes as a significant or potent symbol. It was the Montgomery bus boycott, coming in their early manhood, that had been the decisive event. On the other hand, I have never encountered students so "up" on the law; many of them could literally recite every important court decision since school integration was ordered. Passive resistance and endless legal action were the two political forms with which they were familiar. I was a little surprised to find virtually nothing special—nothing Southern, nothing Negro—in their views of the presidential candidates. A few said they would not vote; a few said they would never again vote Democratic. Many more engaged me in discussions as to the relative merits of Kennedy and Stevenson. Presidential politics seemed to them a universe apart from sitdown, picketing, student solidarity.

For the Negro student these new forms of political activity were a kind of self-testing and proving. Each new sitdown, each day of picketing, each disciplined march, each mass meeting was cause for pride and exhilaration. White students who were willing to participate were welcomed. But I attended two long meetings between Negro and white students at neighboring colleges (most of the students had never met before) and I never heard a Negro ask, or even hint, that whites should join their picket lines. It will be better for *them,* and for us, I was told, if they come unasked. The boy who said this was the same one who had told me that what he wanted was not brotherhood, but a cup of coffee. He was right of course, it is not necessary to feel fraternal towards the man you sit beside at a Woolworth's lunch counter. But what about the man you walk beside in a picket line? For it is there, I believe, on the line, that real equality is finally being won.

—1960

new styles in "leftism"
IRVING HOWE

There is a new radical mood in limited sectors of American society: on the campus, in sections of the civil rights movement. The number of people who express this mood is not very large, but that it should appear at all is cause for encouragement and satisfaction. Yet there is a segment or fringe among the newly blossoming young radicals that causes one disturbance—and not simply because they have ideas different from persons like myself, who neither expect nor desire that younger generations of radicals should repeat our thoughts or our words. For this disturbing minority I have no simple name: Sometimes it looks like kamikaze radicalism, sometimes like white Malcolmism, sometimes like black Maoism. But since none of these phrases will quite do, I have had to fall back upon the loose and not very accurate term, "New Leftists." Let me therefore stress as strongly as I can that I am not talking about all or the majority of the American young and not-so-young who have recently come to regard themselves as radicals.

The form I have felt obliged to use here—a composite portrait of the sort of New Leftist who seems to me open to criticism—also creates some difficulties. It may seem to lump together problems, ideas, and moods that should be kept distinct. If some young radicals read this text and feel that much of it does not pertain to them, I will be delighted by such a response.

The society we live in fails to elicit the idealism of the more rebellious and generous young. Even among those who play the game and accept the social masks necessary for gaining success, there is a widespread disenchantment. Certainly there is very little of the joy that comes from a conviction that the values of a society are good, and it is therefore good to live by them. The intelligent young know that if they keep out of trouble, accept academic drudgery, and preserve a respectable "image," they can hope for successful careers, even if not personal gratification. But the price they must pay for this choice is a considerable quantity of inner adaptation to the prevalent norms: There is a limit to the social duplicity that anyone can sustain.

The society not only undercuts the possibilities of constructive participation, it also makes very difficult a coherent and thought-out political opposition. The small minority that does rebel tends to adopt a stance that seems to be political, sometimes even ideological, but often turns out to be little more than an effort to assert a personal style.

Personal style: That seems to me a key. Most of whatever rebellion we have had up to—and even into—the civil rights movement takes the form of a decision on how to live individually within this society, rather than how to change it collectively. A recurrent stress among the young has been upon differentiation of speech, dress, and appearance, by means of which a small elite can signify its special status; or the stress has been upon moral self-regeneration, a kind of Emersonianism with shock treatment. All through the fifties and sixties disaffiliation was a central impulse both as a signal of nausea and a tacit recognition of impotence.

Now, to a notable extent, all this has changed since and through the civil rights movement—*but not changed as much as may seem*. Some of the people involved in that movement show an inclination to make of their radicalism not a politics of common action, which would require the inclusion of saints, sinners, and ordinary folk, but rather a gesture of moral rectitude. And the paradox is that they often sincerely regard themselves as committed to politics—but a politics that asserts so unmodulated and total a dismissal of society, while also departing from Marxist expectations of social revolution, that little is left to them but the glory or burden of maintaining a distinct personal style.

By contrast, the radicalism of an earlier generation, despite numerous faults, had at least this advantage: It did not have to start *as if* from scratch, there were available movements, parties, agencies, and patterns of thought through which one could act. The radicals of the thirties certainly had their share of bohemianism, but their politics were not nearly so interwoven with and dependent upon tokens of style as is today's radicalism.

The great value of the present rebelliousness is that it requires a personal decision, not merely as to what one shall do but also as to what one shall be. It requires authenticity, a challenge to the self, or, as some young people like to say, an "existential" decision. And it makes more difficult the moral double-bookkeeping of the thirties, whereby in the name of a sanctified movement or unquestioned ideology, scoundrels and fools could be exalted as "leaders" and detestable conduct exonerated.

This is a real and very impressive strength, but with it there goes a significant weakness: the lack of clear-cut ideas, sometimes even a feeling that it is wrong—or worse, "middle-class"—to think systematically, and as a corollary, the absence of a social channel or agency through which to act. At first it seemed as if the civil rights movement would provide such a channel; and no person of moral awareness can fail to be profoundly moved by the outpouring of idealism and the readiness to face danger which characterizes the vanguard of this movement. Yet at a certain point it turns out that the civil rights movement, through the intensity of its work, seems to dramatize . . . its own insufficiency. Indeed, it acts as a training school for experienced, gifted, courageous people who have learned how to lead, how to sacrifice, how to work, but have no place in which to enlarge upon their gifts.

The more shapeless, the more promiscuously absorptive, the more psychologically and morally slack the society becomes, the more must candidates for rebellion seek extreme postures which will enable them to "act out" their distance from a society that seems intent upon a maliciously benevolent assimilation; extreme postures which will yield security, perhaps a sense of consecration, in loneliness; extreme postures which will safeguard them from the allure of everything they reject. Between the act of rebellion and the society against which it is directed, there remain, however, deeper ties than is commonly recognized. To which we shall return.

These problems are exacerbated by an educational system that often seems inherently schizoid. It appeals to the life of the mind, yet justifies that appeal through crass utilitarianism. It invokes the traditions of freedom, yet processes students to bureaucratic cut. It speaks for the spirit, yet increasingly becomes an appendage of a spirit-squashing system.

New Leftism appears at a moment when the intellectual and academic worlds—and not they alone—are experiencing an intense and largely justifiable revulsion against the immediate American past. Many people are sick unto death of the whole structure of feeling—that mixture of chauvinism, hysteria, and demagogy—which was created during the cold war years. Like children subjected to forced feeding, they regurgitate almost automatically. Their response is an inevitable consequence of overorganizing the propaganda resources of a modern state; the same sort of nausea exists among the young in the Communist world.

Unfortunately, revulsion seldom encourages nuances of thought or precise discriminations of politics. You cannot stand the deceits of official anti-Communism? Then respond with a rejection equally blatant. You have been raised to give credit to every American power move, no matter how reactionary or cynical? Then respond by castigating everything American. You are weary of Sidney Hook's messages in *The New York Times Magazine?* Then respond as if talk about Communist totalitarianism were simply irrelevant or a bogey to frighten infants.

Yet we should be clear in our minds that such a response is not at all the same as a commitment to Communism, even though it may lend itself to obvious exploitation. It is rather a spewing out of distasteful matter—in the course of which other values, such as the possibility of learning from the traumas and tragedies of recent history, may also be spewed out.

Generational clashes are recurrent in our society, perhaps in any society. But the present rupture between the young and their elders seems especially deep. This is a social phenomenon that goes beyond our immediate subject, indeed it cuts through the whole of society; what it signifies is the society's failure to transmit with sufficient force its values to the young, or, perhaps more accurately, that the best of the young take the proclaimed values of their elders with a seriousness which leads them to be appalled by their violation in practice.

In rejecting the older generations, however, the young sometimes betray the conditioning mark of the very American culture they are so quick to denounce. For ours is a culture that celebrates youthfulness as if it were a moral good in its own right. Like the regular Americans they wish so hard not to be, yet, through wishing, so very much are, they believe that the past is mere dust and ashes and that they can start afresh, immaculately.

A generation is missing in the life of American radicalism, the generation that would now be in its late thirties, the generation that did not show up. The result is an inordinate difficulty in communication between the young radicals and those unfortunate enough to have reached—or, God help us, even gone beyond—the age of forty. Here, of course, our failure is very much in evidence too: a failure that should prompt us to speak with modesty, simply as people who have tried, and in their trying perhaps have learned something.

Let me specify a few characteristic attitudes among the New Leftists:

1.   *An extreme, sometimes unwarranted, hostility toward liberalism.* They see liberalism only in its current version, institutional, corporate, and debased; but avoiding history, they know very little about the elements of the liberal tradition which should remain valuable for any democratic socialist. And thereby they would cut off the resurgent American radicalism from what is, or should be, one of its sustaining sources: the tradition that has yielded us a heritage of civil freedoms, disinterested speculation, humane tolerance.

2.   *An impatience with the problems that concerned an older generation of radicals.* Here the generational conflict breaks out with strong feelings on both sides, the older people feeling threatened in whatever they have been able to salvage from past experiences, the younger people feeling the need to shake off dogma and create their own terms of action.

There are traditional radical topics which no one, except the historically minded, need trouble with. To be unconcerned with the dispute in the late twenties over the Anglo-Russian Trade Union Committee or the differences between Lenin and Luxembourg on the "national question"—well and good. These are not quite burning problems of the moment. But *some* of the issues hotly debated in the thirties do remain burning problems: In fact, it should be said for the anti-Stalinist Left of the past several decades that it anticipated, in its own somewhat constricted way, a number of the problems (especially, the nature of Stalinism) which have since been widely debated by political scientists, sociologists, indeed, by all people concerned with politics. The nature of Stalinism and of post-Stalinist Communism is not an abstract or esoteric matter; the views one holds concerning these questions determine a large part of one's political conduct: and what is still more important, *they reflect one's fundamental moral values.*

No sensible radical over the age of thirty (something of a cutoff point, I'm told) wants young people merely to rehearse his ideas, or mimic his vocabulary, or look back upon his dusty old articles. On the contrary, what we find disturbing in some of the New Leftists is that, while barely knowing it, they tend to repeat somewhat too casually the tags of the very past they believe themselves to be transcending. But we do insist that in regard to a few crucial issues, above all those regarding totalitarian movements and societies, there should be no ambiguity, no evasiveness.

So that if some New Leftists say that all the older radicals are equally acceptable or equally distasteful or equally inconsequential in their eyes; if they see no significant difference between, say, Norman Thomas and Paul Sweezy such as would require them to regard Thomas as a comrade and Sweezy as an opponent—then the sad truth is that they have not at all left behind them the old disputes, but on the contrary, are still completely in their grip, though perhaps without being quite aware of what is happening to them. The issue of totalitarianism is neither academic nor merely historical; no one can seriously engage in politics without clearly and publicly defining his attitude toward it. I deliberately say "attitude" rather than "analysis," for while there can be a great many legitimate differences of analytic stress and nuance in discussing totalitarian society, morally there should be only a candid and sustained opposition to it.

3. *A vicarious indulgence in violence, often merely theoretic and thereby all the more irresponsible.* Not being a pacifist, I believe there may be times when violence is unavoidable; being a man of the twentieth century, I believe that a recognition of its necessity must come only after the most prolonged consideration, as an utterly last resort. To "advise" the Negro movement to adopt a policy encouraging or sanctioning violence, to sneer at Martin Luther King for his principled refusal of violence, is to take upon oneself a heavy responsibility—and if, as usually happens, taken lightly, it becomes sheer irresponsibility.

It is to be insensitive to the fact that the nonviolent strategy has arisen from Negro experience. It is to ignore the notable achievements that strategy has already brought. It is to evade the hard truth expressed by the Reverend Ralph Abernathy: "The whites have the guns." And it is to dismiss the striking moral advantage that nonviolence has yielded the Negro movement, as well as the turmoil, anxiety, and pain—perhaps even fundamental reconsideration—it has caused among whites in the North and the South.

There are situations in which Negroes will choose to defend themselves by arms against terrorist assault, as in the Louisiana towns where they have formed a club of "Elders" which patrols the streets peaceably but with the clear intent of retaliation in case of attack. The Negroes there seem to know what they are doing, and I would not fault them. Yet as a matter of general policy and upon a nationwide level, the Negro movement has chosen nonviolence: rightly, wisely, and heroically.

There are "revolutionaries" who deride this choice. They show a greater interest in ideological preconceptions than in the experience and needs of a living movement; and sometimes they are profoundly irresponsible, in that their true interest is not in helping to reach the goals chosen by the American Negroes, but is rather a social conflagration which would satisfy their apocalyptic yearnings even if meanwhile the Negroes were drowned in blood. The immediate consequence of such talk is a withdrawal from the ongoing struggles.

4.   *An unconsidered enmity toward something vaguely called the Establishment.* As the term "Establishment" was first used in England, it had the value of describing—which is to say, delimiting—a precise social group; as it has come to be used in the United States, it tends to be an all-purpose put-down. In England it refers to a caste of intellectuals with an Oxbridge education, closely related in values to the ruling class, and setting the cultural standards which largely dominate both the London literary world and the two leading universities.

Is there an Establishment in this, or any cognate, sense in the United States? Perhaps. There may now be in the process of formation, for the first time, such an intellectual caste; but if so, precise discriminations of analysis and clear boundaries of specification would be required as to what it signifies and how it operates. As the term is currently employed, however, it is difficult to know who, besides those merrily using it as a thunderbolt of opprobrium, is *not* in the Establishment. And a reference that includes almost everyone tells us almost nothing.

5.   *An equally unreflective belief in "the decline of the West"*—apparently without the knowledge that, more seriously held, this belief has itself been deeply ingrained in Western thought, frequently in the thought of reactionaries opposed to modern rationality, democracy, and sensibility.

The notion is so loose and baggy, it means little. Can it, however, be broken down? If war is a symptom of this decline, then it holds for the East as well. If totalitarianism is a sign, then it is not confined to the West. If economics is a criterion, then we must acknowledge, Marxist predictions aside, that there has been an astonishing recovery in Western Europe. If we turn to culture, then we must recognize that in the West there has just come to an end one of the greatest periods in human culture—that period of "modernism" represented by figures like Joyce, Stravinsky, Picasso. If improving the life of the workers is to count, then the West can say something in its own behalf. And if personal freedom matters, then, for all its grave imperfections, the West remains virtually alone as a place of hope. There remains, not least of all, the matter of racial prejudice, and here no judgment of the West can be too harsh—so long as we remember that even this blight is by no means confined to the West, and that the very judgments we make draw upon values nurtured by the West.

But is it not really childish to talk about "the West" as if it were some indivisible whole we must either accept or reject without amendment? There are innumerable strands in the Western tradition, and our task is to nourish those which encourage dignity and freedom. But to envisage some global apocalypse that will end in the destruction of the West is a sad fantasy, a token of surrender before the struggles of the moment.

6.   *A crude, unqualified anti-Americanism, drawing from every possible source, even if one contradicts another: the aristocratic bias of Eliot and Ortega, Communist propaganda, the speculations of Tocqueville, the res*sentiment *of postwar Europe, etc.*

7.   *An increasing identification with that sector of the "third world" in which "radical" nationalism and Communist authoritarianism merge.* Consider this remarkable fact: In the past decade there have occurred major changes in the Communist world, and many of the intellectuals in Russia and Eastern Europe have reexamined their assumptions, often coming to the conclusion, masked only by the need for caution, that democratic values are primary in any serious effort at socialist reconstruction. Yet at the very same time most of the New Leftists have identified not with the "revisionists" in Poland or Djilas in Yugoslavia—or even Tito. They identify with the harder, more violent, more dictatorial segments of the Communist world. And they carry this authoritarian bias into their consideration of the "third world," where they

praise those rulers who choke off whatever weak impulses there may be toward democratic life.

About the problems of the underdeveloped countries, among the most thorny of our time, it is impossible even to begin to speak with any fullness here. Nor do I mean to suggest that an attack upon authoritarianism and a defense of democracy exhaust consideration of those problems; on the contrary, it is the merest beginning. But what matters in this context is not so much the problems themselves as the attitudes, reflecting a deeper political-moral bias, which the New Leftists take toward such countries.

Between the suppression of democratic rights and the justification or excuse the New Leftists offer for such suppression there is often a very large distance, sometimes a complete lack of connection. Consider Cuba. It may well be true that United States policy became unjustifiably hostile toward the Castro regime at an early point in its history; but how is this supposed to have occasioned, or how is it supposed to justify, the suppression of democratic rights (including, and especially, those of all other left-wing tendencies) in Cuba? The apologists for Castro have an obligation to show what I think cannot be shown: the alleged close causal relation between United States pressure and the destruction of freedom in Cuba. Frequently, behind such rationales there is a tacit assumption that in times of national stress a people can be rallied more effectively by a dictatorship than by a democratic regime. But this notion—it was used to justify the suppression of political freedoms during the early Bolshevik years—is at the very least called into question by the experience of England and the United States during the Second World War. Furthermore, if Castro does indeed have the degree of mass support that his friends claim, one would think that the preservation of democratic liberties in Cuba would have been an enormously powerful symbol of self-confidence; would have won him greater support at home and certainly in other Latin-American countries; and would have significantly disarmed his opponents in the United States.

We are all familiar with the "social context" argument: that for democracy to flourish there has first to be a certain level of economic development, a quantity of infrastructure, and a coherent national culture. As usually put forward in academic and certain authoritarian-left circles, it is a crudely deterministic notion which I do not believe to be valid: for one thing, it fails to show how the suppression of even very limited political-social rights contributes, or is *in fact* caused by a wish, to solve these problems. (Who is prepared to maintain that Sukarno's suppression of the Indonesian Socialists and other dissident parties helped solve that country's economic or growth problems?) But for the sake of argument let us accept a version of this theory: Let us grant what is certainly a bit more plausible, that a full or stable democratic society cannot be established in a country ridden by economic primitivism, illiteracy, disease, cultural disunion, etc. The crucial question then becomes: Can at least some measure of democratic rights be won or granted?—say, the right of workers to form unions or the right of dissidents within a single-party state to form factions and express their views? For if a richer socioeconomic development is a prerequisite of democracy, it must also be remembered that such democratic rights, as they enable the emergence of autonomous social groups, are also needed for socioeconomic development.

Let us go even further and grant, again for the sake of argument, that in some underdeveloped countries authoritarian regimes may be necessary for a time. But even if this is true, which I do not believe it is, then it must be acknowledged as an unpleasant necessity, a price we are paying for historical crimes and mistakes of the past. In that case, radicals can hardly find their models in, and should certainly not become an uncritical cheering squad for, authoritarian dictators whose presence is supposed to be unavoidable. . . .

Indeed, to nationalize an economy without enlarging democratic freedoms is to create a new kind of social exploitation. Radicals and liberals may properly and fraternally disagree about many other things; but upon this single axiom concerning the value of democracy, this conviction wrung from the tragedy of our age, politics must rest.

—1962

the negroes, the cops, the jews
BAYARD RUSTIN

Let us recall the early days of our struggle when, in 1954, the Supreme Court made its historic decision. A great psychological ferment began to take place, which, as you know, was followed by a period of intense direct action.

It was a time of many sacrifices. People were killed. People were brutally mistreated and beaten. Girls had their hair chopped off and burning cigarettes put into their breasts and down their backs. There was a bombing in Birmingham. Millions of dollars are still tied up in fines and bail, some of which we will get back one day.

Although this was a period of great travail, it involved the simplest kind of social action. It was simple for a very good reason: the whole nation was stirred up about the least fundamental, though the highly important, issue of dignity. I say, least fundamental because dignity cannot spring from civil rights bills. They will help; but finally it is the economic and social nature of our institutions which determines how much dignity people have, how much money they can control, and whether or not they share equitably in the national wealth.

This period of direct action was simple also because attention was focused basically on the desegregation of public accommodations—swimming pools, restaurants, hotels, buses, libraries. And direct action was possible without a single penny being spent by the federal government. Without a single penny being spent, without an act of Congress, it was possible to create sufficient dislocation around these institutions, and a few Negroes demonstrating could both destroy the old institutions and create new ones overnight.

If enough people rode and rode in the buses, finally the bus companies would capitulate. If enough people sat at counters and went back and were arrested again and again, then, finally, restaurants—long before the Civil Rights Bill was passed—would have to begin to integrate. Libraries were closed. So were swimming pools. Sooner or later the people—even white people in the South—became disgusted with not having these institutions, and they were opened up. You will remember the irony of opening up the libraries, at first without chairs, so that everybody had to stand, and then, finally bringing in the chairs.

So it was possible to destroy the old institutions and public accommodations and to build up new ones simultaneously. In Birmingham, even Dr. King himself did not quite know what he was doing when he called for an across-the-board settlement in housing, schools, jobs, police behavior, etc. But after Birmingham we were thrust by the successes of the civil rights movement into an extremely difficult period.

About two and a half years ago, I wrote an article in *Commentary* called "From Protest to Politics." I meant to point out that the movement was now faced with totally different problems, problems we had never been faced with before. Where demonstrations had destroyed and created new institutions, demonstrations now could only do one thing. They could merely call attention to the fact that something is wrong. You cannot demonstrate yourself into a new school system, full employment, or the destruction of slums. That is a *political* job, requiring allies, priorities, and an educational job among the masses of the American people.

But in the new period, for a time, "frustration politics" was to be the order of the day. Now one can dislike this, but to rail against it is not the way to do away with it. Ever since 1954 the great masses of Negroes in the North have found that not all the legislation that was being passed was helpful to them; they discovered, rather, that as the legislation was piled up, their situation did not become fundamentally altered. Since 1954 Negro unemployment has doubled. Unemployment among Negro youth is now three times as high as that of white youth. Unemployment among Negro young women and teen-age girls is several times what it is among whites. The ghettos are larger, with more rats, more roaches, more doopan. More people are being driven off the farms in the South by machinery, piling into Harlem and Bedford-Stuyvesant. And the educational system has increasingly failed to prepare poor Negroes, Puerto Ricans, and other minority people to make a living in a society where automation and cybernation affect most grievously the poor, the unskilled, and the uneducated—breeding disillusionment and hopelessness.

This hopelessness has led to a series of unfortunate conditions, all of which can be labeled "frustration politics." Now this is about the way it goes—and I want to be very graphic here, because if we don't understand this, we understand nothing about what is happening. The young Negro says, "Obviously, as Stokely Carmichael says, if I have been beaten fifteen times, if I have been jailed twenty-eight times, if my buddies were murdered in Mississippi, if I have paid fines of over $8,000, if I have bail on me of over $10,000, and we have made all these sacrifices, but the situation in housing, schools, and jobs gets worse and worse, then there is something wrong with our tactics. The hell with Dr. King and his nonviolence. It's wrong; it's not working."

And then he attacks these people *precisely in the order in which he depended upon them, in which he had faith in them.* To many young people, Dr. King is no longer the Moses. He is the man who promised, with whom they stood when they were treated brutally. And now they turn on him, because the objective situation gets worse.

Next, they say, "What's the matter with Phil Randolph? He's old now. Roy Wilkins is backward. Whitney Young is grabbing money." Who is right? Nobody can be right, because the objective situation is so bad. So they turn on the Jews. And that is precisely because they had faith that the Jews, who had known persecution, would continue to stand with them as they had from the beginning in this fight.

They say, "The Jews have power. They control the unions. They own the banks. They've got power. If they meant business, we wouldn't be in this condition. The hell with them too." Then they turn on the trade-union movement. "If they really meant business," they say, "conditions wouldn't be this way." And then come the white liberals.

But let's remember that all whites except the police and the Jews have deserted the Negro ghetto. What can you expect, when the general attitude is to say, "The hell with all the white people! These conditions get worse and worse and they do nothing about it. They have the power, we do not. We need power." And so Negroes end up with the eloquent frustration called Black Power. Meaningless? No doubt; yet it answers a need. Stokely Carmichael knows the advantage he enjoys, knows he doesn't have to offer a social, economic or political program to get applause. He need only give vent to the despairing anger of the ghetto, and "triumph" over those of us who see no value in anger except as it inspires mobilization for change.

Now when everybody's deserted the ghetto except the Jewish merchants and the police—even if the police behaved like angels and if the Jewish merchants behaved like angels—they would automatically be turned on, for the very simple reason that you can always turn on those who are near you and with whom you do business and about whom you care. The young Negroes are not jumping on Wallace. They don't care about him. But they have a relationship with the police and the Jewish merchants. And the Jews and the police, for the next few years, are going to take all the pressure, all the emotional confusion that many ghetto people feel about whites.

Is the answer, then, that Jews should desert the movement? Isaiah and Jeremiah made it very clear long ago that one is not a Jew because he declines to mix milk and meat in the same pot, or because he's circumcised, or because he follows the law of the Torah. One is a Jew because he stands for social righteousness, is opposed to injustice wherever it is, first of all in himself. That is what we blacks have learned from the Hebrew prophets.

Let's look at anti-Semitism in Russia, which I've discussed in several cities in this country. Even if every Jew in the country told me he didn't need my help, that he hated me, I would have to go on helping just the same. If I was told, "Get out of my way, roll over; this is the day of great Jewish power"—my answer would be simply, "You go straight to hell. I am not going to get out of the movement which I am dedicated to, the movement against injustice, just because right now you are behaving in a frustrated manner." And if every Jew told me to get out, I would still accept every invitation to go and speak about this. And if I didn't get invited, I would speak to people in buses and trains.

The frustration of the Negro community is almost impossible to describe. If we had a graph comparing and measuring the Negroes' aspirations in 1936 and 1966, you would discover that in 1936 Negroes wanted *this* much and the society was prepared to give them *that* much. In 1936 the distance between what Negroes wanted and what society was giving was very non-revolutionary—because there was a very short distance between aspirations and conditions.

Now I know that what this society, in 1966, is prepared to give has risen. And there *has* been great progress over the last thirty years. But that progress is meaningless to those who are trapped in the ghettos, simply because their aspirations have risen higher, up to the ceiling, making the gulf between real conditions and aspirations so vast as to be extremely radical, extremely dangerous.

To the question, "Has there been progress?" my answer is, "Yes, much progress." But this progress has absolutely no meaning for people who in their day-to-day lives are still overwhelmed by enormous problems, who find unemployment doubling and tripling, find the ghettos growing, the educational system not able to meet the needs of their children. That is the basic social and psychological problem we face.

Our society today aids and abets the frustration of a Stokely Carmichael and his followers. And these are not really radical young Negroes. Basically, to judge by their behavior, they belong to the most conservative elements in this country. Because of their despair over not playing a role in real politics, they end up making an unconscious alliance with some of the worst elements in the country, those which helped elect Ronald Reagan governor of California.

Their position in Chicago was, "Negroes, stay away from the polls. Senators Douglas and Percy both stink. Don't vote for either." They did not know they were forming political alliances with the forces that wanted to destroy the man who has done more than any other American to enact social legislation; but that's what they did. They went into California wearing "Boycott, Baby, Boycott" buttons all over the state, with hundreds of young Negroes dissuading people from getting to the polls. If I had turned to Stokely Carmichael and said to him, "What are you doing in alliance with these forces that represent the Birch Society and the conservative wing of the Republican party?" he would have said, "I am not in alliance with them. I detest them." But by keeping Negroes from the polls—out of his desperation and absence of hope that there can be movement in this society—he was in fact cooperating with the right-wing movie star and helping to elect him.

In Maryland, the same thing happened. There we were fighting against a man whose slogan was, "Your home is your castle," by which he meant, "Your home is your castle which Negroes are about to storm.

Live in fear." In this situation we have a compounding factor to Negro frustration, and that is white economic fear.

The Freedom Budget is aware of both these phenomena. It is addressed not merely to the Negro community, but equally to Negro frustration and white fear. In the United States any strategy and tactic that is not addressed both to Negroes and whites in their most desperate as well as in their most creative areas is a useless strategy, for we Negroes are only one tenth of the population.

Let us, therefore, examine the benighted people who attack King, who threw urine on nuns and called them "whores for niggers" as they marched in Chicago. Who are these people? It would be very simple to describe them as bigots and let it go at that. But it should be more profitable to analyze what I call white economic fear.

These people are buying homes in Cicero that cost $25,000 but are only one-third paid for. Yesterday, they were Poles, Hungarians, and Italians who were in ghettos themselves. Now they are trying to leapfrog out. They are saving money to send two children to college, but the burden is great, and therefore the wife goes to work. The minute the wife goes to work, they find themselves not economically better off but worse, because now she must buy a car. So they are paying for two cars. And they fear—if the husband were out of work for a few weeks, the whole economic structure they have built up would be laid waste. And with this fear, you get *the socialization and politicalization of prejudice.*

We will not get rid of prejudice by being nice or by merely passing legislation—but by re-organizing the social and economic order so that we reduce to an irreducible minimum both black frustration and white fear. For this we need an economic program. It is not enough to put up posters telling people to be nice. People will not be nice in situations that encourage being unnice. All of God's children would be charming people if we could contain them within a social order that would make it possible for the best to be brought out of them.

But our economic order makes it possible for the worst to be brought out of people. I'll give you two illustrations. Three days ago, a Negro boy with no talent whatever came to see me for a job. I called one of my friends at the ILGWU who almost always will try to find work for these boys.

Now this young fellow came in and he said to me, "Mr. Rustin, what kind of work is this you're getting me?" I told him, "I don't know; but you are just going to have to go to work. You don't have any skills, and if you stay there for three or four months, maybe I can get you something later where there's some possibility of being upgraded." The teacher's union has taken in about eight or ten boys; they've given them skills to run office machines and once one is graduated, I try to put another one in his place.

I told the boy about this. He looked at me and he said, "No. I will not take a nigger job. I would rather shoot pool in the poolroom and sell numbers on the street before ever again I'll take a nigger job." Now you may say to me, "That's a terrible situation." But part of the revolt of the Negro masses has been the rejection of jobs which this society has for 250 years said are jobs for Negroes only—cleaning toilets, waiting on table, pushing carts through the garment district. More and more, these youngsters will not do that kind of work.

Now if somebody wanted to give me a million dollars to set up classes for these boys, I wouldn't do it, because it would be wasting their money. We have to find young Negroes, who are in the throes of discovering who they are, work that is well paid, and work that has a future. Otherwise many of them will do nothing.

The Freedom Budget attempts to do for the poor today what this society did in the past for the poor who came from Europe to America. That the Jews and the Hungarians and the poor Irish and the Italians lifted themselves up by their bootstraps is sheer mythology. God knows, they had to work long, hard hours in sweatshops, and under terrible conditions. But since the dawn of American history this society has provided steps along which the poor could move, if they wanted to move. But now most of those steps no longer exist and are not accessible to the American Negro. What the Freedom Budget does is to try to establish a new series of steps for our time.

Once there was free land, and millions of poor got a start in this country because this society provided them with free land. It will never do that for the poor today. Once this society provided for the poor, no matter how bestially it treated them, because it was prepared and eager to buy their muscle power. I maintain that an East European Jew who came here in 1900 was not half so prepared to make it in this society as the average uneducated, illiterate Negro out of Mississippi. This Negro, after all, knows something of American culture, and the language of the land is his own.

Then what is the difference? The difference is, the minute that East European Jew got off Ellis Island, this society was ready to buy his muscle power. No head start was needed for him, no special training, no talk of upgrading. Society just bought his muscle power. Today the situation is different for the great masses of Negroes and poor whites. This society is buying less and less muscle power, and people must have a high degree of skill to find work.

Once society was prepared to help the great masses of poor immigrants if only by purchasing their muscle power. And the trade union movement was growing and developing. It therefore could act as an umbrella against extreme capitalism and government, protecting the rights of the workers and uplifting them economically. Today, the trade union movement is not growing at a comparable rate in this country.

The trade unions today cannot afford economically to organize many of the people who need most to be organized. In the old days, it was not merely that Jews were intelligent and had a family life. I maintain that many Jews got from the lower East Side to West End Avenue precisely because the Hatters were being formed and the Amalgamated and the ILGWU, and that the union movement offered the immigrants tremendous protection and possibility of growth.

Another step is no longer available. Somebody's always telling me about how his grandfather had a little shop, and he sold candy and cigars, and the kids lived with the mother in the back. Then, a few years later, he moved upstairs, and then he could have the shop downstairs and the two rooms for the family upstairs; and this goes on and on until he owns Macy's!

But today the failure rate of small businesses is astronomical. Small family retail stores are being squeezed out by the big chain stores, by big business. The corner grocer cannot compete, in the quality or prices of his goods, with A & P. He ends up, ironically, exploiting the people in his own neighborhood. And to get into the larger establishments, you must already have managerial or sales skills.

Today Mr. Randolph is asking this country to provide a series of steps over which people can move out of poverty. It is all there for you to see in the Freedom Budget: full employment, a $2.00 minimum wage, redefinition of work, guaranteed income for those who cannot or should not work, and a new kind of public work—in the building of things that are needed for us all.

The Budget suggests the examination and expansion of the whole area of public services and redefinition of our concept of "work." The Freedom Budget wants to make very clear, we are not taking the position which some people have taken. We call for a guaranteed annual income as a supplement to full employment, not as a substitute for it. We do not see the abolition of work on the immediate horizon. Indeed, we believe that if this nation seriously undertakes to meet our vast unmet social needs, we will find that there is plenty of work to be done. Millions of new jobs would be created. Instead of sending the unemployed slum dweller a check every month, why not give him a job rebuilding his neighborhood?

In Western society a man's dignity springs, fundamentally, from his part in the production of goods and services. Man's work must relate him to the production of goods and services, and therefore we need a redefinition of the concept of work, to make full employment possible.

The Freedom Budget will affect us all, because it calls for putting millions of people back to work, for cleaning up the rivers which are filthy, and cleaning the air which is filthy. There is a need for new schools, new homes. People can be put to work tearing down slums and building new homes. Men could be put to work, without great skills, doing these things. And these things would not merely benefit the poor but would benefit all of us.

These economic steps will alleviate both white fear and Negro frustration. They will make this nation a more beautiful place to live in, with justice in our streets.

—1967

vietnam: strategies for opposition
MICHAEL HARRINGTON

The war in Vietnam has given rise to more agonies of conscience than any conflict in which America has participated during this century.

The reason for this moral anguish is not hard to find. In the First and Second World Wars and in the Korean War, the overwhelming majority of the American people believed that their country was acting in self-defense against German, Japanese, or North Korean aggression and was therefore justified in the use of violence. There was a tiny minority of pacifists who refused service. In World War I, some of them were political opponents of American participation, but in World War II most maintained their position on the basis of a transcendental commitment to abjure the use of force under all circumstances.

With the tragic intervention in Vietnam, however, popular opposition against the war became widespread. It went far beyond the ranks of the religious pacifists and was widely prevalent among the most intelligent and idealistic of the young. (What empirical data we have on the campus activists of the sixties indicates such a correlation between scholarly attainment and political concern.) At this writing, it has spread to the majority of the best students on the finest campuses.

These deeply held, but unpacifist, attitudes toward the Vietnam War could not be contained within the traditional categories which the society had established for conscientious objection. In some cases—the simplest to deal with—this was a legal matter, for the federal statute permitted exemption from military service only to those conscientious objectors who professed a belief in a "Supreme Being." In other, and more complex, instances, students and intellectuals asserted an obligation, under the doctrine proclaimed by the United States in the Nuremburg trials, to refuse any form of support to the military effort, such as paying taxes. Finally, some asserted a right to disrupt the prosecution of the war through nonviolent civil disobedience.

These various issues are obviously related to one another, yet it is extremely important to understand the different questions they pose and to treat each in its turn. What is at stake in all of them is a definition of the relationship between politics and morality in that extreme situation when the state proclaims its right to take life and orders the citizen to execute, or cooperate with, its command. Hopefully, this larger point will become clarified in the course of analyzing the specifics of protest.

My own analysis is based on the following premises:

I reject the proposition that a society's decision to employ violence against its alleged enemies cannot be questioned. That is the conclusion of some absolute forms of judicial pragmatism; it is the faith of the superpatriots. In this context, I take it as a gain for the entire nation that the young have insisted upon the necessity for making a conscientious decision about the political use of violence. As the late John Courtney Murray, S.J., put it, "the Student community is to be praised for having raised a profound moral issue that has been too long disregarded in American life."

But I also oppose the notion that one can easily violate the law in a democratic society. Democracy is an excruciatingly imperfect method of political organization—but the very best there is. In its present form, where legal equality before the law is systematically contradicted by economic and social inequality, the democratic structure must be radically transformed. The best way to do that is through democracy itself, and this requires that the losers abide by the political victories of the winners. If the democratic structure collapses under the strain of its tensions, then politics will take to the street, but probably not in non-violent form. And from the point of view of human freedom, a tragedy will have occurred.

Second, I believe that, in Reinhold Niebuhr's terms, it is "blasphemous" when an individual casually pretends to be the voice of God and thereby places himself above his fellow citizens.

In short, I hold that, even in a manifestly inadequate democracy, the individual is normally obliged to obey the laws but may, under extreme and limited circumstances, be required to break them. In what follows I propose to apply this principle to the very difficult task of defining some important relationships of politics and morality as they have been posed by the horrible war in Vietnam.

The present Selective Service statute should be both reinterpreted and revised in order to provide atheist and agnostic objectors with the same legal status as members of peace churches, and to permit exemption on the basis of moral opposition to a particular war. This would grant federal protection to peace activists, the bases of whose actions are now wrongly considered to be only political and who are therefore excluded from the exemptions provided by the present law.

When the courts and the Selective Service system originally interpreted the present statute, they did so in a literalist, undemocratic and antilibertarian fashion. The language of Congress demanded (wrongly, I believe) that the objector base his claim on belief in a Supreme Being. The government proceeded to insist upon a narrow, textbook definition of that Being and, in effect, restricted the protections of the law to members of the historic peace churches. Atheists and agnostics whose positions were rooted in deeply held convictions about the nature and destiny of man were sent to prison.

This interpretation of the law was, I believe, unconstitutional and, even though the courts have thus far rejected this assertion, I hope they will eventually come to recognize it. Simply put, the First Amendment should apply to religion in a completely nonsectarian way. Definitions of the religious spirit by thinkers like William James and Paul Tillich have already made a persuasive case for extending the concept to any transcendent commitment, earthly as well as heavenly, and this should be the rule of the courts. The effective establishment of theistic religion which has prevailed for more than two decades should be ended as soon as possible.

In recent years there have been some signs that the judiciary is moving in this direction. In the Seeger case, an agnostic objector had been denied even a hearing on the grounds that his lack of religious affiliation *a priori* excluded him from any consideration under the law. The Supreme Court responded favorably to a due-process appeal but not to the substantive issue of whether the "Supreme Being" proviso was constitutional. It held that the question of belief in a Supreme Being was complex and that it was therefore wrong to assume without a hearing that an "agnostic" could not possibly qualify. The local board then gave Seeger an exemption.

The Court's strategy in *Seeger* was to work within the limits of the present statute and to duck the more basic issue of the constitutionality of the "Supreme Being" test. Given the hallowed American tradition of repealing bad laws by intelligent judicial reinterpretations of them, the very phrase, Supreme Being, could eventually be taken as symbolic Congressional language for any deeply held, ultimate principle, and atheists would thus be qualified as objectors under the present rules. It would, of course, be infinitely preferable to have a clear declaration on the unconstitutionality of the current language. But, in any case, it is imperative that the society accept the claims to conscientious objection of agnostics and atheists as well as of Quakers and Mennonites.

But such a reform of the law does not resolve the issue of politics and morality. It is only a first step. For it does not deal with the citizen who, on formal religious or philosophical grounds, refuses to serve because he is against a particular war. Here I would argue that anyone who can show that he is opposed to all wars *or all wars of a certain type* should be granted objector status.

In making this last point, I would distinguish between moral objection to war, *or a war,* and political objection to a war. The moral objector invokes a principle that requires him not to kill at all, or only to kill when certain conditions of a "just war" are present. In the course of coming to his decision, he may well take political considerations into account, *i.e.,* a major Christian tradition requires that the war itself be "just," and a judgment on this criterion will inevitably intermingle politics and morality. But even then, the obligation being stated is a transcendental one in the sense that is requires the objector to refuse combat in any and all situations which fail to meet his criteria. It is not that he is simply politically opposed to the war, but that he maintains a moral position in which such political opposition makes it conscientiously impossible for him to be a participant in that war

Such an attitude can be distinguished from one of political opposition pure and simple. Here I would take the figure of Lenin as an illustration of my point. Lenin was against Russia's case in World War I, heart and soul—he was a "revolutionary defeatist." Yet he did not believe that his political stance required him to refuse military service. Exactly the opposite. Since he believed that the only way to end this war, and war itself, was by the revolutionary overthrow of the existing order, he urged his followers to go into the army precisely because they were antiwar. For, he argued with some prescience, it was in the army that the upheaval would begin.

A relatively small minority of the antiwar young in America today adhere to this Leninist position. I cite this case, not because it is at all typical, but rather to show that political opposition to a war, and moral objection to serving in it, are not the same thing.

But most young political opponents of the war today are, I believe, in a heart-rending dilemma. On the one hand, they are horrified (rightly I would say) by this particularly ugly, futile combat in Vietnam; on the other hand, they are not absolute pacifists and yet they do not have the Leninist hope that being drafted is a worthwhile step toward revolution. They have the worst of all possible worlds.

Under these circumstances, the Selective Service law and administrative practices should be changed so as to allow for principled moral objection to a specific war. Here again, as in the case of atheists and agnostics, it would be possible to sneak into a decent position by juggling with the current phraseology. For that matter, this writer was granted full objector status by a St. Louis draft board in 1951 after clearly enunciating a "just war" position. But it would be much better if American society made an honest, candid decision to broaden the scope of its respect for conscience. For that is what is at issue: whether this nation is going to insist that an entire category of individuals should be under legal compulsion to violate the dictates of their own conscience.

The National Advisory Commission on Selective Service took up this question and, by a majority vote, decided to urge that objector status be reserved for absolute pacifists. I think they were wrong . . . when they said:

> It is one thing to deal in law with a person who believes he is responding to a moral imperative outside of himself when he opposes all killing. It is another to accord a special status to a person who believes there is a moral imperative which tells him he can kill under some circumstances and not kill under others.

The law, in other words, will provide exemption for a conscience formed in the Quaker tradition but not for one educated to traditional Catholic norms. And the Commission apparently believed that a simple statement of the distinction between the two positions was one justification for it. Yet in both cases even the Commission's language admits that the individuals are responding to "moral imperatives." Why honor the one and send the youth obedient to the other to jail?

But there are other reasons asserted beyond this *ipse dixit.* "Moreover," they continue, "the question of 'classical Christian doctrine' on the subject of just and unjust wars is one which would be interpreted in different ways by different Christian denominations and therefore not a matter upon which the Commission could pass judgment." But the Commission is not being asked to pass this judgment on the various advocates of the "just war" position any more than it has to choose between, let us say, Protestant and Jewish versions of absolute pacifism. It is being asked to suggest a public policy toward those who, for whatever serious and deeply held reason, feel themselves morally compelled to refuse service. Indeed, it is precisely the Commission's negative attitude toward selective objection which takes it into the area of making theological judgments. It is in favor of the selective protection of conscience and it uses religious criteria to determine which shall be respected and which shall be outraged.

The Commission also says that "selective pacifism is essentially a political question." In view of the fact that it had held, in the previous paragraph, that this question is taken on the basis of a "moral imperative," I do not take this point very seriously.

Indeed, the one substantive rationale for the majority decision which I found—and with which I disagree—is this:

> . . . legal recognition of selective pacifism could open the doors to a general theory of selective disobedience to law, which could quickly tear down the fabric of government; the distinction is dim between a person conscientiously opposed to participation in a particular war and one conscientiously opposed to payment of a particular tax.

But if there is any real danger of injuring the fabric of government in this Vietnam war period, it comes from *not* recognizing the rights of selective objection. For it is precisely this policy which has caused so much anguish of conscience, made youthful opposition more and more frenzied, and even driven some to voluntary exile in Canada. No political situation in my memory has occasioned so much despairing discontent with the society, and a sophisticated pragmatism should have impelled the National Advisory Commission to provide some honorable alternative for young people who are now required to choose between jail and self-betrayal.

But my own advocacy of selective objection is not based on such pragmatism. I am convinced that there is a principled "just war" position involving transcendental moral obligations which can impose itself upon the conscience of religious, agnostic, and atheistic citizens. I believe that a democratic society should not require its citizens to violate their deeply held principles. And I am convinced that it would be a relatively simple administrative problem to distinguish the committed from the frivolous, the evaders, and so on.

There is in all this, let it be freely admitted, more of a political dimension than is found in absolute, unconditional pacifism. Yet the basic justification for the policy advocated here is the respect that a democratic society owes to the moral convictions of its members.

Legal reform to grant objector status to atheists and agnostics, and to permit selective objection on a moral basis, can easily be justified within the present legal framework of the United States. But the question of tax refusal, on the grounds that the government is engaged in an immoral exercise and that tax payment would implicate the citizen in this guilt, is something else again. For there are indeed those who have accepted the logic of the National Advisory Commission on Selective Service and who have, with radical intent, defended a "general theory of selective disobedience to law." This extends the primacy of the individual moral judgment into political spheres where it has not been recognized in the past. So in terms of the general theme of this chapter it is a case eminently worth examining in some detail.

First of all, it is important to distinguish between the compulsion directed against a soldier, or even a protestor enjoined from marching, and that exercised against a tax payer.

The soldier is being drafted into a situation in which his support of what he regards as an immoral cause will be personal and immediate. He can be ordered to kill or to facilitate killing, and he may himself be executed if he refuses, particularly at the front line. He is therefore being told to give the utmost cooperation to an action which he regards as profoundly wrong. If he does not make his stand before induction, then the price of obeying his conscience, which now includes the possibility of his own death, has risen so high that only the most heroic person will, or can be expected to, accept martyrdom.

A less dramatic, but somewhat analogous, case occurs when a march is enjoined by a court. It may well be, as Martin Luther King, Jr., obviously believed in Birmingham in 1963, that to obey such an order would constitute an irreparable loss to the movement. The precise moment for action may come only once, and a retreat would mean that the group is not simply being asked to postpone a demonstration but to sacrifice its cause. This element of immediacy is made all the more acute when there is a very real possibility that higher courts will reverse the decision of the lower tribunals, or that a federal appeal will overturn a state decision. For all these reasons, deliberate disobedience of the law may become necessary even though those involved are working within the democratic process.

A similar situation arises when the law is being used as a hypocritical instrument of injustice. The use of "trespass" statutes to enforce a *de facto* segregation is a case in point. In the sit-in decisions, the Supreme Court of the United States effectively admitted that normal democratic process had so broken down in the South—or rather, had become an instrument of antidemocratic tyranny—that Negro youth were justified in anticipating a higher federal legality by disobeying a local ordinance. But this retrospective justification of the nonviolent campaign in the lunch rooms and department stores depended partly on the fact that the youth had *correctly* anticipated the federal law.

Now all of these cases are, I submit, much more immediate than the act of paying taxes. But even more to the point, the tax payer who believes the war to be immoral has a clear alternative open to him, one that he can pursue without heroic courage and through the exercise of normal democratic rights. In this he differs from the soldier, marcher, or sit-in activist. He can organize politically and change the government which administers the taxes. During the time that he is involved in this campaign he will not be commanded to do anything as decisive as taking another life; he will not be, through paying taxes, subjected to irreparable harm like the protest marcher; he will not be victimized by a mockery of the democratic process like the sit-in student of 1960.

Second, the rationale for tax refusal usually rests upon the old economics. . . . In the pre-Keynesian days, governments did indeed use tax bills as a means of raising revenues for specific purposes. But even then, there was more than a little deception involved: the bonds which Americans purchased to "buy" tanks, planes, hospital supplies, etc. in World War II were primarily useful in controlling inflation. The military goods would have been produced whether the people purchased the bonds or not. Now, however, Washington has become more frank about its general tax strategy, though it still resorts to patriotic appeals and old-fashioned economics when that is politically convenient (as it has become for Mr. Johnson on the Vietnam question).

The size of the federal budget is now dictated by the general state of the Gross National Product. If the economy has excess capacity, Washington increases its spending in one way or another (through direct public investment, through a tax cut, etc.); if it is operating at full, or over-full, capacity, in theory the government is supposed to hold down demand either through cuts in spending (the favorite solution of the conservatives) or through an increase in taxes.

In this context, President Johnson's 1967 proposal of a tax increase is, despite his politically motivated statements to the contrary, only tangentially related to the war in Vietnam and certainly not "necessary" to the prosecution of that conflict. If there is one certainty in American politics it is that Congress, in a united front of hawks and doves, will send sufficient military supplies to Americans in a shooting war. The real purpose of the tax increase is to act as a damper on the inflationary trends which the Administration economists have discerned.

Now it may rightly be said that these inflationary tendencies were given a considerable impetus by the war in Vietnam—but so was the employment of Negroes, and one would not oppose that. More to the point, if Congress refuses the tax increase, presumably to the cheers of at least some in the peace movement, the result will not be to bring the end of the war in Vietnam any closer but to place the main burden of that conflict upon the black and white poor.

For in the political realities of 1967, the real debate over the tax increase was a liberal-conservative antagonism over what groups should be required to sacrifice most in the fight against inflation. The Right proposed to deal with the problem through cut-backs in social welfare spending, the Left through the utilization of a highly imperfect tax instrument which, for all of its faults, is the most progressive means of fighting inflation the society possesses. Should the antiwar movement, having not yet succeeded in winning a political majority to put an end to the killing, adopt a tactic whose actual effect will be to tax the ghettos and the rural slums? . . .

Most of the people who have been attracted to the notion of tax refusal during the course of the Vietnam War would regard all the foregoing as mere sophistry. Their point of departure is not rational or political, but it is substantial and understandable. Tax paying is one of the few "personal" relationships which the middle-class citizen has with the government. Rightly outraged by a horrible war, many people seek desperately for some way that the individual can communicate his distress to the politicians and the IBM machines. And tax refusal is one of the few means at hand. I sympathize profoundly with those who have taken this position—but I cannot agree with them, and not simply for reasons of economic theory.

One should be careful, particularly in a democratic society, of proclaiming too many "Nuremburg" obligations. The Court of the victors which sat in judgment of the Nazis asserted a natural-law duty of resistance, and even heroic resistance, to clearly immoral military orders. But, and this is a very important point, the country at issue was Nazi Germany, *i.e.,* a fascist dictatorship. Under such circumstances, I would certainly affirm the right of all citizens to civil disobedience and, for that matter, to the violent overthrow of their own government—and the citizen's duty to refuse monstrous commands, even if that meant sacrificing life itself.

But the United States of the Sixties is hardly Nazi Germany; the tax payer is not really being ordered to do anything more specific than to help in maintaining a boom; and there exist alternate methods of bringing the war to an end. . . . Tax refusal may well be personally therapeutic and morally exhilarating; but it does not pass the supreme test, for it contributes little or nothing to ending the immoral war in Vietnam. If an individual feels conscientiously compelled to take this course, I would defend all of his civil liberties, but I cannot agree that he has either enunciated a binding obligation or formulated an effective tactic for bringing the killing to an end.

It is a paradox that, in the fall of 1967 when public opinion polls suggested a majority of the American people were coming to oppose the war in Vietnam, a minority of protesters turned to desperate, anti-political tactics. At the precise moment when the possibility of winning a majority through democratic action had become quite real, these activists chose to move outside of the democratic framework. By far and large their rationale was that the immorality of the government's action was so patent and urgent that the individual was obliged to take direct action to prevent Washington from carrying out its policy. So in this case—the most extreme one to be discussed here—a transcendent ethical duty is assumed to justify, not simply opting-out of the normal political process through tax refusal, but a form of nonviolent sabotage.

As the *New Republic* described this mood in a sympathetic account of a demonstration in October, 1967, aimed at closing the induction center at Oakland, California:

> ... *Stop the Draft Week* represented the transition from "dissent to resistance." It was a recognition not only of a previous failure to change the Johnson Administration's war policy—that was to be expected—but a deeper recognition of a loss of momentum and a failure of nerve in the face of an exhaustion of tactical possibilities. The new technique is political disruption, an attempt to "stop the war machine," entailing a renunciation of violence while still shrinking from a positive recommendation of violence." (Michael Miller, the *New Republic*, 1967.)

In dealing with this strategy and the philosophy that justifies it, one is not confronting any of the traditional cases for pacifist civil disobedience. In Oakland during that week, the first protest was made according to accepted nonviolent rules. Joan Baez and a group of people appeared at the induction headquarters, made no attempt to resist arrest and went peaceably with the police when they were taken into custody. *They were disobeying the law as a witness to the outrage of their conscience but they were not interfering with those who felt otherwise.*

This form of civil disobedience does not disrupt the democratic process. It allows protesters to manifest the intensity of their convictions and in this way to reach out to the consciences of their fellow citizens. It means that the individual is ready and willing to pay the legal price for making his point. (This writer was twice arrested in the course of such demonstrations and is thus obviously sympathetic to the tactic.)

But it is an entirely different matter when it is claimed that the alleged immorality of a government allows the citizen of an imperfect, but still functioning, democratic society to obstruct that government in carrying out its policies and to disrupt the activities of those who agree with that government. This is the right which was being claimed in the fall of 1967. It is not only a rationale for an attack upon civil liberties but could open up an era of intolerance which will victimize the protesters more than those protested against.

Consider, for instance, this statement of Jerry Rubin, one of the organizers of the October 1967 demonstration at the Pentagon. In talking about the coming Democratic party convention, Rubin was quoted by *Newsweek* as saying, "Can't you see it—100,000 hippies all around the hall, smoking pot, faking delegates' cards, tossing smoke bombs." The intention of such words is clear enough. It is not to mount a protest, as was done at the Democratic party conventions of 1960 and 1964 by the civil rights movement, but to disrupt a public meeting. (The middle-class, *épater la bourgeoisie* sources of this fantasy are revealed by the fact that "smoking pot" is put on a par with "tossing smoke bombs.")

The theoretical and practical dangers of this attitude are enormous. In the name of morality, a sort of pacifist, and not so pacifist, *putschism* is justified. And indeed at the antiwar march of the Students for a Democratic Society in Washington in 1965, Staughton Lynd specifically argued for the desirability of a nonviolent *coup d'état* in which the marchers would, on their own nomination, represent the supposedly voiceless majority of a democratic society and take over the buildings of government. The poetic imagery which Lynd had used at that time was to inspire at least a wing of the protesters when some tried to rush the Pentagon in October 1967.

But this is not simply a repudiation of fundamental, and precious, democratic principles contained in the Bill of Rights. It is also an invitation to the American reactionaries to answer in kind. And in response to this challenge, former governor George Wallace of Alabama did indeed propose taking the "bearded professors who tell students they are for victory for the Vietcong" and putting them in jail. Thus, as so often happens, the violation of civil liberties in a "just" cause provokes the "unjust" to violate even more civil liberties. . . .

In summary, the Vietnam War has posed a number of different questions relating to the boundaries of the political and the moral and the interrelationships between the two spheres. It is intolerably anti-libertarian to exclude atheists and agnostics from exemption as conscientious objectors on the grounds that they are not motivated by belief in a "Supreme Being." The courts could, using the prevailing legislative language, make a definition of Supreme Being in the tradition of William James and Paul Tillich and thus bring any deeply held fundamental principles under the operation of this clause. It would be infinitely preferable, however, if this reform were to be a conscious act of the Congress, for that would give the firmest possible foundation to a non-sectarian reading of the First Amendment to the Constitution.

Second, the National Advisory Commission on Selective Service erred when it refused to grant moral validity to the position of objectors to a particular war. In point of fact, the government's denial of this right is doing much more serious damage to the social fabric than its recognition of this position possibly could. In point of principle, the state does not have the philosophical-theological competence to decide that consciences formed in one religious tradition are deserving of respect while those shaped by another religious, or nonreligious, tradition are not. So it would be a gain for the entire society if the political order guaranteed fundamental rights to such principled, selective conscientious objection.

Third, the "Nuremburg" analogy—whereby direct and personal participation in the genocidal activities of a fascist dictatorship is equated with paying taxes for a tragic war undertaken by a relatively democratic society—is too loose to be compelling. Moreover, the very structural evolution of modern government, particularly on questions of fiscal policy, undermines the assumption that there is any relationship between a particular tax and a war policy. Therefore, there does not seem to be a good case for a *duty* of tax refusal, although individuals may make the *tactical* decision to engage in this form of protest as a form of witness. In the latter case, the debate over tax refusal is not principled, but rather will be concerned with the effectiveness of the witness. I personally do not think it is a very useful form of opposition mainly because it is almost inevitably restricted to the middle class.

Finally, I would make a sharp distinction between these three forms of protest and the assertion of an obligation and right to disrupt the activities of a democratic government through *force majeure,* whether violent or not. Such a policy will threaten the very institution of the democratic dialogue; it will invite savage Rightist reprisals; and it will open up the way to violence. Given the fact that many legal political alternatives are available to the protest movement, there is no justification for such an extreme position. And, perhaps most important of all, this is an elitist stance that justifies an attack upon the civil liberties of citizens, and government itself, on the basis of the presumed moral superiority of a minority.

As a last generalization, it seems to me that anyone concerned with morality and politics should be wary of facile claims that the former must prevail over the latter. For as long as there is a democratic process through which laws can be changed, the presumption is in its favor. There are extreme situations—the pacifist ordered to kill; the selective objector commanded to fight in this war—when the individual must place his conscience above the state. But it would be intolerable if this procedure were made the norm. That would not only overburden the conscience of the individual; it would disintegrate the structures of freedom as they are now known.

Those of us who are against this terrible war are, I think, under a special obligation not to claim privileges from the society, not to tear it down because it has the gall not to agree with us, but to change it. And the fact that we can change it is something not to be too lightly dismissed.

—1968

SEVENTIES

We have begun to see that the CIA is only one glacier in an Ice Age of covert operations. Since FDR created the OSS during World War II, a monstrously large American "intelligence community" has materialized. Its parts are dispersed like the limbs of Osiris. . . . How did it all come to pass? A platitudinous but not therefore inaccurate answer is that it was a product of the Cold War. No doubt. In the long run, however, a search for historical origins leads us into an infinite regress. The Cold War had its precedent in President Wilson's Red Raids and, for that matter, in the Alien and Sedition Acts.

Bernard Rosenberg, "CIA, DIA, FBI—and 50 More!," 1975

foreword

DAVID BROMWICH

You can get a fair idea of the writers around *Dissent* only if you think of a group of friends meeting to talk and argue. Allow for rivalries as well as disagreements among these friends; maybe "associates" is a more accurate word. In the middle of a discussion, somebody will say, "We should write about that." Somebody else will wonder aloud, "Who can write it?" The next step is something between a request and a command. Often enough, the writer pressed into service ends up warming to the task.

Not that most *Dissent* articles have ever been command performances. But the atmosphere of a contentious meeting is part of a tone, or texture, at home in the magazine: never more than in the 1970s. Meetings in earlier years were small, irregular, almost domestic affairs, punctuated by the occasional larger discussion open to the public. By 1971, they had settled into a semi-regular schedule, three or four each year, faithfully attended by a dozen or more editors and a few guests.

"Editing a little magazine," Irving Howe said, "is like running a candy shop: you never know when supplies will be short." All the meetings were in someone's living room—Joseph Buttinger and Muriel Gardiner, Simone Plastrik, Deborah Meier. Discussion of the contents of coming issues and the budget was followed by a political talk; and a *Dissent* meeting was not a good place to give a half-baked talk. Everyone seemed to come well-armed with facts and doubts—an impression of coherence largely owing, perhaps, to the shared background of many editors in the European socialist movements and what would now be called European modernism. A high (almost parliamentary) decorum of speaking was maintained: David Spitz, Erazim Kohak, Michael Walzer particularly shone on these occasions. And the visitors were frequently on a par with the rest: Richard Lowenthal, Victor Alba. Strong things were said, in a reasoned tone, that would have ignited permanent enmities in a group less accustomed to impassioned argument.

Remember that when people say the sixties, they often mean the years 1964–73: from the assassination of John Kennedy to the resignation of Richard Nixon. The early seventies felt continuous with the late sixties. *Dissent* in these years had fewer of the freelance polemical essays on culture that had marked its earlier phase; names like Harold Rosenberg, Paul Goodman, and Norman Mailer were less to be seen in its pages now. Regarding the "youth culture" that was rapidly becoming identical with American popular culture and the new rank and file in left-wing politics, the editors tended to be skeptical. The mixing of culture with politics and of politics with theater seemed to touch in them an inveterate nerve of rational suspicion.

Dissent had opposed the escalation of the Vietnam war, but without Martin Luther King's prophetic understanding of its destructive impact at home. And yet, as the seventies took on a distinct character, airily self-centered beside what came before, intimations of regret for a gone era of reform could be felt in essays like the memoir by Michael Harrington reprinted here. By the early 1970s, Harrington would have shared the leading thought of King's great April 1967 oration at Riverside Church, that he could not segregate his protest against the violent injustice of America abroad from his nonviolent protest on behalf of civil rights at home. A gifted younger contributor like Jervis Anderson was able to publish in *Dissent*—at a length and from a point of view unlikely to be congenial elsewhere—a sketch of the predicament of black revolutionists that was at once sympathetic and resonant in its critique.

Politics being so steady an emphasis at *Dissent,* the magazine offered a forum to the branch of the feminist movement associated with rights much more than with cultural identity. Cynthia Fuchs Epstein's article in this respect honors a tendency that would become prominent among contributors during the next two decades. This was a new range of voices. By contrast, a vivid concern with international politics and "contemporary history" has been an inseparable trait of *Dissent* ever since its founding; and Theodore Draper's essay-review on the bad faith of apologists for the Vietnam war is a fine and characteristic example of intellectual polemic. As early as 1967, Draper had published *Abuse of Power,* a conclusive indictment of President Johnson's turn to full-scale war. What strikes him most forcibly now, in looking back on the war, is that its rationalizers, Henry Kissinger and Zbignew Brzezinski among them, have scarcely suffered a loss of prestige for having pursued and justified a ruinous policy. The way to success in the foreign policy establishment of the seventies was to have been wrong about the war, wrong without shame or regret.

a collective sadness
MICHAEL HARRINGTON

Sometimes, Emile Durkheim once remarked, a society develops a collective sadness.

That is obviously the case with America today. The Harris poll, showing a pervasive uneasiness in this country, only confirms what all of us instinctively know. An optimistic and confident nation whose Great Seal proclaims it a New Order of the Ages seems to have lost its nerve. And some of the causes of this mood are painfully apparent. After the elections of 1964 and 1972, the overwhelming majority of the American people who had named Lyndon Johnson and Richard Nixon as their president were forced, almost against their will, to turn upon the man for whom they had voted. Those of us who have always thought of Nixon as a devious, dishonest man sometimes forget the shattering psychological consequences when more than half of the people who voted for him in 1972 want to turn him out of the White House. Implicit in that change is the admission: I was gulled and tricked by a scoundrel who may be, in his own immortal words, a crook as well.

But then Johnson and Nixon are only the names we give to two of the most wrenching and disillusioning experiences in the nation's history: our first truly unpopular war and our greatest political scandal. Add to this some five years of spectacular economic mismanagement carried out by an Administration whose constant prophecies of imminent great success became a horrible joke, like the light at the end of the tunnel in Vietnam that was always being glimpsed during the Johnson years. These people, George Meany remarked, would have said that the Titanic stopped to take on ice. And to make their misery abject, the nation of plenty had to wait in line at the gas pumps last winter and, though most of them are not aware of it, still face massive dislocations because of the outflow of an extra $60 billion from the industrial West to the oil-producing nations.

All of these factors are at work in our collective sadness, but I will not linger over any of them. In an analysis that makes no pretense at being complete, I want to treat three other (but related) aspects of the current malaise. First, there is a cultural crisis that represents the explosion of epochal contradictions within the daily life of just a few years; then there is the impact of what Joan Robinson calls The Second Crisis of Economic Theory; finally, there are new possibilities of political disintegration.

I do not think it personal ethnocentrism if I take the crisis of American Catholicism as the point of departure for an impression of a culture crisis that affects the entire society. Two generations ago, American Catholics were almost all workers and they are still a major element in the labor movement. Today, they are also to be found in a new middle class (with a good number of the Irish in the vanguard) and in newly conscious "ethnic" groups (Italians, Poles, other South and East Europeans). Their experience is unique in that the religious dimensions of the cultural crisis are dramatically present in their case; but they are also typical in that their disenchantment is to be found, in other forms, throughout the working class and sectors of the middle class. Archie Bunker, who sings of the days when there was no welfare state, men were men and Glenn Miller played, is their cousin even though that thought would startle his anti-Catholic prejudices.

For the Catholics, the center of their lives was a belief in God and country. Now both are in doubt and the question arises, by what values does one live?

The religious crisis is characteristic of the sloppiness of history. The death of God was clearly announced more than a century ago and Marxists (and atheistic humanists of every persuasion) predicted the imminent demise of that most Medieval of institutions, the Roman Church. But it did not pass away, especially in America. Here the working class did not defect, as it did in France and Italy, for there was not a nobility, or even a Catholic bourgeoisie of any consequence, on whose behalf the prelates could betray, and repel, the faithful. Here there was a society in which, as Tocqueville understood long ago, religion was an important means of group identity. American Catholicism was democratic in practice and ultramontane in theory; it failed to produce a single heresy of any consequence. Hierarchical and meritocratic, this Church was a center of established truth—of a morality, a world view, a way of life—for tens of millions of citizens, particularly for urban white workers.

And then it seemed that the crisis, which had so perversely delayed its arrival for more than a century, erupted into a decade. Priests and nuns left their vocations—and married and had children—and there was a catastrophic fall in new recruits to the religious life. There was folk music on the altar and new doctrines were preached from the pulpit. And just as the stern old pastors had said before the deluge broke, but not for the reasons they gave, once the morale of the Church went there was no stopping the forces of militant secularism. A Supreme Court appointed by a pietistic Protestant president effectively legalized abortion on demand; pornography came out of the stag parties and into the movie houses; young couples publicly lived in sin together, and starlets had babies out of wedlock; women's liberation and gay liberation challenged the holiest of verities about family structure and sexuality; and on and on. The very ethical fiber of the country seemed rent and torn.

Suddenly masses of rank-and-file Americans, the Catholics most obviously, saw the religious foundations of their personal code begin to crumble. *They did not know what to believe any longer.* At the least, they were not sure. And at more or less the same time, the second pillar of their daily faith—that America is the greatest nation on the face of the earth—began to quake.

The immediate cause was, of course, Vietnam. Those old enough to remember World War II know how extraordinary the events of the '60s were. For in the '40s, the war was genuinely popular. There was a kind of siege comraderie throughout the society. People picked up hitchhikers in uniform and sometimes took them to their homes; the trains and buses were jammed to bursting with millions of men and women who faced constant uncertainty and the possibility of youthful death: yet the spirit was good. We are, Joe Lewis said in one of the popular aphorisms of the time, on God's side.

And then Vietnam. Young people publicly admitted that they were trying to avoid the draft; some fled to Canada, others deserted. An antiwar movement that was absolutely right on the basic issue sometimes delighted in the most infantile contempt for symbols, like the flag, which other Americans took as holy. Gradually, even the hawks were forced to the conclusion that the war was insane. More often than not they did so out of disillusioned militancy rather than dovishness—if we didn't have the guts to nuke Hanoi or Peking, we had no business letting American soldiers die for Saigon. But that still meant admitting that the

United States had lost a war. The myths of our invincibility and righteousness shattered.

I think that all this was experienced most acutely by Catholics because their religious crisis was more extreme than that of other faiths. But I suspect that the factors I have defined here as elements of a particularly Catholic sadness are to be found, in one way or another, among millions of other religionists in this society. People can't believe in either their God or their country the way they used to; people just don't know what to believe in at all.

By far and large, the crisis of God and country took place in the '60s within a prospering economy. The Kennedy-Johnson years witnessed the longest, uninterrupted peacetime boom in American history. So if people were puzzled in the presence of new cultural forces, they could always fall back on that most fundamental of American convictions: next year's living standard will be better than this year's. Then along came a bewildering combination of recession-inflation. Joan Robinson described it in a brilliant address to the American Economic Association a few years back as The Second Crisis of Economic Theory. She was comparing this shock to the First Crisis, the Great Depression of the 1930s. In her opinion it was a fundamental event comparable to the Depression, one that challenged the basic assumptions of the society. She was right.

Two themes abstracted from her intricate argument are particularly relevant to this sketch of America's collective sadness. Within the Keynesian framework, Robinson writes,

> It was sufficiently obvious that if continuous near-full employment was maintained without any change in traditional institutions and attitudes in industrial relations, there would be an irresistable pressure to inflation. I think that in the United States this element in Keynes was somehow swept under the carpet.

And then, later in her essay, she notes that

> experience of inflation has destroyed the conventions governing the acceptance of existing distribution. Everyone can see that his

relative earnings depend on the bargaining power of the group that he belongs to. The professors become quite nervous when they are discussing the earnings of the garbage collectors. Now it is clear that the income from property is not the reward of waiting but the reward of employing a good stockbroker. On top of this a sudden freeze comes down. [Mrs. Robinson's paper was presented the year after the Nixon economic freeze of August, 1971.] If it is successful it is to keep everyone in the position where he happened to be when the scramble for relative gains was brought to a halt and it will perpetuate the division of income between work and property that happened to exist when it set in.

But it does not seem likely that it will be as successful as all that. Rather it will add a political element to the distribution of bargaining power. Perhaps this is going to create a crisis in the so-called free-enterprise economy.

Now we know, of course, that Joan Robinson's prediction was accurate. Nixon lifted the controls, which had come under increasing attack from both labor and business; we are back to a scramble for relative earnings based on bargaining power. In the Robinson analysis, that is a structural tendency of Keynesian economics. It is also, I believe, a source of the collective sadness in our society, for it is often destructive of solidarity, particularly among the great mass of people.

Indeed, this trend sets in motion a process that, with acknowledgment to Daniel Bell, might be called "situs conflict." In the political bargaining going on under the conditions Joan Robinson describes, where a person works becomes extremely important. During the height of the energy crisis in the winter of 1974, for instance, the workers and the owners of the airlines industry felt a common stake in getting fuel for their department of the economy; the truckers made their claims; so did mass transit. In each case, there was a vertical integration of management and the employees in a de facto struggle with the other blocs of management and employees. In a kind of industrial feudalism, men and women become attached to their jobs and function politically, not so much as members of a class, but as partisans of an industry in alliance with all of its members, from the chairman of the board to the janitor.

Then there are more traditional, but now exacerbated, struggles for money that set workers against workers. Policemen in New York fight to get more than firemen. Public employee wage demands seem to be raised, not against the "boss," but against the taxpayers, i.e., in considerable measure against other workers. (The American Federation of State, County and Municipal Employees, one of the most progressive unions in the country, has rightly tried to deal with this problem by linking wage demands to increasing the quality of public service.) The building trades' attempt to keep pace with inflation—and it must always be remembered that the high hourly rates in this sector are necessary because of the seasonal character of the work and the chronic unemployment that results—are seen as an act of hostility toward prospective new homeowners.

Perhaps one of the most significant signs of the time in this area is the switch in policy taking place in the American Federation of Teachers. Under Albert Shanker, its new president, the union is moving away from its earlier social democratic style toward a much narrower, situs-oriented approach that has so long characterized the most conservative forces in the labor movement. As Shanker said during his election campaign for the union's presidency, "I favor building the AFT on *teacher issues—issues which will appeal to all teachers regardless of their political views—*and avoiding politically divisive issues" (emphasis in original). In terms of an old but still quite functional distinction, Shanker here puts the interest of the trade over that of the class. I do not single him out on this count simply because of my disagreements with him on other issues; this kind of thinking will, I suspect, become frequent in the coming period. (Although I must add that the UAW's rejection of a protectionist policy for the auto industry at its convention last June is an encouraging example of the opposite, and to me infinitely preferable, policy.)

All of this has a saddening—and frustrating—effect for a number of reasons. People feel themselves on a tread mill. The auto workers' strike of 1970, for instance, was a bitter struggle to make up for the losses inflation had already caused and to anticipate, and head off, those that might come. The militancy in the public sector is a special case in point: for here workers have had to fight to make up for the generations of second-class economic citizenship that had been forced upon them.

Moreover, there is no clearly defined enemy as there was in the Great Depression. Indeed, one explanation of why American workers in recent years have been so moderate in their wage demands is that they have bought the argument that big increases will only generate higher prices, which will take their new buying power back from them before they have had the chance to use it.

But finally, the most perplexing thing about this situation is that, if one accepts the present distribution of economic and political power as given (and therefore legitimate), then there is no solution to these problems. Forty years ago, the New Deal created a welfare state, which may, or may not, have been accompanied by a very modest redistribution of income. Since then, practically everyone (including the Council of Economic Advisers in their Report this year) agrees, there has been no significant change in the distribution of wealth. The top 20 percent of the American people own 76 percent of the society; the bottom 20 percent have two tenths of 1 percent. Thus the new political power, which the workers and other groups acquired during the '30s, has not been able to affect the relative shares in the economy. It may have staved off a trend toward immiseration, as John Strachey and others have argued, and if that is the case, it is a real accomplishment. But it is also limited.

As long as there were relatively steady increments in the absolute standard of living, most people did not bother about the "abstraction" of fairer shares. But now that we have experienced stagnation, and periods of decline in real buying power (the AFL-CIO estimates that the effective demand of American workers went down by 3 percent in 1973), the distribution issue is posed again. If everyone contributes equally to the fight against, or suffers equally from, inflation, that will perpetuate our intolerable division of wealth. It will also make millions of people feel as if they are riding an endless merry-go-round.

The conservatives are preparing to fight for the status quo, of course. They are arguing that profits are essential to new investment and increased production and must therefore be encouraged; but that wage increases and social spending will augment demand before profits have accomplished their contribution to the common good.

What is obviously required is an offensive by the labor movement aimed, not simply at bettering the position of this or that segment of the working people, but at *changing the rules of the game* so that there can be some kind of rational solution to the inflationary challenge. And indeed most unions have political policies that move in this direction. The problem is that, for a complex of reasons which cannot be analyzed here, the most powerful drive within the labor movement is still that of each group of workers trying their best to fend for themselves in an impossible situation. Let us hope that will change as the full import of the new situation becomes apparent to the union leaders and members.

Right now, however, the dominant mood is one of scrambling to make the best of a bad lot. This corrodes what solidarity does exist; it privatizes social struggles and it makes people sad. It also creates the basis for a similar disintegration in our political life. Here, too, the centrifugal forces seem to predominate, and there are even those, like Dean Burnham, who foresee the end of the American party system.

The reasons for this view are clear enough. Independents now constitute the second largest voting bloc, behind the Democrats but ahead of the Republicans. Then in the 1972 presidential election, nonvoters were a higher percentage than at any time since 1948. The result is that the established model of American political behavior is breaking down—and perhaps the party system with it. According to that model, most elections confirm, or only temporarily deviate from, a basic alignment that lasts for a long period of time (the Republicans from the 1890s to the 1930s; the Democrats from the 1930s to the 1960s). Realigning elections, in which a new majority coalition came into being, were seen as relatively rare occurrences.

But how, on that basis, explain the extraordinarily erratic patterns of recent times? Within a mere eight years, the voters gave landslide mandates to the candidates of different parties—and within a few years of having made that choice, they turned by an overwhelming margin on the man they had picked. In the established model, voting habits—and therefore the party system—were normally consistent and fixed. Now, suddenly, they don't seem to be so at all.

Are the centrifugal tendencies in American politics so great that there is no coherent majority coalition possible and that we will therefore zig and zag into the unforeseeable future? Yes, it is possible. At any given moment these days, as I suggested in *Toward a Democratic Left*, two radically different scenarios seem plausible. In one, the various elements with a stake in social change—the unions, the college-educated constituency, the minorities and so on—unite in spite of their differences; in the other, they fight one another, each placing a particular interest over those of coalition. Clearly something like that happened in 1968 when many in the Kennedy-McCarthy movement failed to rally to Humphrey and in 1972 when George Meany and his associates turned their back on McGovern.

If the politics of disintegration do indeed prevail, then the prospect is for an increase in the collective sadness of American life. We will find ourselves in the unprecedented position of suffering a cultural crisis that shakes the confidence of millions in the values by which they have lived while at the same time confronting a new academic challenge, one that is perhaps more profound, and certainly more elusive, than that of the Great Depression. And all of this under political circumstances where the majority coalition with a democratic Left program, which is so desperately needed, may be impossible.

Clearly, I do not take these things as inevitable. Clearly, my analysis motivates me to action, not despair, to fighting for a "centripetal" strategy that will bring into being that new coalition. But it is important to understand how difficult the task is and to perceive the new anxieties and frustrations that have contributed to our collective sadness.

—1974

the agonies of black militancy

JERVIS ANDERSON

Although black militancy has been one of the veins of American radicalism at least since the abolitionists, it was only during the early sixties that most people started paying much attention to it or even calling it by that name. More people seem to have been militant in the early sixties than ever before. If that is so, however, it suggests something quite important about that stage of the sixties: that it encouraged more hopes of a breakthrough into freedom, and thus stirred more black activism, than any previous period in the century.

When people started speaking of black militancy, they were not naming the tradition of black militant activity itself, but a mode of activism that seemed to be distinctly part of the style and personality of the sixties. And they were referring to black militancy not in the sense of black nationalism but in the sense of a movement whose controlling impulse was to break down barriers that stood in the way of a full and equal participation in American society, barriers that began to seem quite vulnerable at the turn of the decade. However, the style and personality of the sixties turned out to be more perishable than most of us could have foreseen. And part of what perished as well was that spirit we had come to identify as black militancy. The term is still used, to be sure—however quaint a throwback it may sound, however it may have the forced and somewhat square ring of language no longer quite in fashion. People who still use the term are mostly those who think that nothing much has changed, or those who find it the most convenient catchall for whatever goes on in the precincts of black radicalism.

Whatever happened to the black militancy of the sixties, or the mood that sustained it, is precisely what became of the sixties themselves. Though not everybody sees it that way, the sixties do not seem now to have been the best time to inaugurate new things—except, as it turned out, buildings and highways in memory of dead men and murdered hopes. To a large number of people, and mainly the young, the decade seems now to be littered with the ruins of great expectations: many of its more decent commitments dismantled; its moral language largely discarded; its political sensibility held in contempt; its outlook upon the world withdrawn; its racial promises revoked or betrayed; its moral sense driven up against the wall. Some who do not regard it that way, but mourn it nonetheless, see it as a half-finished house on a deserted road: not a nail has been driven in since the bank cancelled its notes; shrubbery has grown up all around it; and vines are climbing over the raw masonry and unpainted woodwork. Some of those who had hoped to find a home in the house have lost faith in banks. Some of them, black militants of the sixties, seem to recall that this sort of thing happened to their forebears several times before. What sense therefore in continuing to believe in promises or in retaining their ties to American idealism?

Anyone who has been raised to respond hysterically to anything with the word black in it—or to find no consoling distinctions between one form of black radicalism and another—may be astonished to hear black militancy associated with the public idealism of the sixties. But such a person should try to remember who were the militants then, what forms their activism took, and what spirit sustained them. They were mostly young people and mostly students. They belonged predominantly to SNCC and CORE, almost the only groups that offered black and white American youth an opportunity to participate constructively in the passions of their time and help set right a society that had long been out of joint. And the tactics they used were sit-ins, freedom rides, disruption of facilities, and a generality of activity described as nonviolent direct action. However irritating most of this may have been to the country, it was somewhat within the American grain. It was certainly what the country seemed to ask of young people then: that they work for change and express their militant energies within the framework of American values. Much of what the young people did then seems rather tame today. But at the time it caused many of their elders in the freedom movement to tear their hair: it was "too provocative" and it could possibly be "counterproductive."

As to the mood that sustained the activism, it was one of optimism—belief that the country was ready and able to respond favorably to demands pressed upon it within the spirit of its own professed ethics. Then came the years between 1963 and 1968 when that belief was shattered by a series of bullets, and the country has not been quite the same since.

Considering whom the bullets struck, they appear to have been aimed directly at the aspirations of the young, the black, and the poor. In any event, most blacks had only one way of seeing it: once again white racism had cast its veto over social and racial progress in America. It does not seem now to be any accident that it was between those years, '63 and '68, that American cities started going up in flames; that young middle-class whites started embracing what have been called un-American heroes and un-American ideologies; that blacks began entertaining—at least expressing—an interest in guns and black power; that the Vietnam war was escalated into a metaphor of contemporary brutality; that this war drove at least half of America out of its skull; that the escape from reality found its most comforting haven in drugs; that almost an entire generation of young people turned to the politics of self-indulgence, self-righteousness, irrationality, violence, and despair.

Today, if there are young blacks who still consider themselves militants, a look at whatever they are "into" will reveal that they are considerably less militant than people who consider themselves something else—people who say that what they are "into" now are things like revolution, liberation, self-determination.

Out of this, where alienated blacks are concerned, two predominant tendencies have taken shape. The first is marked by a set of attitudes which, shared by a variety of individuals and groups, is defined roughly as "nation-building" or cultural nationalism. And the second, a set of political attitudes—roughly described as revolutionary nationalism—is represented most spectacularly by the Panthers.

While it is not the first time that frustration has forced a large number of blacks to withdraw into themselves—and while the black nationalist movement of the twenties was larger than anything that exists today—this is the first time that the withdrawal has appeared so calculated and considered. One cannot recall a time when so many among the educated black young and the lumpen intelligentsia of the streets appeared so utterly at odds with the idea of America, when there appeared to be such a deep and conscious spirit of disaffiliation with the things and processes of the general culture.

Whether it be the movement to salvage and revaluate black history, build up black studies, or talk up the black experience; whether it be the search by young writers and literary intellectuals for a "black aesthetic," different in method, sensibility, spirit, and values from the "white Western aesthetic"; whether it be the claim that black culture is a distinct, independent, and viable element within American society—whether it be any of these, there now seems more intellectual energy and seriousness than ever in the bid to reconsider the blacks' relationship to the society, to define the grounds for dissociating from the culture, and to create "new black men."

Stated simply, perhaps too simply, the black cultural tendency holds a greater feeling for its connection to African cultural forms and roots than for its development within the community of white history and values. Whether such a feeling may have developed in any case—even if blacks had long been accorded what they conceived to be their rightful status in the society—it is hard to say, though it may be worth speculating upon. What seems clear is that the feeling has come about in direct response to a long history of denial in American society.

Much or all of this, however, is in conflict with the ideology of cultural integration held by a more traditional school of black literary and cultural intellectuals. These intellectuals do not so much advocate cultural integration—though the advocacy is clearly implied—as they assert it to be a fact: that there is neither a black nor a white American culture but that the one has been irrevocably shaped and influenced by the other. There are no more articulate and formidable proponents of this point of view than Ralph Ellison and Albert Murray, both of whom operate out of a deep sense of the inescapable interconnections of black and white American life. To them the term black American or Negro American is not merely a convenient political combination, but a fine fusion of culture and consciousness and historical experience.

Ellison's ideas, stated and restated in much of his writings, were recently quoted in part by James Alan McPherson in an article, signed by both men, in the *Atlantic Monthly* (December 1970):

> I think that too many of our assertions continue to be in response to whites. I think that we're polarized by the very fact that we keep talking about "black awareness" when we really should be talking about black American awareness, an awareness of where we fit into the total American scheme, where our influence is. I tell

white kids that instead of talking about black men in white society, they should ask themselves how black *they* are because black men have been influencing the values of the society and the art forms of the society. How many of their parents fell in love listening to Nat King Cole? We did not develop as a people in isolation. We developed within a context of white people. Yes, we have a special awareness because our experience has, in certain ways, been uniquely different from that of white people; but it was not absolutely different. . . . I think . . . that we've looked at our relationship to American literature in a negative way. That is, we've looked at it in terms of our trying to break into it. Well, damn it, *that literature is built off our folklore* to a large extent! I ain't conceding that to *nobody!*

In his book *The Omni-Americans* Albert Murray writes:

White Anglo-Saxon Protestants do in fact dominate the power mechanisms of the United States. Nevertheless no American whose involvement with the question of identity goes beyond the sterile category of race can afford to overlook another fact that is no less essential to his fundamental sense of nationality no matter how much white folklore is concocted to obscure it: Identity is best defined in terms of culture, and the culture of the nation over which the white Anglo-Saxon power elite exercises such exclusive political, economic, and social control is not all white by any measurement ever devised. American culture, even in its most rigidly segregated precincts, is incontestably mulatto. Indeed for all their traditional antagonisms and obvious differences the so-called black and so-called white people in the United States resemble nobody else in the world so much as they resemble each other. And what is more, even their most extreme and violent polarities represent nothing so much as the natural history of pluralism in an open society.

In pointing out these interconnections within black and white culture Ellison and Murray are absolutely right, of course. That certainly seems to be the cultural reality of the United States. But it is not so much the reality itself which troubles those young people who now want to consider themselves cultural nationalists as it is their experience at the hands of the reality. It may be one thing for them to see that American culture is indeed a composite to which blacks have contributed some of the most vital elements. It is quite another thing for them to realize that those who dominate the cultural composite take no more serious and consequential a view of the blacks' part in it than a white household takes of the traditional black help, or a white audience of black entertainment. What most marks the response of whites in such situations is an enjoyment that rests upon a certain fundamental contempt for those who provide it. The general view of such help or such entertainment is that it is after all what blacks do best, almost the only thing they do well, and of considerably less consequence than the role of whites in the life of the culture. As John Corry put it in a recent article in *Harper's*, "One way or another, white America will try to turn blacks into song and dance men."

Not all blacks will oblige. Were they to oblige, it would be almost like saying that one way or another blacks will acquiesce in America's efforts to keep them second-class citizens. That, of course, is not true. And the same smoldering resentment most blacks feel against the effort to keep them second-class citizens marks their refusal to be considered no more than the song-and-dance men of American culture. Not everybody will want to go in the direction of the cultural nationalists; but the effort they make to cut themselves off from the general culture, withdraw into a cultural community of their own, and cultivate the African strains in their historical background, all of this may represent *their* refusal to be seen merely as the song-and-dance men of the culture.

This feeling of tension with the majority elements in the culture is connected not only with periods in the past but also with a tradition of skepticism quite as respectable as the intellectual tradition that supports the idea of cultural integration. As early as the turn of the century, W. E. B. DuBois was expressing the painful contradictions of the black American cultural situation in these words:

He [the American Negro] would not Africanize America for America has too much to teach the world and Africa. He would not bleach his Negro soul in a flood of Americanism, for he knows that Negro blood has a message for the world. He simply wishes to make it possible for a man to be both Negro and American, without being cursed and spit upon by his fellows, without having the doors of Opportunity closed in his face.

And almost two decades later, during the Harlem Renaissance, Alain Locke noticed a cultural reaction similar if not identical to that of today:

This deep feeling of race is at present the mainspring of Negro life. It seems to be the outcome of the reaction to proscription and prejudice; an attempt, fairly successful on the whole, to convert a defensive into an offensive position, a handicap into an incentive.

While neither of these reactions implies or advocates cultural separation, they have a good deal in common with the reaction of those who today are in effect crying out as DuBois did against the agony of being an integral part of a culture that nevertheless spits in one's face and declares one not yet worthy of being taken seriously.

Why, anyway, is it blacks who are constantly being reminded that American culture is a composite? Are there not others who appear to be in greater need of the reminder? Why is it that most whites are able to get away with forgetting it? Why is it that remembering it does not seem to make much difference in blacks' experience? Why—since American culture is so "patently and irrevocably composite"—have the experiences and contributions of blacks been ignored, distorted, or otherwise treated so shabbily in American history books? Why has it been left to blacks to salvage much of their past and their pride from the cutting-room floors of white historians? The answer may well have something to do with power, particularly with those who have it: the power of the majority culture to see as it pleases; to define and impose standards; to promote values and pass judgment; to determine what is of consequence and what is not. Whites "do in fact dominate the power mechanisms of the United States," Murray says. They certainly do. And those mechanisms include culture, which in turn includes the power to dominate and influence the shape of a minority's sense of itself.

The point of all this is not that cultural nationalists are justified in their attempt to withdraw into a cultural enclaved of their own or that this is even possible in America. One cannot by sheer fiat or a simple act of will undo the complexities and continuities which have been in process since blacks were transported into the Western experience. The point is, though, that there has been a good deal of anguish felt and a good deal of contempt suffered by blacks while trapped in the cultural crucible of these centuries. The point too is that they are entitled to bawl, and deserve to have some attention paid to the cause and nature of their pain.

"There is also," Ellison writes, "an American tradition which teaches one to deflect racial provocation and to master and contain pain." That may be true—though God knows it is hardly a tradition one would choose if he had anything to say about it. But what one knows as well is that experience also teaches us that pain cannot or should not be contained forever, and that a continual deflection of racial provocation may well be achieved at the cost of some awareness of and regard for who and what one is. One can well understand how deep-seated in the white American imagination is the image of silent and noble black endurance—in fact we know this because it is one of the perceptions forced upon us by the power of the majority culture. But it is simply another fantasy built upon wishfulness and contempt. And, even more important, it is a fantasy that has done its part, a very large part, in helping to maintain the status of race relations in this country and the contradictions in the social and political experience of blacks and whites.

It's time we all stopped believing it. It's time we all realized that humanity may consist more in giving utterance to one's suffering than in containing it, resisting racial provocation than in deflecting it, raging against an unjust status than in accepting it.

If it turns out—and as it appears—that no viable rearrangements are possible within the present reality of American culture, the function of intellectual leadership may well be to speak compassionately to that condition, to provide the rationales by which blacks may confront the stubborn irony of it and make some tragic peace with it.

There is hardly anything to be said about the Panthers that hasn't already been said or that everybody doesn't already know. Whatever insufficiencies the Panthers have been victimized by, they do not include an insufficiency of publicity. Almost everyone has heard about their founding in Oakland; of their claims to be the vanguard of an armed black revolution; their breakfast programs and shoot-outs with the police; their alleged connections with international Communist conspiracies; their trials in and out of court; the fascination they hold for rich ladies in pants suits; and their cerebration by the intellectuals of chic, machismo, and cultural fashion. Much of what describes the reaction of the cultural nationalists may be applied politically to the Panthers. Only one aspect of this resemblance will be considered here.

At the latest stage in the continuum of black radicalism, the Panthers are as much in reaction against the society's continued frustration of black hopes as against the failure of the civil-rights protest movement to fulfill these hopes. This is of course a hard position to take against the protest movement, since the power of that movement is simply to persuade and not to act. It is also a position that ignores the solid accomplishments of the protest movement in the early sixties, accomplishments that dramatically widened the frontiers of black freedom. To be a part of the radical spirit of today, however, is to share in the ideology of instant gratification and to hold a contempt for strategies and tactics that may achieve gratification a twinkling later.

Thus—although almost every bit of racial progress this century has been achieved by the civil-rights movement—it is now held to have temporized and compromised too much, to have wasted its time fighting for integration, to have bitten its tongue in the presence of the white establishment, to have asked for what it could get rather than demand what it was entitled to, to have sold out on black manhood. Thus too it has come to appear that one of the principal issues around which the Panthers are in motion is the issue of black manhood. An inordinate amount of their rhetoric seems aimed at expressing the essential quality of black manhood which has been denied—a certain mixture of bravery and arrogance. Bravery and arrogance express themselves in a kind of existential revolutionary theater: living dangerously, threatening destruction, cultivating extreme experiences, risking themselves in extreme situations. Since the slave rebels, only a handful of black men have felt the call to live this way—politically. Cleaver: "We shall have our manhood or the earth shall be leveled in our attempts to gain it." Or as someone less prominent said more recently, the only thing young blacks are prepared for in this country is to destroy it.

The last time that black radicalism was so strident in tone—though more intelligent, more thoughtful, and less sanguinary—was in the years between World War I and the middle twenties when the black economic radicals led by A. Philip Randolph attacked American society and the traditional black leadership with a racial militancy and an ideological vehemence that probably still has not been surpassed. And perhaps it was way back there that the possibilities for rational radical action among blacks began to be exhausted, because the black radical movement of the twenties turned out to be pretty much a spectacular failure. If this is so, then, perhaps the country only has itself to blame that the only possibility for the continuation of black radicalism today lies in the areas of irrationality and violence, or—as Joseph Conrad said in a book that has some relevance to our present political experience— madness and despair. Victories in these areas are measured in martyrdom, in suicide, and in how much of the society a rebel takes with him at the moment of his destruction.

As the seventies grow older, this could even get worse. Who's to say what attractions young and embittered black soldiers returning from Vietnam may find in the Panther movement? How many young exconvicts may be inspired and emboldened by the revolutionary examples of Cleaver and George Thomas? Urban guerrilla warfare led by Panthers, the young black lumpen proletariat, embittered exsoldiers and exconvicts may be a nightmare from which it could take a long time to recover—and which many, of course, *many of us* may not survive.

Finally, as periods of black politics have followed periods of intense radical or protest activity, so may the Panther period, as it has been christened by admirers, give way to renewed political activity among many young blacks. Not immediately, of course, for the memory of the more recent frustrations are still too fresh in our minds. The majority of the black population itself represents no more encouragement to the prospect of a revolutionary radical future than America itself does. "The Negro mind," wrote Alain Locke in 1925, "reaches out as yet to nothing but American wants, American ideas."

Ironically, the opportunities for political involvement to which a large number of young blacks may yet turn in the seventies were created by the efforts of the much maligned civil-rights movement. The increase in registered voters, the training of young people as political organizers, the striking down of many of the legal obstacles blocking the way to an open society, the continued if incomplete integration and democratization of the trade-union movement, the election of black candidates to political offices across the nation—all of these have been enabled by the limited but genuine accomplishments of the civil-rights movement. They have also created more space in which blacks can maneuver themselves to the levers of American power. One only has to look at LeRoi Jones's political activities in Newark and his new proximity to the levers of power in that city to realize the uses that may increasingly be made of conventional political avenues to power.

One last word, though, about the Panthers. Even those who believe that blacks can at best share equally and democratically in American power, rather than seizing it, are in no position to carp too cheaply at the Panthers. They are paying an enormous human cost in madness and despair. But madness and despair were not embraced voluntarily; they are precisely where the American experience has driven youthful idealism and activism for the foreseeable future. People like the Panthers are witnessing to the madness that all blacks have felt at one time or another—and to the despair that many of us have avoided only by dint of some tragic and incredibly hopeful conception of the world and of our experience.

—1971

perspectives on the woman's movement
CYNTHIA FUCHS EPSTEIN

The current woman's movement is unique in the American experience. This movement, multidimensional in character, is striking toward change in the structure of our major institutions, in the quality and content of our culture, and at the level of interpersonal dynamics. Not even a decade old, it has permeated the fabric of modern life.

Women, forever intimate and integrated with men, have been subservient to them, to a greater or lesser extent, in all societies. The women's movement is without precedent because of the special ambivalences that mark the relationship of women to men—the components of attraction and withdrawal; love and hate; need and distaste—which have not been characteristic of other subordinate groups. Furthermore, through the current movement women have sought to do more than demand greater access to the resources of society; they have wanted redefinition of who they are and what they are worth both in private relationships and in public ones.

It is difficult to analyze the extent of these changes within American society. One can look at the data—statistics that indicate rates of change in terms of numbers of women who now work in fields they never worked in before; numbers of women entering business and professional schools. Such changes are extensive if one measures what has happened since the beginning of the woman's movement in the mid-60s. But statistics do not indicate the cause of change, or whether it is rooted or ephemeral.

Because more has happened to alter the position of women in the past ten years than for a score of decades before, I think it is safe to assume that the woman's movement was the driving force. Neither past changes in the economy nor the two world wars, which utilized womanpower as never before, caused real alterations in women's roles. Although "the pill" surely made a large difference, contraception was widely used prior to its invention, and fertility, which increased or decreased according to the impact of other experiences, showed in general a downward trend.

Although millions of women had left home to take jobs during World

War II, traditional ideology convinced them to yield these jobs to male veterans after the war. And while there is some debate as to whether women left factory jobs voluntarily or were laid off because of low seniority, veterans' job priorities, and the closing of war-producing factories, women did not assert their "right" to jobs previously defined as men's work. They were also persuaded that their first commitment was to the home, whether or not they worked. Myth conquered reality, and few recognized that a growing proportion of the labor force—close to one-third and increasing every year—were women. "Should or could women work?" was the eternal debate, while in fact women were working.

Most social commentators agree that Betty Friedan's book *The Feminine Mystique* provided the ideological underpinning for a woman's movement.

In writing *The Feminine Mystique,* Friedan became a Tom Paine for women. It was an analytic book, and it had popular appeal. In it Friedan sketched the problems women faced in a society that judged itself by the degree of equality it offered its citizens while excluding women from that judgment. The problems of black people were obvious to all—even to those who chose not to do anything about them. But whether women had a problem, or how important it was, seemed unclear to women themselves.

Friedan's book described a malaise, "the problem that had no name." She gave form to women's distress, and provided sound social structural reasons for it. She indicated how women's powerlessness drove them to lives of vicarious fulfillment, and how as consumers but not producers they were playing a frustrating role, but one necessary for the continuation of the economic system.

Friedan translated ideas into action when she organized the National Organization for Women (NOW) in 1966, and ever since she has been at the forefront of the enterprise, from the organization of the Women's Political Caucus to the first women's bank, and currently the Economic Think Tank on Women.

Friedan does not follow any "great man" model of leadership. Lacking both conventional charisma of person and the charisma of family or office, but with a compelling intensity, she became a person with a message to be reckoned with, at a time when conditions in the economy and the ideological structure of the society were ripe for change.

We have no model of leadership for women; there is only the model of the ideal woman whose qualities of dedication to demure service and soft nurturance are inconsistent with the demands of a leader's office. Men might fight for liberty, but women were to defend only the sanctity of the home and morality; liberty, with its connotations of self-realization, was not deemed her province.

While Susan B. Anthony, Elizabeth Cady Stanton, and others who organized the first woman's rights conference in Seneca Falls, New York, in 1848 were regarded as revolutionaries and insurrectionists, Friedan has drawn fire from both the Left and the Right—accused both of middle-class reformism and disruption of the family. Part of the attack is directed at the alleged impropriety of her personal style and appearance.

How curious that not only is the leader of the woman's movement judged by how well she fits the acceptable modes for a proper lady, but so too is the *movement itself*! Polls indicate a growing sentiment in support of more equality for women, but they show that women not associated with women's groups do not care to be thought of as "women's lib" types. In fact, a current poll by the Roper organization shows that 57 percent of the women questioned favored efforts to strengthen their status, an increase over the figures reported in 1971 and 1972 by Louis Harris, in which 40 percent and 48 percent expressed support. But in 1972, 49 percent were still unsympathetic with efforts of women's liberation groups.

Perhaps it is characteristic of subjugated groups to become convinced that they have little right to question the views of their "betters." It has certainly been true of women, who, in public debate and in philosophical and psychoanalytic tracts, have accepted such definitions and the rationales supporting them. The antiegalitarian views—the Old and New Testaments; the writings of Nietzche, Freud, and even of political theorists such as Jefferson—have gained popular support through time while competing views—those of John Stuart Mill, Charlotte Gilmans Perkins, and later Karen Horney—did not.

I suggest that this is not because the competing ideas were less philosophically or scientifically sound, but because the gatekeeping, both formal and informal, of the males in power created support for the explanations they preferred. Furthermore, the longer these views were supported and adopted by a majority of people, the more "normal" they appeared to be.

The change of the feminist movement at the turn of the century from a radical ideology demanding change throughout society to one of relative moderation was probably caused by the powerlessness of women. Earlier, just getting the vote had been dismissed by Elizabeth Cady Stanton as "not even half a loaf; . . . only a crust, a crumb."

Getting the vote did not even put women into the *political* mainstream. Aside from pressure in the 1920s, which led to protective work legislation, women did not create focused political interest or do much lobbying. Under pressure from the Catholic bishops, Congress had by 1929 cut appropriations for the Women's Bureau and the Children's Bureau. The vote became like money in the bank that its owners were afraid to spend even as it lost value through inflation. At most, women's suffrage may have put a brake on the further enactment of regressive legislation.

If women were not exercising political power, they were moving into the labor market in increasing numbers and played active nontraditional worker roles during the two world wars. A general movement toward mass primary and secondary education, and then toward higher education for many students, meant that women were no longer confined to the home. The home may have been where their heart was, or was expected to be, but their feet were often off and running.

Yet each bit of advancement was met with severe opposition. Educating women or opening opportunities to work have not necessarily been indicators of public sentiment supporting women's *rights* to equality. What made the women's movement in the U.S. unique was that changes in behavior and attitudes were demanded, not only in the society but in personal life as well.

In that way American women were more avant-garde than their sisters in the East European countries. We know that Soviet women physicians (75 percent of all doctors) must also perform household duties unassisted by husbands, and without the mechanical aids available to American housewives. The Soviet grandmother is the chief child-care institution in that country, as she is still in Italy, France, Germany, and, to some extent, in the United States. Child care and housework still seem to be assigned to women universally, and this checks their ability to assume commanding positions in other areas of life, even where they constitute dominant numbers. In all countries, and in the "socialist" ones too, despite the ideological claims of writers from Engels to Mao, entrenched habits of mind linked with the vested interests of men in power have kept women assigned to roles men don't respect or wish to perform. In no country has women's equality yet been accomplished, or has there been complete reevaluation of modes of thought that define women's capacities and roles.

To return to the American situation: in initiating a new woman's movement in 1966, Betty Friedan took a step that was to raise the consciousness of millions of American women and result in the formation of thousands of groups, both formal and informal. Moving swiftly, organizations such as NOW and WEAL (Women's Equity Action League) sought to implement the Civil Rights Act of 1964. This act, intended to stop discrimination against minorities, was amended to include sex in a last-minute effort by Representative Howard W. Smith (D. Va.) who thought the added word might send the entire act to defeat. Not only did the act pass, it provided the major foundation for movement activity. The combination of law and the organization of women was powerful. There were other allies. The Equal Economic Opportunities Commission (EEOC), which before had handled only cases of discrimination against minority people, established guidelines for compliance with Civil Rights Act provisions relating to women. It was the EEOC and a number of feminist lawyers who took on the American Telephone and Telegraph Company, the largest employer of women in the world, and won a landmark agreement forcing AT&T to provide goals and timetables for the hiring and promotion of women and minorities. AT&T was also forced to pay $15 million in back pay to persons who had been denied promotion because of discrimination and $23 million in immediate annual pay increases to women and minority males who were deemed underpaid in their job classifications.

The EEOC action against AT&T not only demonstrated that women had power if they cared to use it, but that there was support for their position in and out of government. Contrary to critics who labeled the women's movement an enterprise of privileged white middle-class women, the AT&T case proved that women working for women were working for women at all levels of the socioeconomic pyramid. It showed that women were oppressed as a class and that legislation giving middle-class women an opportunity to be hired as lawyers also gave lower-income women the opportunity to be promoted as supervisors in factories and businesses.

Middle-class women had louder voices than lower-income ones; perhaps because their aspirations were spurred by rising opportunities they were more discontented. Many of the women most involved in "causes" were drawn from those who had been active in the civil rights movement or had been student activists. In the late 1960s these women started realizing the extent to which they themselves were victims of discrimination. Assigned to the kitchen to cook for striking students in Columbia University; hooted off the platform at the SDS national convention for introducing women's liberation resolutions; mocked by Stokely Carmichael in his classic remark that the only position for women in the movement was "prone"—young women, finding themselves somehow excluded from all social reform programs, sought focus for their rights.

Splinter groups broke away from NOW in the late 1960s over issues of radical politics and on the role of lesbians in the movement. As Friedan was asking for women to be "in equal partnership with men," some women's groups were campaigning for separatism. A few groups argued that women should join together in their own communities, away from man, the enemy. Lesbianism, in this context, was seen politically as a way of life for women who could express their sexuality apart from men. In fact, sexuality and sexual activity became targets of attack. Beliefs concerning women's sexuality had long been used to legitimate their second-class status. Biology, it turned out, was more politics than science. New freedoms in sexual morality, which gave women permission to discard the ideal of chastity, had their repressive side. Young men expected them to be more available sexually outside of marriage and the women felt a compulsion to comply. There were no longer unequal costs to women for having sexual relationships, and some were beginning to initiate them, but sexual equality, women soon found out, was not necessarily linked to equality in other spheres.

Although sexual mores had been changing toward greater liberality since the Victorian period, the talk about sex still seemed radical to many Americans. It was one thing to be for equal pay for equal work. It was another thing to be in on the discussion about the "big O," Women's liberationists campaigned for the clitoral orgasm as Freud, in his way, had campaigned for the vaginal orgasm. Women were insisting on their right to orgasm in reaction to older claims that women weren't as capable of sexual fulfillment as men. Here, as in other spheres, new freedoms created backlash. It was claimed that men not only disliked all this talk about sexual rights for women, but were "turning off" and becoming impotent in response to these sexually emancipated women. All changes in the direction of emancipation effected by the women's movement could expect to be sabotaged in newer and more subtle ways.

Before the modern woman's movement existed, Philip Wylie was complaining that "Momism" was killing the manhood of American men, and indeed there was a spate of scientific studies that "proved" mothers were responsible for traits ranging from juvenile delinquency and homosexuality to aggressive achievement motivation. Now American women were reminded of their responsibility for maintaining the intensity of sexual drives in men. So vulnerable were men, it was claimed, their very sexuality was dependent on women's submissive behavior. Science also provided a number of studies to back up that notion and showed case after case where female animals had to present themselves submissively to males in order for sex to work.

Intellectual and political arguments over sexual capacity, sexual etiquette, and sexual "rights" were fought in the laboratory, movement meetings, the media, and in the bedroom. But it was clear that whatever truths were discovered, their interpretation could be used to serve any side of an issue. Science, like alcohol, can apparently make people sexier by loosening their inhibitions, or frigid by depressing them. Science had still not provided the answer to who was fit to make decisions in society.

The women's movement meanwhile was working steadily and expanded into academic and professional organizations of all types. Formally excluded from male societies, women sometimes had formed separate professional associations (which had low prestige and little power) or served peripherally in service roles in the "integrated" organizations. In the past six or seven years, however, these major associations have had to cope with emergent women's caucuses, which pressed for representation in decision-making committees and offices. (A recent count showed women's units within 67 professional organizations as diverse as the Society for Cell Biologists and the American Management Association.) These organized professional women were instrumental in increasing the representation of women in professional and graduate schools.

As women became more vocal in these male domains, they also insisted that sexism was embodied in the work of the professions and that it be identified and routed out. Thus women in medicine urged more respect for women as patients and the more serious study of diseases associated with their sex. There was pressure for demystification of the male medical establishment by feminists and young male physicians who had become alert to the problems of minority groups in getting good medical care. Many women had felt physicians often treated them as hypochondriacal half-wits whose gynecological pains seemed less worthy of medical concern than pains associated with more androgenous zones of the body. Young feminists formed self-help clinics and recruited sympathetic women doctors, although there were few to choose from. Quotas on women in medical schools, like those in law and business schools, had been kept at a fairly constant 3–10 percent from the first opening of the doors to women until the late 1960s. Feminists also analyzed medical texts in current use and exposed stereotyped characterizations of women's psychological makeup which had no basis in reality, in the same way they monitored the media and schoolchildren's texts for stereotyping of women in classic housewife roles.

In law, a number of vigorous women students' associations were formed. Slowly, the barriers to admission of women eased. That change did not come about by feminist effort alone. The movement was gaining strength in a context of concern with civil rights and it was also the time of debate over the Vietnam war. Women found it easier to get into law schools, not because the doors were opened in immediate accord with their demands, but because there were fewer male applicants (draft exemptions were not granted for law school). Furthermore, young women were beginning to feel that by going to law school they could "be something"—a lawyer—an experience few could have had after earning a degree in history or literature.

Young women lawyers (as well as interested male researchers) learned that in a number of states women offenders were likely to receive stiffer sentences than men for the same crimes, because women's criminality was perceived as more threatening to the moral structure of society than men's. The attitudes of judges and other lawyers toward women clients and attorneys became the target of feminist attack.

Still there was evidence that in some professions the study of women or problems relating to women was not considered as serious as study of other problems. Family matters, or any areas related too closely to women, have always been at a disadvantage in the prestige structure of the professions; to be a marriage and divorce lawyer always meant to be less of a lawyer, as to be a family sociologist meant to be of lower rank than a sociologist of organizations.

Certainly, word was spreading throughout the U.S. Although much media news about women's endeavors to improve their situation was tinged with derision and humor, and often only the dramatic and radical activities gained attention (picketing and those oft-cited but infrequent bra-burning demonstrations), women throughout America were reporting that they were reassessing their roles as housewives and mothers. They were becoming sensitive to the discrimination they were facing in getting jobs, getting credit, the dependency problems they had in marriage and the disorienting anomie that divorce created in their lives. Consciousness-raising groups started in suburban neighborhoods with middle-aged women following the models set by young, college-aged women in urban centers. In fact, college-aged women, infused with a sense of the waste they saw as the tragedy of their mothers' lives, seemed to be turning more toward planning careers that could be held (still in conjunction with marriage) throughout life.

Women not counted among the many thousands in feminist organizations were nevertheless following feminist principles even as they rejected the "taint" of identification with the movement. A 1974 poll reported that almost half (46 percent) the women polled in a national sample preferred a marriage "where husband and wife share responsibilities more—both work, both share homemaking and child-care responsibilities."

Still, large questions remain. The great fear of feminists is that the movement's apparent great strides will turn out to be token changes or the result of fads. There are also fears of the repercussions that may result from entrance of very large numbers of women into professions where they were virtually absent before. Now that many law schools have classes that are nearly half female, the question remains whether substantial numbers will be able to get jobs. Law firms often were pleased to hire a few exceptionally able women attorneys; and the few women engineers who graduated in the early 1970s can pick and choose among companies looking for minority recruits. But feminists are aware that affirmative-action programs in these organizations are the motivating factor in their hiring and not a sudden appreciation of women's talents.

Increasingly tight economic conditions create another source of trouble. Employers may feel freer to retreat to older hiring practices, especially when their token group has been completed. In 1970, 65 percent of American women polled by Gallup believed they got as good a break in life as men, and the 1974 Roper poll reported that three out of four women interviewed said that being a woman has not prevented them from doing the things they wanted to do in life. There is always the chance that having won more equality in a few areas, as women did at the time they won the vote, they may lower their guard and their militancy.

It is too early to be certain of the lasting consequences of the women's movement. We can, however, sketch some areas of major change and others where change is significant but countered by other conditions.

- Item: While women have increased their percentages in law (from 3 percent to 4.9 percent between 1960 and 1970) and medicine (from 7 percent to 9 percent), this has not substantially affected the generally unchanging sex-division of labor. There continue to be tendencies toward creating boundaries between "men's work" and "women's work."
- Item: While more women are now getting jobs in the male-dominated professions, they are still being directed into types of work considered "suitable" for women, and avoiding, or being kept out of, male preserves. In the legal profession, for example, women could only find work in the trusts and estates divisions of large firms, or had specialties in divorce, child custody, and real-

estate work in smaller firms. Today women lawyers are "choosing" specialities that seem largely the same or their equivalent. For example, newly created women's firms are dealing with "women's matters" (such as sex discrimination and rape as well as divorce) and thus come to be professional ghettos.

The "ghetto" phenomenon is manifested in other ways. Many new women professors in law schools are asked to teach "women and the law" courses and find they are often lecturing mainly to women.

- Item: More women have entered graduate schools of business administration and are then getting management trainee positions in government and business. But it is clear that many of them are made assistants to senior executives, or administrative assistants in charge of personnel or affirmative-action programs. Although these are "management" positions (and thus count on the charts monitored by government agencies) and pay executive-level salaries, these jobs are not on the track to high administrative offices. Women, like blacks, are given separate work, apparently equal to male executive jobs but unequal in career potential.

- Item: Many more women seem to be running for political office. Those who are elected are highly visible and some (Bella Abzug and Shirley Chisholm) have spectacular images. An important qualitative change over the past is that a growing number of women in political life seem to have made their mark without attachment to a male politician. It was not so in the past. Becoming a widow of a congressman or senator was a common route for women in American legislative life. Yet Ella Grasso, just elected governor in Connecticut, or Congresswomen Bella Abzug, Shirley Chisholm, and Elizabeth Holtzman of New York, and Yvonne Braithewaite of California all seem to be their "own women."

- Item: The woman's movement gained strength during a time of high employment and a vigorous economy. There is great fear that a depression would destroy the now uneasy balance between the feminists and the gatekeepers of the opportunity structure. Young men, now seen as more egalitarian than their elders, may become more conservative as they face the competition of increasing numbers of women for a limited supply of jobs. At the level of middle management, men express fears that they are increasingly deprived of chances for upward mobility because blacks and women are favored for promotions. The statistics do not substantiate these fears, but it is certainly possible they may be realized as more women become trained.

· Item: Women are going to work at all levels of the economic pyramid, and married women, even with preschool children, have become more firmly attached to the labor force. The number of working mothers whose youngest child is in the age group from three to five rose by 13.2 percent since 1960; it is now 38.3 percent of employed women. Those with children under three went up to 29.4 percent.

An increasing number of female heads of households, both black and white, have no choice but to work. And as inflation puts a greater strain on family incomes, it creates a need for both spouses to work. Currently 56 percent of husband-wife families are multiple-worker families, an increase over the present 47 percent of 1963.

All of these factors create new conditions for the playing-out of the ambiguous commitment Americans have to women's equality. Clearly, backlash is mobilizing in many forms. Employers are protesting the economic costs of special training for women. (The whole notion of the need for special training may be a bugaboo. It seems clear that women need jobs more than training, especially because most work is learned on the job.) Many groups are protesting what they regard as preferential treatment for designated minorities. The reaction of some Jewish groups against quotas (e.g., the DeFunis case) speaks to the sensitivity caused by competition between minority groups for a limited number of places.

There is also the insidious backlash many women are experiencing in their personal relations with men. Although most men today find it necessary to indicate a commitment to the ideals of equality, the translation of it into their personal lives is difficult and often cumbersome. Marriages seem ever more fragile under the new assaults of the incongruent needs for autonomy and privacy, for rest and support on the part of both partners.

Any set of freedoms creates problems of disharmonies between the rights and needs of the individuals involved. Not only the men, the women too, tire of the battle and may retreat into traditional models of marriage to reestablish equilibrium in their lives. But even this is often no solution because neither partner is really convinced of the ideological worthiness of the compromise.

All movements need momentum, and an ever-militant corps who will unceasingly maintain pressure. Many women are consolidating the gains they have achieved in the struggle for equality by uncovering myths, by advancing in their work, without letting a sense of defeat stop their efforts. But there is often little time for movement activity if they have a job and are also doing the dishes and being the mothers in a society still unresponsive to the needs of women for household assistance and child care.

Furthermore, there is some indication that attention directed toward improving the status of women is now being diverted into other realms. Energy and the economy have the headlines. With a sense that enough has been done, government and the private sector may lean back and lessen their efforts.

There is indication that the issue of women's equality is still a joke at high levels. Witness President Gerald Ford's first address to a joint session of Congress on August 12, and his egregious assertion that he would be "the President of black, brown, red and white Americans, of old and young, of women's liberationists and male chauvinists and all the rest of us in between. . . ." But consider the uproar he would have generated had he asserted he fell somewhere "between" the racists and egalitarians. The next day, his wife, when questioned on her views of women's liberation apparently felt it a thorny issue, and only committed herself as far as "equal pay and equal opportunity" were concerned.

The achievements of the women's movement are not a joke, nor are those women who are committed to winning full equality. The swiftness with which they have advanced probably acts in their favor. Many remember the quality of life and work before (was it only ten years ago?), and none will forget the hard work that went into changing them.

None will easily let the new freedoms slip away. Today there is enough organizational structure in local communities and nationally, in business and the professions, to keep movement projects going and recruit new adherents. A major recession would hurt everyone and probably minority groups most, but this society's general acceptance of the idea of equality will make it difficult substantially to undo the work of these past ten years.

—1975

ghosts of vietnam
THEODORE DRAPER

The Vietnam war was beyond doubt the most demanding test of American foreign policy and its makers since the Second World War. The war in Vietnam was not just another crisis in 30 years of successive crises; it was by far the most costly and most stultifying. It lasted longer than any other war and ended in the most humiliating failure in American history. It resulted in over 210,000 American casualties, including almost 57,000 dead and over 150,000 wounded. The monetary cost has been officially estimated at from $180 billion to $210 billion. This bill for the war ignores all the indirect costs, such as the corrosive economic inflation it stimulated and the feverish social turmoil it provoked. As for the havoc inflicted on North and South Vietnam, it belongs to a different order of magnitude. No wonder that the memory of Vietnam is so oppressive that Americans seem to want to stuff it away in their collective unconscious.

One might well assume that the present custodians of American foreign policy had been chosen because they were proven right in their judgment of the war. It could come as a surprise that, in order to rise to the top of the post-Vietnam American political system, it was almost necessary to be wrong, hopelessly and certifiably wrong. Yet, in some odd way, this is what happened. The false counsellors were rewarded with more power than they had had before they made their ghastly mistakes about the war.

President Jimmy Carter consistently supported the war and was saved from making his support too conspicuous only by his relative obscurity in national politics. Secretary of State Cyrus Vance was another proponent of the war, also sheltered from too much public notice by his inability or unwillingness to speak out very forcefully about anything. Both of them seem to think that it was enough for them to say, "Sorry, folks, we were wrong about the war," to gain political absolution. They were more fortunate than Professor Zbigniew Brzezinski and his predecessor as national security adviser, Dr. Henry Kissinger. Kissinger managed to find bad reasons to support what he knew was a bad war; Brzezinski hit on essentially the same reasons for what he thought was a good war. And now, as the most influential member of his staff and his closest confidant, Brzezinski has with him Professor Samuel P. Huntington, one of the hardest of prowar hardliners and the least repentant.

In one respect, the problem of the Vietnam war resembled that of the Korean war. Since American interests in both Korea and Vietnam were minimal, other reasons had to justify American intervention. In the case of Korea, American policy-makers considered North Korea to be nothing but a Soviet puppet ordered by Moscow to attack South Korea as the opening move in a larger strategy to "probe for the weakness in our armor," as former President Truman put it, in order to start a process of disintegration in the entire American structure of allies and dependents throughout Europe and Asia.

Fighting Russia in Korea was what made the war seem necessary and worthwhile. According to this reasoning, the Soviets should have taken advantage of their success in bogging down the bulk of American armed forces in Korea for three years, particularly at the time of the crushing defeat of General MacArthur's forces by Chinese armies across the Yalu River at the end of 1950, which was presumably what the wire-pullers in the Kremlin had been waiting for. Instead, the Korean war increasingly lived a life of its own. The original rationale for getting into it became dimmer and dimmer, and all that remained was to get out of it as gracefully and cheaply as possible. The Korean war turned out essentially to be a *Korean* war, which ultimately made it tangential to America's larger interests and preposterously expensive for what we could get out of it. Whatever the Russian role might have been, and we still know little for sure about it, the Korean war was far more a feint than the real thing.

The Vietnam war followed the same general course. In the beginning, the Truman administration injected itself into the French imbroglio in Indochina with vast amounts of financial assistance and military equipment, ostensibly to bolster French pride and stability and to gain French support for American defense plans in Europe. After the outbreak of the Korean war, the struggle in Indochina took on a wider connotation as part of a worldwide Communist "conspiracy." With the defeat of France in 1954, the Eisenhower administration took over responsibility for South Vietnam, now split off from North Vietnam by the Geneva accords, on the ground that loss of all of Vietnam would inevitably bring about the loss of all the other "dominoes" in Southeast Asia, including Thailand, Malaya, Burma, and Indonesia. In the stage of massive, direct American intervention during the Johnson administration, the real enemy in Vietnam became China, a point of view put forward most extravagantly by then former Vice-President Richard M. Nixon in 1965 and with monumental obtuseness by Secretary of State Dean Rusk in 1966 and afterward. Without superimposing a larger framework on the Korean and Vietnam wars, American policymakers would have been forced to acknowledge that essentially they were civil wars—civil wars with outside backing but still primarily localized civil wars—and not the opening shot of the Final Conflict. We might still have been drawn into them, but at least we would have known what we were doing and what they were worth to us.

How difficult it was to justify American intervention in Vietnam intellectually is strikingly shown by the travail of two outstanding foreign-affairs intellectuals—Henry Kissinger and Zbigniew Brzezinski. If they could not think up better reasons for supporting the war, no one could.

Kissinger's position on the war made its first public appearance in *Look* magazine of August 9, 1966, in the second year of massive American intervention. In an article written after he had made two trips to Vietnam at the invitation of then Ambassador Henry Cabot Lodge, Kissinger set forth two principal propositions. One was that the war could not be won by military means. The other was that it had to be settled by negotiation. In effect, he succeeded in establishing some distance between himself and both the extreme hawks and extreme doves. Kissinger had clearly learned enough during his two tours of Vietnam and from his Pentagon sources to make him extremely cautious about committing himself to anything that might be called "victory."

After outlining this equivocal approach, Kissinger fell silent on the issue of Vietnam for almost two years, an uncharacteristic reticence that his friendly memorialists have had great difficulty explaining.

Kissinger broke his silence on Vietnam in the summer of 1968, by which time even the inner circles of the Johnson administration had given up the war as a lost cause. At a conference on Vietnam in Chicago in June of that year, sponsored by the Adlai Stevenson Institute of International Affairs, Kissinger savagely criticized American policy, especially its "concepts"—military concepts, traditional liberal concepts, balance-of-power concepts, indeed the entire "American philosophy of international relations." If American policy was that bankrupt, one might imagine that the best thing to do would be to get out of the war as soon as possible at the least possible cost. But Kissinger did not offer any new concepts or policies himself; he merely called for a "prayerful assessment" of the procedures and concepts that had landed us in such a mess.

Kissinger saved his own conceptual prescription for the speeches that he composed for Governor Nelson Rockefeller in the presidential campaign that summer and for an article in *Foreign Affairs* written in his own name in the same period. The basic idea—or, to use Kissinger's favorite term, "concept"—was that of a negotiated settlement, hardly a novel one at the time. More important were the conditions that Kissinger attached to such a settlement. It had to be arrived at in such a way that it did not shake "confidence in American promises" or compromise American "credibility," "prestige," or "steadiness." The key word was "honorably"—the war had to be ended "honorably." He conceived of doing so by means of a U.S.-Soviet-China "subtle triangle," whereby the United States would improve its relations with the two leading Communist powers and thereby achieve or at least advance an honorable settlement in Vietnam through them.

By this time, the United States in essence had no other stake in Vietnam than its "honor." Here again, the hard questions were evaded. What if the United States could not end the war "honorably" without paying an exorbitant price for the attempt, and then not succeed anyway? What if the road to peace in Vietnam did not run through Russia and China? What if Russia and China themselves were to work at cross purposes in Vietnam and elsewhere? Kissinger's honorable settlement in Vietnam was fitted into his rickety new "global, conceptual approach," which presupposed that Russia and China could restrain North Vietnam and that the Thieu regime in South Vietnam could be made capable of defending itself without American armed forces. Without these presuppositions, it would have made no sense for the Nixon-Kissinger policy to drag the American people through four more years of a war emptied of all meaning but that of getting out of a trap into which the United States should never have fallen.

When did Kissinger awake to the realities of the war? His friend Professor John G. Stoessinger tells us that it took Kissinger until the fall of 1971, all of three long, bloodstained Nixonian years, to realize that "Hanoi would not compromise." In 1972, Kissinger thought that he could get a Soviet "linkage" to a Vietnam settlement through the grain deal, which gave hundreds of millions of dollars worth of American wheat to Russia at bargain prices at the expense of the American consumer, a price that, Kissinger argued, "was well worth a Vietnam settlement." Again he was disappointed. Finally, on the day that Saigon fell in the spring of 1975, Kissinger told Stoessinger: "Vietnam is a Greek tragedy. We should never have been there at all. But now it's history." As an epitaph on this war, "We should never have been there at all" may never be excelled.

Unlike Kissinger, Brzezinski was at first much less circumspect. He was one of the first of the most militant defenders of the prowar faith; he supported the war aggressively in a notable television debate in which his opposite intellectual number was Professor Hans Morgenthau, who was never taken in by the war. Brzezinski's service in behalf of the war helped to get him an appointment in 1966 to the State Department's Policy Planning Council. *Newsweek* hailed him as "one of the fastest-rising stars in the Johnson Administration" and "one of the architects of U.S. foreign policy" after only four months on the job. As for "his hawkish position on Vietnam," the magazine's piece entitled "Diplomacy: The Thinker," went on, "he is apt to act as though he had a monopoly of the truth." The cheering was premature; Brzezinski returned to Columbia University after two years in Washington, apparently sorely disillusioned with the exercise of planning without power.

In this period, Brzezinski had little sympathy with antiwar demonstrators. In an article in *Foreign Affairs* of July 1966, he put them down as "a manifestation of a psychological crisis inherent in modern society." Vietnam, he wrote scornfully, was merely "an outlet for basic cravings and fears, and if that issue did not exist, some other one would provide an excuse for the expression of personal and political alienation." This was one way of exonerating the Vietnam war of blame for the widespread popular unrest and widespread opposition to the war.

By 1968, Brzezinski's attitude toward the war showed signs of unbearable strain. On the one hand, he gave up a clear-cut victory in Vietnam; he was now satisfied with denying victory to the enemy, though he never explained how the no-victory-no-defeat for either side was going to be calibrated. On the other hand, he told the *U.S. News & World Report* of February 26, 1968, that he wanted the United States to make it clear that it was willing to continue to fight in Vietnam for 30 years in order to prove to the enemy that "we have the staying power" and "happen to be richer and more powerful." He gave as his reason for such a long-range projection that the United States could not "commit itself to the extent it has, and 'chicken out.'"

By now, there was little or nothing in Vietnam that made 30 years of war advisable or necessary, even to a hitherto fervent supporter of the war; it was the American "commitment" itself that condemned us to an almost unimaginably interminable bloodletting. Thirty years of war was so breathtakingly long that Brzezinski might as well have said "forever." And all this for not even victory. Rereading this interview, one cannot take it seriously. What it suggests is that even as sharp and knowledgeable a specialist in foreign affairs as Brzezinski had completely lost his way and no longer made sense when he talked about the Vietnam war.

By 1969, Brzezinski himself must have realized that he had to find his way back to some kind of sanity about the war. Richard Nixon was now president and vast demonstrations all over the country for a Vietnam "moratorium" had just taken place. In these circumstances, Brzezinski advised Nixon to pledge the removal of American forces from Vietnam "by a particular date (say, two years)." In this statement to the *New York Times* of October 17, 1969, Brzezinski forgot about the 30-years war and neglected to make clear why it was better to "chicken out" in two years rather than immediately.

After this, Brzezinski apparently decided that it was the better part of valor to leave the Vietnam war alone. While the country was in an uproar over it during the first Nixon administration, he turned his attention to other matters—the "technetronic era," Japan and Africa. This intellectual flying-trapeze act took him out of the line of fire and broadened his horizon in preparation for bigger things to come. It was also an admission that the war had become too much for even its most ardent and hardened supporters. It had become intellectually insupportable and even unmentionable.

Brzezinski's advice against "chickening out" and Kissinger's emphasis on ending the war "honorably" were essentially similar in motivation. We were supposed to go on fighting to prove something to ourselves or to the world at large, not to achieve anything of material or political interest in Vietnam. Brzezinski's temporary aberration of fighting on for 30 years was the logical outcome of this line of reasoning. If we could not end the war "honorably" and could not "chicken out," it had to go on and on indefinitely. Brzezinski's bravado was thus the *reductio ad absurdum* of the Vietnam war. Even he seems to have realized it in time.

In the end, Kissinger blamed Watergate and a failure of nerve for the debacle in Vietnam. The American people, Congress, South Vietnam, North Vietnam and the Soviet Union had all conspired to let down Henry Kissinger. The implication that his own people had failed him suggests that Kissinger's understanding of warfare left something to be desired. A good general—and even a good lieutenant—assesses his own strength as objectively as that of the enemy; he does not go into battle without taking into account what his own forces are capable of accomplishing and, in the particular case of the American people, what they are willing to fight for and at what cost. It was violation of this cardinal rule of warfare, not failure of nerve, that brought about the dishonorable end of the Vietnam war. It was the very nature of the war— a hopeless war in a land where we should never have been at all—that made its continuation so intolerable and its end so ignominious. There was no good way of getting out of the Vietnam war but the worst way was to pay the price of getting out later rather than sooner.

In effect, Kissinger and Brzezinski, two celebrated intellectuals who lent their considerable talents to a prolongation of the war, gave up the job of justification when they fell back on ending it "honorably" and not "chickening out." If they could do no better than that, the job was hopeless. Or so it seemed until now.

For we have just been offered a book that promises to relieve the American people of a sense of guilt for the Vietnam war and to absolve

the United States of "*officially condoned* illegal and immoral conduct."
The book is *America in Vietnam,* by Professor Guenter Lewy of the University of Massachusetts at Amherst. The work comes recommended by
Charles B. MacDonald, a military historian, as "a sober, objective answer to polemicists on all sides" that "should enable the Vietnam veteran at last to hold his head high." Has Lewy succeeded where Kissinger
and Brzezinski failed?

It should be said at once that those who read this book in order to
assuage their guilt over the war are doomed to disappointment. The
idea that it will enable a Vietnam veteran to hold his head high is utter
rubbish. It does not attempt to answer "polemicists on all sides"; it
polemicizes almost exclusively against the antiwar "polemicists." The
author, his admirers, and his publishers may have made a mistake in
presenting the book as if it were a wholesale apology for the war. This
presentation may be enough to arouse curiosity but it does an injustice
to the book as a whole.

It is a schizophrenic book. In large part, it made me writhe all over
again at the willful stupidity and obdurate delusions with which the war
was prosecuted. An almost unrelieved recital of mistakes and misdeeds
fills pages and pages of the book. There are two Lewys in this work—one
makes an admirable effort to get the facts straight; the other wants to
give the United States a clean bill of health or at least the benefit of the
doubt. Thus the book lends itself to different conclusions or interpreta-
tions depending on what chapter and even what paragraph one chooses
to cite. The scholar and the advocate struggle for supremacy; sometimes
one wins, sometimes the other.

It would be a mistake, therefore, for critics of the Vietnam war to
reject Lewy's work *in toto* because he betrays a special animus against
them, sometimes unfairly, or for hard-core supporters of the war to
accept it with glee because he seems to favor them from time to time.
Much of the book is the result of serious and painstaking research. If I
had to draw up a list of a half dozen books worth reading on the war, I
would put this one among them, despite its flaws.

But does the author make good his claim that "the sense of guilt
created by the Vietnam war in the minds of many Americans is not
warranted"? That is what the argument over this book is likely to
be about.

The answer partly depends on the answer to another question—guilt about what? There may be justifiable guilt about some things and not about others. Lewy never makes the distinction clear. He himself contributes the most damaging evidence that American officialdom was disastrously guilty of misconceiving and mishandling the war; he also attempts to clear it of some specific varieties of guilt on a most selective basis. Yet his generalizations would make it appear that the United States has no need to feel guilty at all about anything. Here and elsewhere, Lewy undermines his own book by overreaching and overstating.

For example, the American forces in Vietnam deliberately pursued a policy of "the encouragement and creation of refugees." This meant that combat operations, crop destruction, and "specified strike zones" were utilized to drive Vietnamese peasants from their homes in the hundreds of thousands. The most cruel and senseless practice for "generating" refugees or as it was also called euphemistically, "relocating populations," took the form of "free-fire zones." An American commander would simply decide to designate an area, often a huge one, as such a zone so that anyone who remained in it was arbitrarily considered an enemy and thereby subject to annihilating artillery or air bombardment. This policy was pursued on a large scale for at least five years. Only in 1968, after over two years of this practice, were commanders in the field advised that they should not generate refugees "needlessly and heedlessly," with little effect on the actual tactics employed; and only in February 1969 were commanders officially instructed to give at least 72 hours notice to civilians in the areas, as if Vietnamese peasants in far-flung areas were likely to receive and understand such notices or do more than save their disrupted lives if they did.

Lewy knows what was wrong with this horror. He lists seven "inherent weaknesses," including the fact that it was militarily useless and even played into the hands of the enemy. The vast majority of those driven from their homes were old people, women and children; few refugees were males of military age. Even so, the battlefield was not cleared, because refugees persisted in returning to their hamlets. The political madness of the policy comes out in his words: "Not surprisingly, attitude surveys showed a high degree of correlation between forcible evacuation and pro-Communist attitudes." He acknowledges that the crop-destruction program made the local people, not the Vietcong, suffer. He reveals that the American crop-destruction missions were disguised as South Vietnamese activity because the damage obviously could not be limited to the enemy forces to conform with the Army's own manual of land warfare.

Lewy documents more of the same. The fatuous policy of "body counts" encouraged the indiscriminate lumping of combatants and noncombatants, with the result that the killing of villagers could give as much credit as the killing of enemy soldiers, and the only ones really deceived were the Americans themselves. The strategy of attrition was an abject failure. The villagers turned against the United States because American military doctrine called for methods that were insensitive to political and human costs; the South Vietnamese and Korean allies trained in that doctrine behaved even more abominably. American commanders often gave only "token compliance" to orders from above to restrain their excessive use of fire power, so that "the worst features of the traditional mode of operation persisted." Corruption in the South Vietnamese army was so great that it enabled the enemy to purchase supplies in South Vietnamese cities, obtain war materiel and food from South Vietnamese officials and officers, and buy positions as hamlet and village chiefs. The once highly touted South Vietnamese land reform was no more than an "empty gesture." American brigade and division commanders falsified reports to hide their persistent utilization of an unauthorized herbicide agent. Lewy also retells the story of the secret bombing of North Vietnam, based on fictitious enemy-action reports, which brought about the demotion and retirement of General John D. Lavelle, commanding officer of the Seventh Air Force. He has an entire chapter on American "atrocities" in Vietnam, one of which was the My-Lai "massacre," using these very terms—"atrocity" and "massacre." He also describes the leniency of court-martials that dealt with these "war crimes"—again in this context his term.

The single American who comes off worst in Lewy's book is no ordinary officer or soldier. He is General William C. Westmoreland, chief of U.S. forces in Vietnam from 1964 to 1968, when he was recalled to become Army Chief of Staff. Lewy seems to hold Westmoreland most responsible for keeping to the disastrous strategy of "the big-unit war of attrition" long after it had been proven futile and self-defeating. In his most scathing indictment of Westmoreland, Lewy goes so far as to doubt that the general could defend himself against the charge that he was guilty of "dereliction of duty," because he should have known that American "violations of the law of war" were bound to take place in the circumstances of Vietnam and should have taken the necessary measures to prevent them.

If one sought to make a devastating condemnation of the Vietnam war, one could do so out of Lewy's book, as I have just done. But such an exercise would reflect only one side of the work. In another, the author seeks almost desperately to muffle his blows on the war and even to lead the unwary reader into believing that he is rushing to its defense.

One way Lewy tries to make a bad war look better is the soft reproach.

For example, President Johnson told reporters after the decision was made to use American troops in Vietnam that he knew of "no far-reaching strategy that is being suggested or promulgated." Lewy's comment is: "Needless to say, Johnson here was being less than candid." Needless to say, Lewy is being less than candid; Johnson knew that a far-reaching strategic change had been initiated and had deliberately misled the reporters and the American people. Or Lewy demonstrates that the so-called Rules of Engagement, ostensibly designed to minimize the destruction of civilian life and property, were extensively and sometimes wantonly disregarded in practice. Lewy's comment is that "this level of familiarity was obviously less than satisfactory." He might have said more satisfactorily that the level of familiarity was grossly unsatisfactory and even culpably negligent.

Sometimes Lewy likes to have it both ways. He raises the question whether South Vietnam could have survived if U.S. aid had not been cut off in 1975. His first answer tends to be highly pessimistic—"there is reason to believe that, everything else being equal, internal weaknesses on the part of the South Vietnamese armed forces alone might have been sufficient to cause defeat in 1975." A few pages later, however, he seems to backtrack. The odds were still against the South Vietnamese but their defeat was not a "foregone conclusion." If President Nixon had been able to dissociate himself from the Watergate burglars and had been able to reintroduce American military power in Vietnam as he had promised; if Congress had been persuaded to provide South Vietnam with adequate military supplies; if the OPEC nations had suffered an early breakup and oil had continued to be cheap; if the North Vietnamese had made a few major mistakes; if South Vietnamese nationalists and anti-Communist sects had been able to overthrow the Thieu regime. . . . After this long string of "ifs," Lewy concludes: "None of these events was impossible, and if their occurrence in combination was unlikely, this was no more so than the combination of opposite events which did in fact take place." In this way, Lewy cuts the ground from under his own work. He has spent most of his book making quite credible the combination of events that in fact took place, with particular emphasis on the internal weaknesses of the South Vietnamese armed forces. Then he turns around, belies his own work, and makes the historical record no more likely to have happened than the conveniently early breakup of OPEC. This is not the only instance where he seems to flinch from the implications of his own findings.

What, above all, gives Lewy the air of being a defender of the prowar faith is his criticism of the Vietnam war's critics. He always refers to them with a particularly wrathful peevishness. Sometimes, his tantrum gets in the way of elementary fairness.

I will offer myself as a case in point.

My book *Abuse of Power* was published in 1967. It was based on work done in the previous year and a half or so. Since Lewy's book has come out in 1978, 11 years later, it would be odd if he had not consulted material not available to me or to other critics a decade ago. In any case, Lewy decided to teach me a lesson about a major turning point in the war—President Johnson's decision in February 1965 to initiate large-scale bombing of North Vietnam.

To justify this momentous step, the State Department issued later that month a White Paper entitled *Aggression from the North: The Record of North Viet-Nam's Campaign to Conquer South Viet-Nam*. The thesis of the White Paper was—North Vietnamese forces had invaded South Vietnam in such numbers that the previously officially regarded civil war had turned into a foreign "aggression." The question naturally arose whether the incursion of North Vietnamese forces was large enough to justify the massive intervention of American ground forces. The White Paper was a propaganda flop because it failed to sustain the claim of a large-scale invasion from the North. Lewy admits the "weakness" of the White Paper. But then he goes on:

> Theodore Draper alleges that at the time the bombing of North Vietnam started, Hanoi had only 400 regular soldiers in the South. The U.S. converted this into an "invasion" in order to have a justification for its own escalation.

The footnote goes even further and changes the "allegation" into a "canard." An allegation implies a statement without supporting evidence; a canard means an unfounded and especially a false report. Could my treatment of the issue fairly be described as either a mere allegation or an outright canard?

I devoted almost eight pages to the question of the North Vietnamese infiltration southward. I related that Secretary of State Rusk had claimed that the entire 325th Division had been moved into South Vietnam by January 1965. But I noted that the White Paper the following month had not even mentioned the 325th, as it might have been expected to do. I also pointed out that Secretary of Defense McNamara, who should have known best, had in April 1965 confirmed the presence of only one battalion, estimated by him at 400 to 500 men, of the 325th in the south. Over a year later, in June 1966, Senator Mike Mansfield, the Democratic majority leader, had publicly repeated the number of "only about 400 North Vietnamese soldiers" in the South at the time of "the sharp increase in the American military effort" in early 1965. An enquiring reporter had subsequently learned that Senator Mansfield had obtained his figure from the Pentagon. Other evidence pointed in the same direction.

After laying out all the available information, I commented:

> Clearly we cannot be sure whether a battalion or a regiment or all of the 325th Division crossed into South Vietnam by January 1965 or at any other time. We could not be sure even if Secretaries Rusk and McNamara agreed, and their disagreement adds a dash of farce to what was otherwise one of the most grievous moments of the war. The most we can conclude from the available evidence

is that it was extraordinarily necessary for the Secretary of State to have an "invasion" of South Vietnam by a North Vietnamese organized unit at least as large as a division before the United States began its systematic bombing of the North in February 1965.

Thus I did not even foreclose the question of the number of North Vietnamese regular soldiers in the South in February 1965. I rather emphasized the official disparities, which at that time would have led any fair-minded observer not to know what to believe. My final word was: "We may still not know much about the elusive 325th, but we can know a great deal about how it was bandied to and fro by high American officials who could not even convince each other." Nor did I say that the United States had converted the smaller number of North Vietnamese regulars into an "invasion"; I said that Secretary Rusk, the only one who then vouched for the presence of an entire North Vietnamese division in the South, had shown an extraordinary need for at least a division to justify the U.S. bombing campaign in the North. My very point was that leading officials of the United States were divided in their pronouncements on the subject.

Can my treatment be fairly described as an "allegation," as if I had picked out a number without reason, or as a "canard," as if I had spread a demonstrably false, unfounded rumor? The real authors of the report about the 400 North Vietnamese regular soldiers in the South were Secretary McNamara and Senator Mansfield, no inconsequential authorities on such a matter, and their information had clearly come from the Pentagon. The most that could be said at the time was that Secretary Rusk and the State Department claimed to know better.

Lewy, however, has triumphantly brought forth a new source of intelligence on what I called "the elusive 325th." It comes from a "Working Paper of the U.S. State Department on the North Vietnamese Role in the War in South Vietnam," issued in May 1968. According to this "working paper," which did not appear in print in the United States until 1969, 4,000 North Vietnamese regulars went south by February 1965 and another 1,800 by March 1965. If the ultimate source was South Vietnamese, Lewy himself, in other connections, tells us how unreliable this source was; and if the data was provided two or three years after the event, it would be even more suspect.

Lewy's use of this "working paper" is so uncritical that it betrays his anxiety to defend the U.S. bombing at all costs.

- First, it appeared in 1968, almost three and a half years after the event and a year after I had shown what unholy confusion had attended the whole matter. Obviously, I could not have known of a 1968 "working paper" in 1967. Neither could Secretary Rusk have based himself on it in 1965.
- Second, the 1968 paper originated in the Department of State, not in the Department of Defense. There was nothing new about the State Department claims. I had already made known similar claims by Secretary of State Rusk in 1965. The problem arose because Secretary Rusk was controverted by Secretary of Defense McNamara and Senator Mansfield. A fair treatment would not have taken something put out by the State Department years later and subsequently generally ignored as if it were the last word on the subject; the discrepancy between the State Department and the Pentagon was the real question worth looking into, but Lewy chooses to ignore it.
- Third, the reason I was struck by the remarkably dissimilar versions of North Vietnamese infiltration by February 1965 was the inordinate importance attached to it as the justification for America's massive intervention. Whatever was the number of North Vietnamese regular troops in the South in 1965, the U.S. combat force in South Vietnam was already far greater. The U.S. force increased from 23,000 at the end of 1964 to about 125,000 in the summer of 1965. Even if the 1968 "working paper" is taken at face value, the number of North Vietnamese troops in the South increased from 2,000 at the end of 1964 to 7,000 by September 1965. The "working paper" itself alluded to the "relatively slow pace of the [North Vietnamese] buildup" in all of 1965. It was already clear to me in 1967 that the American decision to intervene on a large scale was based "on South Vietnamese weakness rather than North

Vietnamese strength." After all his pious protests against my "allegation" and "canard," Lewy ends by agreeing with me on this point. Somehow, a mere "allegation" and an outright "canard" had enabled me to reach the right conclusion.

I have gone into this example of Lewy's polemics against the "polemicists" because it shows how lacking in sobriety and objectivity he can be. It was necessary to go into it in some detail because the present reader could not be expected to have Lewy's book and mine at hand to refresh his memory regarding the background and significance of the question at issue. In effect, Lewy's book sometimes suffers from an excess of zeal, especially in his frequently intemperate dismissal of premature critics of the Vietnam war.

The heart of the matter is the peculiar strategy that Lewy employs to relieve Americans of a sense of guilt created by the Vietnam war and to dismiss from their consciences "charges of *officially condoned* illegal and grossly immoral conduct." He convinced me that this form of apologia is as doomed as the American war effort in Vietnam.

It is important to be clear about what Lewy defends. He does not defend the American way of war in Vietnam. He condemns its "obtuseness and mistakes in judgment." All that he affirms is that these were not the result of "culpable negligence." If the negligence was not "culpable," no war crimes were committed. He is operating here on a very narrow defensive front. The only sense of guilt he seeks to relieve is that for very legally circumscribed, intentional "war crimes."

The word "intentionally" plays a crucial role in his brief for the defense. He is willing to admit that "the rather free use of napalm and attacks upon fortified hamlets with artillery and air strikes can be criticized on humanitarian grounds"—to put it mildly in view of his own account of the ruthless, senseless devastation wrought by the "free-fire zones." Yet he can still find it "morally significant" that the tactics employed "did not intentionally aim at inflicting casualties upon the civilian population." Nevertheless, he had previously shown that, year after year, almost all the casualties brought about by these tactics were inflicted on the civilian population. He had previously shown that these casualties had been remorselessly inflicted on the civilian population because Vietnamese civilians and enemy soldiers or agents had been stupidly, arbitrarily, and indiscriminately lumped together. What in these circumstances is the meaning of "not intentionally"? What makes it so remarkably different for our sense of guilt from "intentionally"?

On one page, Lewy's apologia reveals its essential hollowness and heartlessness. His conclusion to a chapter on "American Military Tactics and the Law of War" begins with a general absolution:

> The American record in Vietnam with regard to observance of the law of war is not a succession of war crimes and does not support charges of a systematic and willful violation of existing agreements for standards of human decency in time of war, as many critics of the American involvement have alleged.

But the first sentence of the very next paragraph goes this way:

> If the American record is not one of gross illegality, neither has it been a model of observance of the law of war.

Here we have Lewy trying to have it both ways again. The second time around he merely absolves us of "gross illegality." How gross is "gross"? We can now see why Lewy italicized two words in his formulation of unwarranted charges of "*officially condoned* illegal and grossly immoral conduct." The conduct may be illegal but it is not all that bad unless it is *officially condoned;* it may be immoral but not anything to feel guilty about unless it is *grossly* immoral. How far up in the military hierarchy did illegal conduct have to go in order to be officially condoned? The "free-fire zone" horror was not merely officially condoned; it was officially conceived and carried out at the very top. It was persisted in by the American military command despite what Lewy calls its lamentable "cost-benefit equation." Lewy's tricky formulas do not white-wash illegal or immoral conduct; they defend it only from the most extreme accusations of such conduct.

In fact, Lewy betrays a guilty conscience of his own. In the very last paragraph of the same chapter, he draws back from making his entire case depend on the "law of war":

In the final analysis, of course, law alone, no matter how comprehensive and carefully phrased, cannot assure protection of basic human values. Back in the seventeenth century, Hugo Grotius, the father of modern international law, quoted with approval the advice which Euripides in *The Trojan Women* put into the mouth of Agamemnon addressing Pyrrhus: "What the law does not forbid, then let shame forbid." This counsel retains its moral worth. While the law of war is an extremely important means of mitigating the ravages of war, it cannot be considered an adequate and sufficient measure of human decency.

The implication is clear: Americans who read *Americans in Vietnam* should not feel guilty; they should feel ashamed. This substitution of terms is really the core of Lewy's case; it may make some readers feel better. It is a continuing shame, however, that the shamefulness of this war should be incidentally mentioned in a book designed to cover up the shame by taking refuge in narrow and dubious legalisms. I said at the outset that this was a schizophrenic book; it is never more schizophrenic than in a chapter that starts by seeking to acquit us of violating the "law of war" and ends by implicitly condemning us to shame.

I have thought it necessary to deal at some length with *America in Vietnam* because it is the most ambitious effort to decontaminate the American role in Vietnam. It is a vain, self-defeating effort. It will serve a useful purpose only if it makes us more acutely aware how stupid, miserable, and costly that war was.

The main reason for the predicament of Kissinger and Brzezinski in the past and Lewy in the present is that they had difficulty fitting the Vietnam war into a larger framework. The war was never worth fighting for Vietnam alone; it always had to be made subsidiary to a larger purpose. The trouble was that it did not quite fit any of those imposed on it.

Kissinger's reason for going on with the war made the entire American position in world affairs and even world peace depend on an "honorable" ending. "What is involved now is confidence in American promises," he wrote in 1968, and "ending the war honorably is essential for the peace of the world." In the end, an "honorable" settlement came to mean the preservation of the South Vietnamese regime or the frustration of a North Vietnamese victory, which amounted to the same thing. Thus the survival of a regime that almost all Americans in positions of authority regarded as hopelessly corrupt and hopelessly weak was endowed with a value and importance out of all proportion to what it could bear. The tangibles of national strength and stability were sacrificed to intangibles such as American "prestige" and "honor." Estimable as the latter may be, they were not worth the price that had to be paid for them in real assets. Even worse, honor went when power failed.

Kissinger's rationale for continuing the war betrayed a basic misunderstanding of both the world and the American people. It was darkly said that America's allies in Europe would lose all faith in American commitments if the United States let down South Vietnam. In fact, America's allies were increasingly alarmed at the frittering away of American resources in Vietnam and the social turmoil in the United States that threatened to escalate out of control. Ominous fears were also expressed as to what the American people might do if and when they woke up to the reality of a lost war, as if Nixonian America were Weimar Germany. When the war ended as badly as a war could possibly end, at least for the South Vietnamese, the popular American reaction was one of relief and fatigue. If it had been otherwise, former President Nixon would have been driven out for the sins of Vietnam instead of for the crimes of Watergate. The American people were not interested in an "honorable" end, whatever that might have been; they were interested in the end.

In his fighting-on-for-30-years period, Brzezinski made a similar miscalculation. He thought it was necessary to prove to the enemy "that we have the staying power" and "happen to be richer and more powerful." It was wrong for the United States to "chicken out," he said, because "the consequences of getting out would be far more costly than the expense of staying in." By 1968, when this rationalization was made, it was already abundantly clear that the riches and power that we had were not the right kind for a war in Vietnam and that we would be much less rich and far less powerful the longer we stayed. It was ludicrously wrong to have made the consequences of getting out far worse than the expense of staying in. These terrible consequences were supposed to have beset the United States in the world at large, not in

Vietnam, and all the world did when we got out was to heave a sigh of relief.

Ten years later, Lewy knows better than to bewail our loss of "honor" or "prestige." His problem is to explain the American failure in Vietnam, not to prevent it. He hints at an explanation without reflecting on what its implications might be.

Lewy twice uses the same phrase—that the United States and its allies in Vietnam failed "to understand the real stakes in a revolutionary war." He never explains what he understands by an American "revolutionary war" in Vietnam or how we could possibly have waged it. But the suggestion is dropped, and it is worth considering.

To have waged a revolutionary war in Vietnam, we would have needed a revolutionary South Vietnamese regime. Lewy has no illusions about the corruption and unpopularity of the Thieu regime. He even quotes a statement, with which he says many agreed, that "if Thieu wants to eliminate corruption in the army he must fire himself." Lewy also recognizes: "The war not only had to be won in South Vietnam, but it had to be won by the South Vietnamese." In effect, the United States could not have made it a revolutionary war even if it had wanted to do so. The politics of this war, which was decisive, was essentially decided by the Vietnamese themselves. The dilemma that this situation presented was: the war could not be won if it was not revolutionary, and it could not be revolutionary if it was up to the South Vietnamese.

Lewy also makes clear why the American armed forces were incapable of fighting a revolutionary war in Vietnam. He reports "the growing disdain for the Vietnamese people among U.S. military personnel in Vietnam." So many American soldiers were killed or wounded by mines and booby traps in or near hamlets that "it became the prudent thing to doubt the loyalty of every villager." The result was: "Some soldiers began to adopt the so-called mere-gook rule, the attitude that the killing of Vietnamese, regardless of sex, age, or combatant status, was of little importance for they were, after all, only gooks." Elsewhere, Lewy changes "some" to "many" soldiers who lived by this "rule," which helps to explain the high civilian casualties, civilian inclusion in the inflated body counts, and the deliberate "generation" of a vast horde of refugees. A survey of marines in 1966 in one province revealed that 40 percent disliked the Vietnamese; small-unit leaders ranked highest in their "negative attitudes." Fewer than 20 percent of noncommissioned officers had "a positive attitude" toward the South Vietnamese armed forces.

A "revolutionary war," then, was and is a political pipe dream. The Vietnam war could not be put into a revolutionary any more than it could comfortably be put into a larger international framework. When Kissinger at long last saw the light and told his friend Professor Stoessinger that "we should never have been there at all," he was saying only part of the depressing truth. The rest that needed to be said was that we should have decided to get out of the war as soon as possible, to cut our losses as soon as possible, to stop killing Vietnamese and Americans and wasting our national substance as soon as possible.

Of course, if the Carters and Vances and Kissingers and Brzezinskis had said all this prematurely, that is, when it needed to be said, they might not be where they are today. All they might have is the dismal satisfaction of knowing that they were right.

—1979

EIGHTIES

In Russia one of the jailers admitted to me in a moment of intimacy, "I would put all writers, without exception and independent of their greatness—Shakespeare, Tolstoy, Dostoevsky—into one big madhouse, because writers only disturb the normal development of life." I think this man is somehow right in his own way. He is right in that the writer, by the mere fact of his existence, introduces a kind of anxiety into the social system. . . . For such authors, as for dissidents in general, there exists a special juridical term in the Soviet Union: "especially dangerous state criminals." I personally fell into this category, and I hope to remain to the end of my days, in the eyes of Soviet society, an "especially dangerous state criminal."

Andrei Sinyavsky, "Dissent as Personal Experience," 1984

foreword
MAXINE PHILLIPS

For me the political tone of the eighties was set the night I invited a friend over to watch the 1980 presidential election returns. I popped the popcorn, arranged the television for easy viewing, and settled in. But our evening was over before it had started. We had no sooner gotten comfortable than the networks called the election for Ronald Reagan.

Irving Howe titled his 1980 election analysis in *Dissent* "How It Feels to Be Hit by a Truck," and his words were prescient. The gloom hadn't lifted when I joined *Dissent* in 1985.

My first impression of *Dissent* was, however, not of its politics but of the European-born widows who played such an important role in its day-to-day operation: business manager Simone Plastrik, a Polish-born French woman with deep roots in the socialist movement; Hedwig Pachter, who spoke five languages and proofread the journal as a volunteer; and Edith Tarcov, who had lost both parents in the Holocaust, been widowed young, and served as the magazine's exacting managing editor, a position I would assume in 1986.

Simone Plastrik imparted much of the *Dissent* culture around the lunch table. The magazine in those years, as Mitchell Cohen notes in his introduction, was run from her dining room in a no-nonsense but warm environment. She constantly warned me and the other part-time staffers, Brian Morton and Mark Levinson, that there was no need for such frills as an in-house copier, a fax machine, an extra phone line, a computer. We joked that she ran *Dissent* the way a frugal French housewife would run her home. No expense was too small to escape her eye.

Early in the decade, *Dissent* underwent a subtle shift. Irving Howe became visibly concerned about mortality. He worried out loud about who would continue the magazine when his generation of *Dissent* writers and supporters died out. He had reason to worry. In the 1980s *Dissent* lost not only co-founder Stanley Plastrik, but also Henry Pachter, Joseph Clark, Brendan Sexton, Jack Rader, Robert Lekachman, and Michael Harrington. The loss of so many writers who not only could make complex ideas accessible but were able to write on a variety of subjects was a body blow to Howe. At every board meeting he bemoaned the narrowness of the writing in so many of the manuscripts we re-ceived. The increasing specialization in the academy and alienation of so many young writers from a life of *engagement* had, he believed, made things worse for *Dissent.*

In any decade Howe would have found the absence of writers willing to take risks and move across disciplines anathema, but in the 1980s it was particularly infuriating for him. *Dissent* saw the challenges the Reagan administration presented as the worst the country had faced since the 1950s. The president's extravagant inauguration and his open admiration for Calvin Coolidge, whose portrait he made a point of hanging in the Cabinet Room, seemed like a bad joke. But it was clear that Reagan was not joking. He was prepared and able to act on his beliefs, and it showed with his firing of the nation's 11,600 air traffic controllers when they struck in 1981, his stereotyping of the poor as "welfare queens," his willingness to spend billions on an unproven Star Wars defense system, and his invasion of Grenada.

For *Dissent* the question in the 1980s was never what to write about. It was how to write about the Reagan years without sounding like Chicken Little complaining that the sky was falling. The essays that appear in this section reflect the balance we tried to achieve. In "Culture in an Age of Money" Nicolaus Mills sees the Reagan administration's obsession with a culture of triumph as permeating every facet of the decade, but he also sees "the low-cal Reaganism of George Bush" strain-ing to maintain what came naturally to Ronald Reagan. In "Blips, Bites, and Savvy Talk" Todd Gitlin describes the deadliness of a television political culture obsessed with spectacle and punditry, but he makes the point that this television political culture did not arise spontaneously: it was a product of a series of calculated media decisions. In "Good Schools Are Still Possible" Deborah Meier acknowledges how bad factory-like, urban schools can be, but she also makes a case—based upon her own experience as the founder and director of an experimental public school in East Harlem—that maverick schools sensitive to the children they serve can survive when the right combination of admin-istrators and teachers comes together. In "Why the Sandinistas Lost" Paul Berman analyzes the failures of the Nicaraguan revolution in terms of the Sandinistas' authoritarian inflexibility, but he also argues that over time "grass-roots democratization" can succeed in a country like

Nicaragua, despite the hostility any genuinely revolutionary Nicaraguan government is likely to encounter from the United States. In "The Feminization of Poverty" Barbara Ehrenreich and Frances Fox Piven document the widespread increase in poverty among women that has been going on since the late 1960s, but they end their essay by emphasizing how women are now leading the way in resisting the attempt to destroy the welfare state as we know it.

Small wonder then that when the Berlin Wall fell and the triumph of the West was proclaimed, *Dissent*'s editors were not out dancing in the streets. It was not that the end of the Soviet Union's hold on Eastern Europe was not worth celebrating. Since it began, *Dissent* had made a point of refusing to turn a blind eye to the suffering the Soviet Union had caused, and in the 1980s articles on Poland, Hungary, Czechoslovakia, and the Soviet Union itself had regularly appeared in our pages. But in 1989 there was, we believed, a long way to go at home and abroad before we could feel comfortable with the country's new, unparalleled power.

Looking back, I think we were right about the inheritance the 1980s left us with. Our mistake was in underestimating the difficulties our new, unparalleled power would produce by the turn of the century. In the wake of the 1980s, we did not imagine how much worse things could get.

culture in an age of money
NICOLAUS MILLS

In early 1981, as the Reagan administration was getting under way, its first cultural controversy began. Nancy Reagan wanted new china for the White House. The cost of the china was the problem. The Lenox pattern with a raised gold presidential seal in the center that the president's wife chose came to $209,508 for 220 place settings. At a time when her husband was talking about cutting welfare eligibility and the misery index (inflation plus unemployment) was over 20 percent, Nancy Reagan's desire for new china seemed like an idea borrowed from Marie Antoinette.

Democrats rubbed their hands in glee. What they failed to understand was that a new era was starting. American culture in the 1980s would be a culture based on triumph—on the admiration of power and status—and nothing would be more important to that culture than its symbols. Especially at the start, they were what allowed the president to insist, "We have every right to dream heroic dreams."

The America that the Reagan administration inherited was an America still in shock from a decade of humiliation. The country had lost the longest war in its history. A president had resigned in disgrace. The economy was in shambles. Only a quarter of the voting age population felt the government could be trusted to do what was right most of the time. New White House china would not erase these past humiliations, but like the president's pledge "to make America proud again," new china would be a start in the right direction. During his final year in office, Jimmy Carter had talked about the country's "malaise." But for the Reagans, triumph would be the watchword. "The cynics were wrong. America never was a sick society," Ronald Reagan declared. In the 1980s his America would not look or act like a weakling nation. The president and his guests would eat off china that proclaimed, "The era of self-doubt is over." The demeaning humility of a Jimmy Carter, who allowed Iran to hold Americans hostage for 444 days and insisted he liked peanut butter sandwiches, was past.

Two decades earlier, John Kennedy had made social commitment seem glamorous, and what followed was a counterculture in which civil rights, the antiwar movement, and Woodstock all had their place. Ronald Reagan's version of Camelot was Disneyland, and what followed was a culture in which the "magic of the marketplace" replaced the Magic Kingdom. Yuppie, upscale, privatization: these were the key words for the 1980s, and they signaled a culture with an insatiable need to proclaim its triumphs. Even the act of charging (thanks to the $300 American Express platinum card) became a way of asserting status.

Businesses no longer just bought up other businesses. The 1980s became the decade in which the hostile takeover was made possible by the leveraged buyout and the junk bond, when greenmail was paid to avoid a takeover, when companies were attacked by raiders and saved by white knights, and fired executives floated into retirement on golden parachutes. Only those labeled cynics by the Reaganites or the special interests (a labor union, the civil rights movement) would oppose such a culture. As Secretary of Education William Bennett bragged to the Heritage Foundation in a 1986 address, "American conservatism now sets the terms of our debate. It does so because, without in the least abandoning its principles, it has succeeded in identifying itself with the quintessential American appetite for new challenges and new opportunities."

In foreign policy the most dramatic indication of the new culture of triumph was reflected in the revival of an imperial America committed to showing its power. Between 1980 and 1987 the military budget more than doubled, climbing to $282 billion annually. But the real change was in the country's inner psychology, its abandonment of what Ronald Reagan called our "Vietnam syndrome." The Grenada invasion of 1983 would show how serious the President was when he insisted Vietnam "was, in truth, a noble cause." The invasion would come less than seventy-two hours after Lebanese terrorists killed 241 Marines in their Beirut barracks, and it would refocus attention on a part of the world that had been an American sore spot ever since the Nicaraguan revolution of 1979.

The fighting itself was over in days. The casualties were light: nineteen killed, 115 wounded. The army would, nonetheless, give out 8,612 medals, and for the country there would be an enormous release of tension. We were no longer a helpless giant. It was now clear what the president meant when during the 1980 campaign he declared, "There is a lesson for us all in Vietnam . . . let us tell those who fought that war that we will never again ask young men to fight and possibly die in a war that our government is afraid to let them win."

The philosophical groundwork for such interventionism had been laid in 1979 by Jeane Kirkpatrick (later Reagan's United Nations ambassador) in an article entitled, "Dictatorships and Double Standards." Now such thinking had a base in reality. After Grenada it became easier to reimagine Vietnam as a war that America could have won. No longer did the Vietnam vet have to be a 1970s figure like the sensitive, crippled hero John Voight played in *Coming Home*. The vet of the 1980s could be Sylvester Stallone's John Rambo, whose rage and muscularity argue that we did not lose Vietnam on the battlefield and who on going back to rescue his POW buddies asks the perfect Reagan question, "This time do we get to win?"

The domestic equivalent of Rambo was the Wall Street buccaneer, the takeover artist that financier Asher Edelman sought to cultivate in his Columbia Business School course, "Corporate Raiding—The Art of War," when he offered a hundred-thousand dollar bounty to any student who found a company he could acquire. The real economic hero of the culture of triumph would, however, be the dream consumer, the yuppie. It was the yuppie lifestyle that the Reagan administration had in mind when it adopted the logic of the Laffer curve, which said that if tax rates, especially at the upper level, were lowered, the rich would try to get even richer and in so doing improve the economy and government revenues.

There would, of course, be jokes about the materialism of yuppies and their passion for brand names. But the yuppie was someone the 1980s culture quickly learned to love. As the popular television sitcom, *Family Ties*, showed, the yuppie was the button-down kid who knew the path to the good life. His 1960s baby-boom parents might not understand his ambitions, but they could not help being impressed (particularly when he was as likable as Michael J. Fox's Alex Keaton) with how good he was at looking out for number one.

For Ronald Reagan the roots of an America in which patriotism and prosperity reigned supreme lay in the Revolution. There we had established our independence. There, as he told the nation in a July 4th radio address, we "began with a tax revolt." The key was to go back to the future. "Our new beginning is a continuation of that beginning created two centuries ago," the president declared in his second inaugural. He would not, however, rely on rhetoric or legislation alone to define the "Second American Revolution" he was after. As he knew from his Hollywood days, the essence of modern America was image.

For Reagan and the culture of triumph, the extravaganza thus became the crucial public event of the 1980s. Nothing else so clearly dramatized what both were about or showed what the President meant when he said, "When I spoke about a new beginning, I was talking about much more than budget cuts and incentives for savings and investment. I was talking about a fundamental change . . . that honors the legacy of the Founding Fathers."

The first inauguration with its $8 million price tag for four days of celebration set the tone for the extravaganzas that would follow. It began with an $800,000 fireworks display at the Lincoln Memorial, followed by two nights of show-business performances presided over by the Reagans, and, finally, on the fourth day, nine inaugural balls that conjured up the image of an American Versailles. From Almaden Vineyards came 14,400 bottles of champagne. From the Society of American Florists $13,000 worth of roses. From Ridgewell's caterers 400,000 hors d'oeuvres. "When you've got to pay $2,000 for a limousine for four days, $7 to park, and $2.50 to check your coat at a time when most people in the country can't hack it, that's ostentation," Senator Barry Goldwater groused. Goldwater had missed the point. The extravaganzas of the 1980s, like the culture of triumph, would not be concerned with the work ethic of small-town America. They were advertisements for America the Grand, and their aesthetic, as Reagan-era historian Sidney Blumenthal shrewdly observed, was one in which the beautiful was the expensive, the good was the costly.

The inaugural aesthetic would be repeated at the 1984 Olympics in Los Angeles. The president did not attend the games, instead contenting himself with urging the American team to "Do it for the Gipper." But in every other respect he was the dominant Olympic figure. His "new patriotism" was reflected in the crowds chanting "USA, USA" every time an American athlete competed. Most of all, the "resurgence of national pride" that the president wanted the country to feel was captured in the $6 million opening and closing ceremonies directed by Hollywood producer David Wolper. "The tone of the opening ceremony is going to be majesty," Wolper promised, and what followed were the most political Olympics since 1936. Wolper's plan to have an eagle take off from the west rim of the Coliseum and soar down onto the field during the playing of the national anthem was cancelled at the last minute. But everything else went like clockwork. Church bells rang throughout the city. A plane wrote "WELCOME" across the sky, and a cast of nine thousand—including 125 trumpeters, three hundred placard bearers, and eighty-four pianists playing "Rhapsody in Blue"—performed on cue.

The peak in extravaganzas came two years later, on July 4, 1986, with the hundredth anniversary of the Statue of Liberty. It was the perfect Reagan moment, an occasion to match the politics of restoration with the restoration of a national monument. On opening night as the faces of the president and his wife were superimposed on the image of the relit statue, he took the tribute in stride, as if such a blending of iconography were only natural. Later he would speak of his tax bill putting a smile on Liberty, but here, as at his inaugural, the president knew that the best way to be effective was to play a role. The spectacle of Liberty Weekend, like that of the Olympics, was left to David Wolper to orchestrate. With a $30 million budget and no athletes to worry about, Wolper had few constraints. Television rights for the weekend went to ABC for $10 million. Millions more came from sponsors paying to use the statue in their advertising. Like the candy makers who carved a fourteen-foot chocolate replica of Liberty or the caterer who molded her likeness out of sixty pounds of chopped liver, Wolper was free to let scale dictate choice.

On Thursday a 1.4 million-watt series of laser beams shot across New York harbor to illuminate the relit statue for the first time. On Friday, following the largest assembly of ships since the end of World War II, the evening concluded with the largest fireworks display in U.S. history (twenty tons of materials, 40,000 projectiles computer coordinated to music played aboard the carrier John F. Kennedy by the Marine Corps band), and on Sunday the greatest spectacle of all at Meadowlands Stadium in New Jersey: a cast of 12,000, including two hundred Elvis Presley impersonators, three hundred Jazzercise dancers, and an eight-hundred-voice chorus, performing on a twenty-tier stage with five waterfalls. The extravaganza's message was again unmistakable. To be American was to be powerful and to be powerful was to be rich.

What about the homeless, whom Los Angeles police had continually swept off the streets during the Olympics? Or the poor, whom the Statue of Liberty welcomed but who were not welcome at Liberty Weekend? "The social safety net for the elderly, the needy, the disabled, and the unemployed will be left intact," the president promised. But the crucial point was that such a safety net, like the safety net for the circus aerialist, was to be kept out of sight. The problem with our concern for the poor, both the Reagan administration and the culture of triumph held, was that in the past it had crippled them. In his influential 1984 book, *Losing Ground,* conservative Charles Murray of the Manhattan Institute described how, as a result of relaxed welfare standards and liberal court rulings, the 1960s had made it easier for the poor to get along without jobs and get away with crimes. For Ronald Reagan, the Murray view of poverty offered the perfect reason to cut back on aiding the poor. "Federal welfare programs have created a massive social problem," he insisted. "Government created a poverty trap that wreaks havoc on the very support system the poor most need to lift themselves out of poverty—the family."

"Reagan made the denial of compassion respectable," New York governor Mario Cuomo would complain. "He justified it by saying not only that the government wasted money, but also that poor people were somehow better off without government help in the first place." The country was, however, in no mood to listen to Cuomo or bother with figures showing that in the 1980s the living standard of the bottom fifth of the country dropped by 8 percent while that of the top fifth rose by 16 percent. Indeed, the kind of denial Reagan and Charles Murray had made respectable with regard to the poor was part of a much larger pattern of denial that was inseparable from the culture of triumph.

Irangate, the stock market crash of 1987, the scandals at the Environmental Protection Agency, the influence-peddling trials of White House aides Michael Deaver and Lyn Nofziger might easily have changed the country politically. But the culture of triumph made dwelling on such negatives a repudiation of what was best in America. We had gotten ourselves into trouble during the 1970s by imagining we were weak when we were not, Ronald Reagan insisted. There was no point in going through that again. In the president's words, "We've stopped looking at our warts and rediscovered how much there is to love in this blessed land."

A powerful counterculture might have challenged such a selective approach to events, but even at its best the counterculture of the 1980s found itself checked by the culture of triumph. The precedent set in 1980 when the mourning for John Lennon's Christmas-season assassination was quickly overshadowed by the first Reagan inaugural would continue throughout the decade. Two years after its installation, Maya Lin's elegiac, black granite Vietnam Memorial was sharing space in Constitution Gardens with Frederick Hart's bronze statue of three battle-weary infantrymen. In even less time, Bruce Springsteen's *Born in the USA* album, with its haunting portrait of a young vet trying to eke out a living in a declining industrial town, became the musical inspiration for Chrysler automobile's upbeat "Made in the USA" commercial.

Most important, the liberal tradition that might have provided the counterculture of the 1980s with a political base collapsed. When accused of being a liberal during the 1988 presidential debates, Michael Dukakis complained about being labeled, before declaring weeks later that he was a liberal in the tradition of Franklin Roosevelt and John Kennedy. But the damage was done. By the end of the second presidential debate, the liberalism of Dukakis and the Democrats lay exposed as a narrow proceduralism—"scolding," Congressman Barney Frank would call it—that made upholding the law the remedy for everything from crime in the street to Irangate.

In the end the 1980s would have no antidote for the cult of success that the culture of triumph made its centerpiece. When the public extravaganzas of the Reagan administration ended, the private extravaganzas of the super-rich replaced them. In the summer of 1989 Wall Street financier Saul Steinberg's $1 million fiftieth birthday party was not even the event of the season. That honor went to publisher Malcolm Forbes for a $2 million seventieth birthday party in Morocco. There he and 800 guests (flown from the United States on three jet airplanes) were entertained by 600 acrobats, jugglers, and belly dancers, had an honor guard of 300 Berber horsemen, and consumed 216 magnums of champagne in toasts.

"How do you defend it? I don't try to defend it," Forbes would say of his party. A few years earlier, shortly before his conviction for insider trading, Wall Street arbitrager Ivan Boesky put the same sentiments in even blunter language. "I think greed is healthy. You can be greedy and still feel good about yourself," Boesky told the press. Over the course of the 1980s, such thinking would apply to the arts as well. "Plutography," Tom Wolfe's neologism for "the graphic depiction of the acts of the rich," would become the decade's guiding aesthetic. Plutography would define novels like Wolfe's own best seller, *The Bonfire of the Vanities,* with its portrait of Sherman McCoy, a Wall Street broker who lives in a world where at forty you are either making a million a year or you're an incompetent. In an even more obvious way, plutography would define television's hit series. *Dynasty* and *Dallas* would make family money wars the heart of weekly programming and pave the way for Robin Leach's *Lifestyles of the Rich and Famous,* which would take viewers on shopping trips along Rodeo Drive and into the homes of the wealthy. Even the fine arts were not immune from the 1980s cult of success. Soho art dealer Mary Boone became as well known as the artists in her stable (among them David Salle and Julian Schnabel) for her ability to sell their work to the right collectors (those with museum connections), then promote it so that its secondary market (resale) value skyrocketed.

The ultimate link between consumerism and high art would, however, be the Bloomingdale's–Metropolitan Museum alliance. In 1980 both turned their attention to aristocratic China and what the Bloomingdale ads called "forty centuries of opulence." But the link would not end here. What Bloomingdale's was packaging as fashion the Met was packaging as art. Robes from the Met's "Costumes of China" exhibit were first shown to the public at Bloomingdale's along with the reproductions the store was selling. Then, on being returned to the Met, the robes were displayed on mannequins dressed by Met curator and former *Harper's Bazaar* fashion editor Diana Vreeland. The problem, as critics were quick to point out, was that the Met mannequins were not dressed in accord with Chinese custom. What dictated their layered look in the museum was what had dictated their look at Bloomingdale's: the illusion of fashionable luxury they could be made to convey.

The same fascination with success and wealth would be more pronounced in the decade's personal fashion. While the Met's Chinese costume exhibit was going on, the *New York Times Magazine* carried an article by Francesca Stanfill, "Living Well is the Best Revenge," that heralded the arrival of an era in which the successful "have no fear of ostentation, nor are they inhibited by the pressure of discretion that often characterizes those with old fortunes." The article was about Oscar and Françoise de la Renta, but it was no less applicable to the Reagans. The president in his jodhpurs and Nancy Reagan in her $25,000 worth of inaugural gowns ($46,000 for the second inaugural) were once again paving the way for the culture of triumph. As novelist and style critic Alison Lurie observed, "The rich need to look secure now, and to look secure you need to look rich." Before the decade was up, even the stores selling the new elegance would figure out ways to flaunt it. To make its flagship store in New York fit its clothes image, Ralph Lauren's gutted the inside of the 1898 Rhinelander mansion, changing it to look like a cross between an English country house and a gentleman's club.

Nor would the changes stop here. The 1980s were not only the decade of the power lunch and the power tie, but the power physique. A decade earlier the middle class had jogged its way to health. In the 1980s it powered its way to health with the Nautilus machine, and when that didn't work, there was always liposuction. As the Calvin Klein Obsession for Men cologne ads—with their muscular male and female nude models—showed, the point of the new elegance was to make it clear that what lay below all the surface luxury was raw power.

Even romance would be unable to resist the success ethic of the culture of triumph. The essence of romance in the 1980s became the successful marriage. (By 1989 even *Playboy* founder Hugh Hefner had remarried.) In the age of AIDS, such a change made sexual sense, but nothing fueled the change so much as money and the vision of a home in which husband and wife were proven wage earners. As Mike Nichols's 1988 film, *Working Girl*, showed, even office romance was different.

The Staten Island-born secretary of *Working Girl* proves herself lovable not by being helpless but by being a financial wiz. When her Wellesley-educated boss gets hurt in a skiing accident, she substitutes for her and pulls off a takeover that wins the heart of her future husband, a Wall Street broker. What dazzles him is that she is better in business than he. He can marry her with the assurance that rather than taking a financial risk he is forming a partnership that will leave him better off. At the end of the film, there is no romantic talk about babies or housework. As music floods the soundtrack, we see the former secretary, now with an office and secretary of her own, starting her work day confident that she has at last arrived where she wants to be.

"They called it the Reagan Revolution, and I'll accept that, but for me it always seemed like the Great Rediscovery: a rediscovery of our values and our common sense," Ronald Reagan would declare in his farewell address. The president's valediction was a perfect description of the way in which the culture of triumph that he championed throughout the 1980s managed to legitimize its aims and delegitimize those of its opponents. Far less gifted politicians than the president learned from his example that if the past could be appropriated, it was a powerful weapon. Attorney General Edwin Meese would justify his attacks on the Warren court by charging that it had violated the "original intention" of the Constitution. Secretary of Education William Bennett would oppose the liberalization of college curriculums on the grounds that it disregarded "the American common culture." Even the media found that they could gain new legitimacy by wrapping themselves in the past. Trying to regain readers it had lost to the feminist movement of the 1960s and 1970s, *Good Housekeeping* magazine would appeal to a woman it called the "New Traditionalist." "She's a contemporary woman," the *Good Housekeeping* ads declared, "who has made a new commitment to the traditional values that some people thought were old fashioned."

The *Good Housekeeping* ads could be written off as self-promotion. But the nostalgia of the president and men like Meese and Bennett was another story. It was rooted in the kind of historical absolutism that prompted the president's favorite televangelist, Jerry Falwell, to call America "back to biblical morality, back to sensibility, and back to patriotism." What lay behind such calls to action was the belief that the foundations of contemporary precedent were shaky. They could be challenged wherever they conflicted with the country's authentic past. There was no need for the modern conservative to adopt traditional conservative restraint.

The legal consequences of such thinking were immediately apparent in the willingness of the Reagan appointees to the Supreme Court to overturn precedents established a decade earlier in affirmative action and abortion rights. But the most dramatic indication of what the historical absolutism of the culture of triumph meant for the 1980s would come with the Bush administration's response to a Supreme Court decision it did not expect: the 1989 ruling upholding flag burning as symbolic speech protected by the First Amendment.

"The flag represents and reflects the fabric of our nation—our dreams, our destiny, our very fiber as a people," the new president declared angrily as he called for a constitutional amendment to make flag desecration illegal. His language, his insistence that the fabric of the flag and the fabric of the country were the same, was pure Reaganism, as was the backdrop, the Iwo Jima Memorial, he chose for his speech. But the moment was also one that summed up how much the culture of triumph, with its symbolism and claims on the past, had come to dominate American life in the 1980s. Even the low-cal Reaganism of George Bush could not escape its hold. In the final year of the decade, it was no longer hubris, as far as the president was concerned, to think that what the Founding Fathers really meant by the First Amendment needed to be spelled out with another amendment.

—1990

blips, bites & savvy talk

TODD GITLIN

In the pilot film for the 1987 television series *Max Headroom*, an investigative reporter discovers that an advertiser is compressing television commercials into almost instantaneous "blipverts," units so high-powered they can cause some viewers to explode. American television has long been compressing politics into chunks, ten-second "bites," and images that freeze into icons as they repeat across millions of screens and newspapers. The 1980s were saturated with these memorialized moments. Think of Ronald Reagan at the Korean DMZ, wearing a flak jacket, field glasses, keeping an eye on the North Korean Communists; or in the bunker at Omaha Beach, simulating the wartime performance he had spared himself during the actual World War II. Think of the American medical student kissing American soil after the troops had evacuated him from Grenada. Think of Star Wars animation and Oliver North saluting. The sense of history as a collage reaches some sort of twilight of the idols when we think of the 1988 election. There it is hard to think of anything *but* blips and bites: the Pledge of Allegiance; George Bush touring the garbage of Boston Harbor (leaving aside that some of the spot was shot elsewhere); the face of Willie Horton; the mismatch of tank and Michael Dukakis. The question I want to raise is whether chunk news has caused democratic politics to explode.

Although I pose the question in an extreme form, it is hardly alien to 1988's endless campaign journalism. Indeed, the journalists were obsessed with the question of whether media images had become the campaign, and if so, whose fault that was. That obsession is itself worth scrutiny. But consider first the coverage itself. According to the most relentless of studies as well as the evidence of the senses, the main mode of campaign journalism is the horse-race story. Here is that preoccupation—indeed, enchantment—with means characteristic of a society that is competitive, bureaucratic, professional, and technological all at once. The big questions of the campaign, in poll and story, are *Who's ahead? Who's falling behind? Who's gaining?*

This is an observation only a fool would deny. I recall a conversation

I had with a network correspondent in 1980. I criticized the horse-race coverage of the primaries. "I know," he said. "We've been trying to figure out what we can do differently. We haven't been able to figure it out." To a great though not universal extent, the media still haven't. They can't. The popularity of unexamined military and sports metaphors like "campaign" and "race" shows how deep the addiction runs. This is a success culture bedazzled by sports statistics and empty of criteria other than numbers to answer the question, "How am I doing?" Journalists compete, news organizations compete—the channeled aggression of the race is what makes their blood run. In the absence of a vital polis, they take polls.

By 1988, the obsession had reached new heights, or depths: one night, ABC News devoted fourteen minutes, almost two-thirds of the news section of the newscast, to a poll—a bigger bloc by far than was given to any issue. In a perverse way, the journalists' fancy for polls is a stratagem directed toward mastery. Here at least is something they know how to do, something they can be good at without defying their starting premise, which is, after all, deference. Their stance is an insouciant subservience. They have imposed upon themselves a code they call objectivity but that is more properly understood as a mixture of obsequiousness and fatalism—it is not "their business" in general to affront the authorities, not "their place" to declare who is lying and who is right. Starting from the premise that they haven't the right to raise issues the candidates don't raise or explore records the candidates don't explore, they can at least ask a question they feel entitled to answer: "Who's ahead?" How can racing addicts be chased away from the track?

By 1988 the fact that the horse race had become the principal "story" was itself "old news." Many in the news media had finally figured out one thing they could do differently. They could take the audience backstage, behind the horse race, into the paddocks, the stables, the clubhouse, and the bookie joints. But this time horse-race coverage was joined by handicapping coverage—stories about campaign tactics, what the handlers were up to, how the reporters felt about being handled: in short, *How are the candidates trying to do it to us, and how are they doing at it?* Anxiety lay behind this new style—anxiety that Reagan really had pulled the Teflon over their eyes, that they had been suckered by the smoothly whirring machinery of his stagecraft. So handicapping coverage was a defensive maneuver, and a self-flattering one: the media could in this way show that they were immune from the ministrations of campaign professionals.

The result is what many people call a postmodern move, in two senses: enchantment with the means toward the means and ingratiation via a pass at deconstruction. There is a lot of this in American culture nowadays: the postmodern high culture of the 1960s (paintings calling attention to their paintedness, novels exposing their novelistic machinery) has swept into popular culture. An aspirin commercial dizzyingly toys with itself ("I'm not a doctor, though I play one on TV," says a soap opera actor); an Isuzu commercial bids for trust by using subtitles to expose the lies of the overenthusiastic pitchman; actors face the audience and speak "out of character" in *Moonlighting*. Campaign coverage in 1988 reveled in this mode. Viewers were invited to be cognoscenti of their own bamboozlement.

This was the campaign that made "sound bite," spin control," "spin doctor," and "handler" into household phrases. Dukakis handlers even made a commercial about Bush handlers wringing their hands about how to handle Dan Quayle, a commercial that went over far better with hip connoisseurs than with the unhip rest of the audience who had trouble tracing the commercial to Dukakis. This campaign metacoverage, coverage of the coverage, partakes of the postmodern fascination with surfaces and the machinery that cranks them out, a fascination indistinguishable from surrender—as if once we understand that all images are concocted we have attained the only satisfaction the heart and mind are capable of. (This is the famous Brechtian "alienation effect" but with a difference: Brecht thought that actors, by standing outside and "presenting" their characters, could lay bare social relations and show that life could be changed; paradoxically, campaign metacoverage, by laying bare the campaign's tactics and inside doings, demonstrates only that the campaign is a juggernaut that cannot be diverted.) Thus, voiceovers explained knowingly that the candidate was going to a flag factory or driving a tank in order to score public relations points. Here, for example, is ABC's Brit Hume narrating the appearance of George Bush at a flag factory on September 20, 1988: "Bush aides deny he came here to wrap himself in the flag, but if that wasn't the point of this visit, what was it?"

In the same vein was the new postdebate ritual: the networks featuring campaign spin doctors, on camera, telling reporters why their respective candidates had done just fine, while the network correspondents affected an arch superiority and print reporters insisted that the spin doctors couldn't spin *them*. Meanwhile, the presumably unspinnable pundits rattled on about how the candidates performed, whether they had given good sound bite—issuing reviews, in other words, along with behind-the-scenes assessments of the handlers' skill in setting expectations for the performance, so that, for example, if Dan Quayle succeeded in speaking whole sentences he was to be decreed a success in "doing what he set out to do."

These rituals exhibited the insouciant side of insouciant subservience—reporters dancing attendance at the campaign ball while insisting that they were actually following their own beat. Evaluating the candidates' claims and records was considered highbrow and boring—and potentially worse. For to probe too much or too far into issues, to show too much initiative in stating the public problems, would be seen by the news business as hubris, a violation of their unwritten agreement to let the candidates set the public agenda. Curiously, the morning shows, despite their razzmatazz, may have dwelt on issues more than the nightly news—largely because the morning interviewers were not so dependent on Washington insiders, not so tightly bound to the source cultivating and glad-handing that guide reportage inside the Beltway. It was a morning show that discovered that the Bush and Dukakis campaigns had hired the same Hollywood lighting professionals to illuminate their rallies. (Possibly the Dukakis handlers had learned from Mondale's blunder in turning a 1984 debate lighting decision over to Reagan's more skilled people, leaving Mondale showing rings under his eyes—so Michael Deaver told Mark Hertsgaard, as reported in Hertsgaard's *On Bended Knee.*)

As befit the new and sometimes dizzying self-consciousness, reporters sometimes displayed, even in public, a certain awareness that they were players in a game not of their own scripting; that they could be had, and were actively being had, by savvy handlers; and that they were tired of being had. The problem first acquired media currency with a tale told by Hedrick Smith, in his 1988 book *The Power Game,* about a 1984 campaign piece by Leslie Stahl. Here is Stahl's own version of the story as she told it the night after the election on ABC's *Viewpoint:*

> This was a five-minute piece on the evening news . . . at the end of President Reagan's '84 campaign, and the point of the piece was to really criticize him for—I didn't use this language in the piece— but the point was, he was trying to create amnesia over the budget cuts. For instance . . . I showed him at the Handicapped Olympics, and I said, you wouldn't know by these pictures that this man tried to cut the budget for the handicapped. And the piece went on and on like that. It was very tough, and I was very nervous about going back to the White House the next day, Sam [she is talking to fellow panelist Sam Donaldson], because I thought they'd never return my phone calls and they'd keep returning yours. [This is Exhibit B on factors inhibiting press criticism: the competition of the pack, which can produce protracted press honeymoons and pile-ons.— T.G.] But my phone rang, and it was a White House official [presumably Michael Deaver, the propagandist-in-chief], and he said, "Great piece, Leslie. " And I said, "Come on, that was a tough—what do you mean, 'great piece'?" And he said, "We loved it, we loved it, we loved it. Thank you very much. It was a five-minute commercial, you know, unpaid commercial for our campaign." I said, "Didn't you hear what I said? I was tough." "Nobody heard what you said. They just saw the five minutes of beautiful pictures of Ronald Reagan. They saw the balloons, they saw the flags, they saw the red, white and blue. Haven't you people figured out yet that the picture always overrides what you say?' "

The 1988 answer was, apparently not. For the networks and the candidates (successful candidates, anyway) share an interest in what they consider "great pictures," that is, images that evoke myths. Curiously, the famous cynicism of journalists does not keep them from being gullible. Indeed, in this setting, cynicism and gullibility are two sides of the same con. The handlers count on the gullible side when they gamble that cameras, to paraphrase the ex-president's masterful slip on the subject of facts, are stupid things. That is why the Reagan staffers were proud of their public relations triumphs; their business was to produce what one of them called "our little playlets"—far-flung photo opportunities with real-life backdrops. Print reporters, meanwhile, were unable or unwilling to proceed differently. Although the pressure for "great pictures" doesn't apply, at least in the establishment press, the print people are unwilling to cede the "playlets" to television; they compete on television's terms, leaving the handlers free to set their agendas for them.

What is not altogether clear, of course, is whether the Reagan staffers were right to be proud of their public relations triumphs. We don't know, in fact, that "the picture always overrides what you say." Possibly that is true for some audiences, at some times, in some places, and not for others. What is clear, though, is that when the picture is stark enough, or the bite bites hard enough, journalists, especially on television, are unwilling to forgo the drama. To be boring is the cardinal sin. Embarrassed by their role as relay stations for orchestrated blips and bites, even amply rewarded journalists purport to resent the way Reagan's staff made megaphones of them; at the least they have become acutely self-conscious about their manipulability. The White House and the television-led press have been scrambling for relative advantage since the Kennedy administration; metacoverage was the press's attempt to recoup some losses.

Too Hip for Words

But to make sense of metacoverage I want to look at the dominant form of political consciousness in a formally open but fundamentally depoliticized society, which is savviness.

Already in 1950, David Riesman in *The Lonely Crowd* described what he called the inside dopester—a consumer of politics who

> may be one who has concluded (with good reason) that since he can do nothing to change politics, he can only understand it. Or he may see all political issues in terms of being able to get some insider on the telephone. [In any case] he is politically cosmopolitan. . . . He will go to great lengths to keep from looking and feeling like the uninformed outsider.

The goal is "never to be taken in by any person, cause, or event."

Over the past forty years, Riesman's inside dopester has evolved into another type: a harsher, more brittle and cynical type still more knowledgeable in the ways in which things really work, still more purposefully disengaged, still more knowledgeable in a managerial way, allergic to political commitments. The premium attitude is a sort of knowing appraisal. Speaking up is less important—certainly less fun—than sizing up. Politics, real politics, is for "players"—fascinating term, for it implies that everyone else is a spectator. To be "interested in politics" is to know how to rate the players: Do they have good hands? How do they do in the clutch? How are they positioning themselves for the next play?

Savviness flatters spectators that they really do understand, that people like them are in charge, that even if they live outside the Beltway, they remain sovereign. Keeping up with the maneuvers of Washington insiders, defining the issues as they define them, savviness appeals to a spirit both managerial and voyeuristic. It transmutes the desire to participate into spectacle. One is already participating, in effect, by watching. "I like to watch" is *the* premium attitude. If you have a scorecard, you can tell the players. The ultimate inside dopesters are the political journalists.

Today, both advertising and political coverage flourish on, and suffer from, what Mark Crispin Miller has called "the hipness unto death." Miller argues that television advertising has learned to profess its power by apparently mocking it, standing aside from vulgar claims, assuring the viewer that all of us knowing types are too smart to be taken in by advertising, or gaucherie or passion of any kind. In the same way, the postmodern savviness of political coverage—whether in the glib version of a Bruce Morton or the more sedate version of MacNeil/Lehrer—binds its audience closer to an eerie politics of half-truth, deceit, and evasion in which ignorant symbols clash by night. If the players evade an issue, the savvy spectator knows enough to lose interest in it as well.

Coverage of the horse race and metacoverage of the handicappers both suit the discourse of savviness. They invite and cultivate an inside dopester's attitude toward politics—vicarious fascination coupled with knowing indifference.

It might well be, then, that Leslie Stahl's 1984 piece, like many others, was really three pieces. A critical audience got her point—Reagan was a hypocrite. An image-minded audience got the White House's point—Reagan personified national will and caring, even as the nice-guy martyr to wise-ass Eastern commentators. And inside dope-sters got still another point—Reagan, master performer, was impervious to quarrelsome voiceovers.

Perhaps, too, there was a fourth piece—the backstage drama in which the White House made a point of showing Leslie Stahl her place. This must be humiliating for any reporter so old-fashioned as to want to take the measure of images against realities. Stahl's story reveals that the only alternative to complicity would be the damn-it-all spirit of an outsider indifferent to whether the handlers will favor her with scoop-worthy tidbits of information the next time. While telling Stahl that she's been had, the White House knows that, given her understanding of her job, she's going to be coming back for more stories; Deaver, the public relations man, knows that the surest way to make a reporter complicit is to treat her as an insider. As long as the agenda is set by the White House, or the campaign, the watchdog is defanged.

An Audience for the Spectacle

More must be said about what I just called the image-minded audience. For 1988 was not only the year of metacoverage; it was the year of the negative commercial, the bite, the clip, the image-blip. In theory, these chunks are television's distinct forte: the emotion-laden image in which an entire narrative is instantly present—Willie Horton, the flag, Bush with his granddaughter. The image is what rivets; the image is what is remembered. Research done by Ronald Lembo in the sociology depart-ment at Berkeley shows that some television viewers are inclined to follow narrative while others, disproportionately the young, pay more attention to distinct, out-of-context images.

What professional handlers and television journalists alike do is find images that condense their "little playlets," images that satisfy both lovers of story and lovers of image. Then blip-centered television floods the audience with images that compress and evoke an entire narrative. The 1980s began with one of these: the blindfolded American featured on the long-running melodrama called "America Held Hostage," sixty-three weeks of it during 1979–81, running on ABC at 11:30 five nights a week, propounding an image of America as a "pitiful helpless giant" (in Richard Nixon's phrase). Those were the months when Walter Cronkite signed off at CBS night after night by ticking off "the umpty-umpth day of captivity for the American hostages in Iran." In this ceremony of innocence violated, the moment arose to efface the national brooding over Vietnam. Now it could be seen that the Vietnam trauma had eclipsed the larger truth: it was the anti-Americans who were ugly. In the 1980s the American was the paleface captive of redskins. It was the anti-American blindfold that disfigured him. The image cried out for a man to ride out of the sagebrush on a white horse into the White House. The script for the Teheran playlet was not written by the Reagan handlers (although it is possible that they promised weapons to Iran's Revolutionary Guards in exchange for their keeping the hostages until election day), but they certainly knew how it would end.

We know how adept Reagan was at performing his playlets—he'd been doing them all his life. For eight years we heard endlessly, from reporters rushing about with spray cans of Teflon, about the mysterious personal qualities of the Great Communicator-in-Chief. But the mighty Wurlitzer of the media was primed for a figure who knew how to play upon it. The adaptability of the apparatus is exhibited by the media success of even so maladroit a figure as George Bush during the 1988 election. Having declared that Bush's central problem was to lick the wimp image, the media allowed him to impress them that once he started talking tough he turned out "stronger than expected." In their own fashion, Bush and his handlers—some of them fresh from Reagan's team—followed. Their masterwork was a Bush commercial that opens with a still photo on the White House lawn: Reagan to the right, at the side of the frame; Gorbachev at the center, shaking hands with the stern-faced Bush. The camera moves in on the vice president and Gorbachev; Reagan is left behind—having presided, he yields gracefully to his successor, the new man of the hour. As the camera moves closer, the stern face and the handshake take over, while the voiceover speaks the incantation: "strong . . . continue the arms control process . . . a president ready to go to work on day one." The entire saga is present in a single image: Bush the heir, the reliable, the man of strength who is also savvy enough to deal.

An American Tradition

How new is the reduction of political discourse to the horse race, the handicapping, the tailoring of campaigns to the concoction of imagery? What is particular to television? How good were the good old days?

Tempting as it is to assume that television has corrupted a previously virginal politics, the beginning of wisdom is history. As the campaigns invite us to read their blips, alarm is amply justified—but not because American politics has fallen from a pastoral of lucid debate and hushed, enlightened discourse to a hellish era of mudslinging and degraded sloganeering. Television did not invent the superficiality, triviality, and treachery of American politics. American politics has been raucous, deceptive, giddy, shallow, sloganeering, and demagogic for most of its history. "Infotainment" is in the American grain. So is reduction and spectacle—and high-minded revulsion against both.

Is negative campaigning new? In 1828, supporters of Andrew Jackson charged that John Quincy Adams had slept with his wife before marrying her, and that, while minister to Russia, he had supplied the Czar with a young American mistress. In turn, pro-Adams newspapers accused Jackson of adultery, gambling, cockfighting, bigamy, slave-trading, drunkenness, theft, lying, and murder. Jackson was said to be the offspring of a prostitute's marriage to a mulatto. Papers accused Jackson's previously divorced wife of having moved in with him while still married to her first husband. Not that all mud sticks. Some mud makes the slinger slip. In 1884 a Protestant minister called the Democrats the party of "Rum, Romanism, and Rebellion" as the Republican James G. Blaine stood by without demurral—which may well have cost Blaine the election.

Is the preference for personality over issues new? Once elected president, Andrew Jackson set to wiping out Indian tribes—but this was not an issue in the campaign that elected him, any more than the New Deal was an issue in the campaign that elected Franklin Roosevelt in 1932. (Roosevelt campaigned for a balanced budget.)

Are the blip and the bite new? "Tippecanoe and Tyler Too," the leading slogan of 1840, does not exactly constitute a Lincoln-Douglas debate. That year, according to Kathleen Hall Jamieson's *Packaging the Presidency*, followers of William Henry "Tippecanoe" Harrison carried log cabins in parades, circulated log cabin bandanas and banners, gave away log cabin pins, and sang log cabin songs, all meant to evoke the humble origins of their candidate—although Harrison had been born to prosperity and had lived only briefly in a log cabin. A half century later, in 1896, Mark Hanna, McKinley's chief handler, was the first campaign manager to be celebrated in his own right. Hanna acquired the reputation of a "phrasemaker" for giving the world such bites as "The Advance Agent of Prosperity," "Full Dinner Pail," and "Poverty or Prosperity," which were circulated on posters, cartoons, and envelope stickers, the mass media of the time. Hanna "has advertised McKinley as if he were a patent medicine!" marveled that earnest student of modern techniques, Theodore Roosevelt. In that watershed year, professional management made its appearance, and both candidates threw themselves into a whirl of public activity.

I draw the information about Hanna from an important book by Michael E. McGerr, *The Decline of Popular Politics: The American North, 1865–1928.* McGerr presents considerable evidence that from 1840 (the "Tippecanoe" campaign) through 1896, vast numbers of people participated in the pageantry of presidential campaigns. Average turnout from 1824 to 1836 was 48 percent of eligible voters; but from 1876 to 1900, it was 77 percent. During the three decades after the Civil War, mass rallies commonly lasted for many hours; there were torchlight parades; there were campaign clubs and marching groups. "More than one-fifth of Northern voters probably played an active part in the campaign organizations of each presidential contest during the '70s and '80s," McGerr writes. And with popular mobilization came high voter turnout—up to 84 percent of the eligible (all-male) electorate in 1896 and 1900 before it slid to 75 percent during the years 1900–16 and 58 percent in 1920–24. (It rose again in the 1930s, with the Great Depression and the New Deal, and then started sliding again.) Arguably the mass mobilization and hoopla turned out the vote; voting was the consolidation of a communal ritual, not an isolated act by which the isolated citizen expressed piety.

In the age of professionalization, reformers recoiled. What developed in the 1870s and 1880s, with a push from so-called "educated men," was a didactic politics, what McGerr calls an "elitist" politics. The high-minded reformers insisted on a secret ballot; they approved of social science; they wanted enlightened leaders to guide the unwashed. Under their leadership, they worked toward a new-style campaign: a campaign of education. Independent journalism helped—newspapers no longer under party management. Alongside the waning partisan press, two new kinds of newspapers emerged: the high-minded independent paper with its educated tone, cultivating political discernment; and the low-minded sensational paper with its lurid tone, cultivating antipolitical passion. The way is already open to our contemporary bifurcation: the *New York Times* and the *New York Post;* Arthur Sulzberger and Rupert Murdoch; MacNeil/Lehrer and Geraldo Rivera. This split corresponds to the highbrow/lowbrow cultural split that developed around the same time, as traced by Lawrence W. Levine in this recent book of that title.

The sharply bifurcated media help divide the public: to oversimplify, a progressive middle class takes politics seriously while a diverted working class is for the most part (except for the Great Depression) disaffected. Although it took decades for this process to develop, and there were exceptional periods of working-class mobilization along the way, the lineaments of the modern campaign were already in place at the turn of the century: emphasis on the personality of the candidate, not the party; emphasis on the national campaign, not community events; a campaign of packaging, posed pictures, and slogans. Politics as a discretionary, episodic, defensive activity for the majority alongside moral politics for the few. In short, the politics of the consumer society.

The radio hookups of the 1920s made the campaigns still more national, made it possible for candidates and presidents to reach over the heads of the party apparatus directly to the electorate. The parties became gradually more redundant. Some of this was welcomed by reformers, and properly so: gradually, candidates found it harder to whisper to white southern voters what they were afraid to proclaim out loud in the north. Above all else, though, the powers of the new media made it necessary for candidates and parties to manage them. Professionally concocted newsreels played a part in the defeat of Upton Sinclair's 1934 "End Poverty in California" gubernatorial campaign. A documentary newsreel spliced together at the last minute to counter a Dewey effort probably helped Truman squeak through in 1948.

But only with television and the proliferation of primaries did media management become central and routine to political campaigns. In 1952, Eisenhower, whose campaign was the first to buy television spots, was reluctant to advertise. After 1960, when Kennedy beat a sweating, five-o'clock-shadowed Nixon among those who watched the debate while losing among those who heard it on the radio, the handwriting was on the screen. The time of the professional media consultant had arrived. When his hour came round again in 1968, the new Nixon had learned to use—and submit to—the professional image managers. Nixon, the first president from southern California, moved advertising and public relations people into his high command. And not just for the campaign. The president in office could use the same skills. Haldeman and Ehrlichman, with their enemies lists and provocateur tactics, were the founding fathers of what Sidney Blumenthal later called "the permanent campaign"—a combination of polling, image-making, and popularity-building strategy that Reagan developed to the highest of low arts.

The pattern seems set for the 1980s: metacoverage for the cognoscenti, spurious pageantry for the majority. *The McLaughlin Group* for the know-it-all; Morton Downey, Jr. for the know-nothing. As the spectacle becomes more scripted and routine—the nominating conventions are the obvious example—more of the audience turns off. The spectacular version of politics that television delivers inspires political withdrawal along with pseudosophistication. As the pundits and correspondents pontificate in their savvy way, they take part in a circular conversation—while an attuned audience, wishing to be taken behind the scenes, is invited to inspect the strategies of the insiders, whether via the chilly cynicism of a Bruce Morton or the college-try bravado of a Sam Donaldson. Savviness is the tribute a spectacular culture pays to the pleasures of democracy. Middle-class outsiders want to be in the know, while the poor withdraw further and don't even vote. Politics, by these lights, remains a business for insiders and professionals. While the political class jockeys, the rest of us become voyeurs of our political fate—or *enragés*. Can it be simple coincidence that as voting and newspaper reading plummeted in the 1980s, Morton Downey, Jr. arrived with his electronic barroom brawl, and talk radio shows proved able to mobilize the indignant against congressional salary raises? Probably not. The vacuum of public discourse is filled on the cheap. Passions are disconnected from parties, moral panics disconnected from radical or even liberal politics. The talk show hosts did not mobilize against a tax "reform" that lined the pockets of the corporate rich.

Can This Generation Be Saved?

And the future? As the artist Folon says, "I work at forgetting I'm a pessimist." Ronald Lembo's research suggests that younger viewers are more likely, when they watch television, to pay attention to disconnected images; to switch channels, "watching" more than one program at once; and to spin off into fantasies about images. Of all age groups, the young are also the least likely to read newspapers and to vote. Do we detect a chain of causation? Does a fascination with speed, quick cuts, ten-second bites, one-second "scenes," and out-of-context images suggest less tolerance for the rigors of serious argument and the tedium of modern political life? Has the attention span been shrinking; and if so, is television the cause; and what would this prophesy for our politics? Is there, in a word, an MTV generation? Future apparatchiks of the media-politics nexus are assuming it: the politicians, the Deavers, the publishers of *USA Today* and its legion of imitators. David Shaw of the *Los Angeles Times* writes (March 15, 1989):

> In 1967, according to the National Opinion Research Center at the University of Chicago, 73% of the people polled said they read a newspaper every day; by last year, the number of everyday readers had fallen by almost one-third, to 50.6%. During that same period, in the 18 to 29 age group, the number of "everyday readers" dropped by more than half, from 60% to 29%.

While 26.6 percent of *Los Angeles Times* readers are aged 18 to 29, 36.2 percent of *USA Today* readers are that age. And whereas young people used to acquire the habit of newspaper reading as they aged, this is apparently no longer happening. To recoup their loses, newspapers are trying to woo the young with celebrity profiles, fitness features, household tips.

In 1988, the Department of Education published a report—a summary of research hither and yon—on television's influence on cognitive development. The widespread publicity placed the emphasis on television's harmlessness. The Associated Press story that ran in the *New York Times* was headlined: "Yes, You Too Can Get A's While Watching 'Family Ties.' " But the report itself, by Daniel R. Anderson and Patricia A. Collins of the Department of Psychology at the University of Massachusetts, is inconclusive on the question of whether television watching affects the capacity to pay attention. "The possibility that rapid pacing may produce effects over longer exposure has not been examined," reads one typical hedge. "There does . . . appear to be some effect of TV on attention, yet the importance, generality, and nature of the effect is unknown": that is the summary sentence. Someday the grants may flow for the research obligatorily called for. But pending research, one still feels entitled to the pessimism that one must then work to forget. Television may not have eroded all possibilities for democratic political life, but it has certainly not thrown open the doors to broad-based enlightenment.

I have tried to show that there is precedent for a shriveled politics of slogans, deceit, and pageantry. But precedent is nothing to be complacent about when ignorance is the product. And the problem, ultimately, is not simply that Americans are ignorant. On this score, the statistics are bad enough. According to a 1979 poll, only 30 percent of Americans responding could identify the two countries involved in the SALT II talks then going on; in 1982, only 30 percent knew that Ronald Reagan opposed the nuclear freeze; in 1985, 36 percent thought that either China, India, or Monaco was part of the Soviet Union. But ignorance is sometimes a defense against powerlessness. Why bother knowing if there's nothing you know how to do about what you know? Why get worked up? What is most disturbing is not ignorance in its own right but, rather, the coupling of ignorance and power. When the nation-state has the power to reach out and blow up cities on the other side of the world, the spirit of diversion seems, to say the least, inadequate. Neither know-it-alls nor know-nothings are likely to rise to the occasion.

—1990

good schools are still possible

DEBORAH MEIER

I came to New York City in the fall of 1966, and began teaching in Central Harlem a few months later. Within the next two years the schools were embroiled in two strikes. Parents were organized and vocal; teachers believed their recently won powers to be threatened; the city was divided by race and class. And yet there was a lively sense that the old system was done for: change of some sort was on the agenda. Decentralization, pedagogical innovations, parent control, teacher empowerment, accountability, public access, increased state and federal monies. These were the slogans of the day.

At their worst, the city's schools were never bad in quite the way the public imagined. My friends used to marvel that I had the "courage" to teach in a Harlem public school. They imagined schools disorderly and chaotic, filled with violence, knives flashing. Such things could be seen from time to time, but most of us taught in moderately orderly schools, with generally benign, even at times overly docile, though uninterested, children. It was tension rather than actual violence that wore down most school people. Our working conditions were often intolerable, but in ways that seemed either hard to explain or trivial to outsiders.

The real issues that concerned us were rarely noticed by the press, the politicians, the parent organizations, the school boards, or even by our own teachers' union. Instead, ersatz issues were endlessly addressed, and they exhausted us. Violent children and low reading scores were the symbols everyone agreed to talk about; these made for drama and slogans but little understanding.

Absence of respect for the people who made up the roster of school life—parents, kids, teachers, principals—was what was really driving us crazy. Schools reflected this in many ways—mostly trivial, cumulatively devastating. Inventively humiliating procedures began the moment one applied for a job, as one wandered down the Central Board corridors of 110 Livingston Street hoping not to get scolded as one tried to untangle endless Catch-22s. The headline battles ignored the participants' experiences and their perceived complaints. The conversations that teachers, and parents as well, held among themselves remained private, as though even they thought them unworthy of exposure, of "serious" people's concern. There was the state of the school toilets as well as the required daily lesson plans, the time-clock and the endless interruptions.

We were never the carriers of our own stories. We never trusted our own voices. Reforms came, but we didn't make them. They were invented by people far removed from schools—by "experts." And somehow teachers were never considered experts. Such reforms bypassed the kind of school-by-school changes, both small and structurally radical, that teachers and parents might have been able to suggest—changes that, however slow, could have made a powerful difference.

Fundamental school-based reform has been the major casualty of the post-1960s reforms. By the early 1970s both teachers and parents, the new actors of the 1960s, had retreated to their more familiar postures. Parents withdrew to their workplaces and teachers once again closed their doors hoping only to be left alone. The "experts" rushed in. Every time a fault was found, a system-wide solution was offered. And only those changes that could be translated into system-wide, replicable programs seemed worth discussing. If it couldn't be marketed on a grand scale, it was hardly worth exploring. The kind of detailed specificity that teachers could offer seemed a mere nuisance to the policy makers.

And so the proposed solutions led teachers to be treated like interchangeable parts. A rule that made sense in one setting had to cover all settings. Every apparently good protest gave birth to a new mandate, a new piece of legislation, a new contractual clause, a new pedagogical or curriculum prescription. And with every "reform" we encountered new nightmares.

Let me be specific.

Our concern for improved literacy (sparked by the exposure of low test scores) created a mammoth drive to improve test scores. Improved test scores, alas, are best achieved by ignoring real reading activity. School libraries were gradually closed and the librarians eliminated in favor of remedial teachers and remedial reading "labs" filled with expensive prepackaged kits and reading programs rather than real books. Federal funds earmarked for libraries were now spent on "software"— filmstrips and computer programs. District reading coordinators focused on finding the "best" reading system and training teachers to "operate" it, rather than on understanding how children learn to read and the value of being literate. As the curriculum began to imitate the tests, the test-coaching programs became school norms. Children rarely met books intended to be read from front to back. Paragraphs replaced chapters; predictable multiple-choice questions replaced conversation about books. Reading scores went up; literacy collapsed.

There were exceptions. Many good teachers kept doing what they knew was right, and brave principals plugged ahead at educating kids (they would coach for the tests at the last moment, hoping that their scores would not fall hopelessly behind their neighboring "competitors"). A few decentralized districts used newly won local control to unleashed talent, to support teachers and principals with ideas, to encourage parent/teacher collaboration. But they did so amid a system that was becoming increasingly test-driven, prepackaged, and bureaucratized.

And then, in the mid 1970s, the schools experienced a major trauma—equal in impact to the late 1960s battles for community control. The city laid off more than 15,000 teachers in response to its financial crisis. A stunning blow—though, as critics noted, no one in the mammoth Central Board offices was laid off.

The impact of this layoff has been virtually undiscussed. In a highly personal profession, the sudden disappearance of so many people, and the attendant reassignment of thousands of others, caused pain and then a kind of numbing. Although it's true that money alone won't buy change, the idea that a system can both ruthlessly cut back on its teaching staff and make educational breakthroughs is absurd. Teachers' salaries were frozen during this period of steady inflation. Class sizes went up, support for the remaining teachers was cut, and school principals were hopelessly mired in new administrative tasks.

There was no one to lead an effective fight to save our schools. The United Federation of Teachers (UFT—the American Federation of Teachers local) tried to assume this role. From the 1950s to mid-1960s the UFT had pioneered a whole array of proposed structural reforms. But the community control fight had both undercut the union's educational position and split apart the city's pro-education coalition. Under attack from all its usual allies for not minding its own business—traditional bread-and-butter demands—the UFT had accepted the more modest posture of factory-style adversarialism. This had not won it friends either. Nor, in face of layoffs, was factory-style militancy useful. In turn, the union's inability to avert such massive layoffs had an impact on teacher self-confidence, as it did on organized parent groups, who saw years of work destroyed overnight. New York's racial minorities had already lost their 1960s enthusiasm and militancy, and were suffering the first stages of official "benign neglect." They too were largely silent. There was no fight left in anyone.

We were back to business-as-usual, but one legacy of the 1960s remained. No one could now publicly acknowledge that "some children" might be less "teachable" than others. This powerful critical idea was, however, translated, as usual, into a simple-minded mandate. All must now score above-grade (however ludicrous such an idea might be statistically)—regardless of race, color, or social class (although class was rarely mentioned). And, as the social problems of families increased, so did the school's burdens—even though the accepted view of the school's role remained strictly "cognitive." Cognitive got translated into "measurable," which led back to test scores.

In this disheartening atmosphere I found a haven in a maverick school district, where a charismatic young superintendent, Anthony Alvarado, supported by the East Harlem political establishment, was unleashing a miniwave of real reform. He called upon teachers to make their own local revolution. Within ten years District 4 established twenty small alternative schools led by innovative teacher-directors. As these twenty were gradually established, they sparked change also in the now less-populated neighborhood schools. Although not all the changes were educationally first-rate, they provided opportunities for teachers and children and a welcome feeling of optimism. Alvarado argued, cajoled, manipulated. He attracted talent, he made schooling seem an adventure. He never downplayed professionalism, didn't knock teachers, avoided looking for villains. He didn't mandate one universal top-down system for improvement. He was a maverick who enjoyed mavericks, and he gave many of them a chance to explore—without pressure for quick results or an eye on the media. In fact, he kept things quiet for us, and thrived on minimal confrontations with the outside world. He was also rare in his calm expectation that he would be with us for a long time. (Few of the city's thirty-two district superintendents have lasted more than a few years.)

During those ten years we lived in a protected world, doing our work—steadily and sturdily. Five teachers and I founded Central Park East (CPE) in the fall of 1974 as a progressive school at a time when everyone claimed such an "open" style was dead. We began a second school (CPE II) in 1979 and a third (River East) in 1982. In 1986, under Alvarado's successor, Carlos M. Medina, we opened a secondary school, thus providing East Harlem with a progressive educational institution for youngsters all the way through high school.

During this same period, the city got a new chancellor, Frank Macchiarola. He took an opposite tack. Macchiarola handled politicians, corporations, foundations, and news reporters marvelously well. He promised big changes—always system-wide. We had grown accustomed to federal and state accountability schemes attached to various funded programs, but Macchiarola promised a new citywide accountability system. Teachers were the workers, Macchiarola boasted, and students the products. Our products should roll off our assembly line classrooms in uniformly proper condition—with plenty of inspections along the way. In reality, the new systems were mainly more of the same: more tests, more officially sponsored coaching, plus undisguised warnings that test scores better go up.

By hook or crook, most of us complied. It was pretty straightforward, and only seemed "crooked" to those who remembered that good assessment devices should not be taught to or coached for. (Any more than an eye exam—which loses value if examinees are "too well" prepared.) In fact, in the "old days" such test-specific coaching had been rigorously prohibited.

Since we now used exactly the same reading tests every year from grades 2–8, teaching to the test was fairly easy. Many schools did virtually nothing but test practice from January through April. With no new ideas, larger class sizes and the same old teachers, the city's scores experienced a remarkable and steady rise. (By 1986 most New York elementary school students were scoring above average!)

Yet no one in the city's high schools praised us for sending them better readers. In fact, things got worse in the high schools. By the mid 1980s a majority of black and Hispanic youngsters were dropping out without diplomas. But Macchiarola managed the news well enough to keep this data out of the public eye until after he departed in the spring of 1983.

At the same time, new regulations for special educational services for the handicapped were creating an ever larger and more expensive bureaucracy, requiring lots of testing and record keeping to stay in legal compliance. Over 10 percent of the city's pupils were soon labeled "handicapped"—nearly 120,000 children! Thousands of social workers, psychologists, and educational evaluators (former teachers) were hired, not to remediate, not to assist teachers, parents or kids, but simply to screen—to test, assess and prescribe. At the end of expensive (but shoddy, by average professional standards) evaluation processes, children were neatly labeled, and specific written school goals set:

> "Given ten two-digit addition examples, the student will use concrete materials to solve eight correctly"; or "given teacher supervision, praise and positive reinforcement, the student will attend to difficult assignments for five minutes, three times out of four, as recorded by teacher." (Taken from the Division's Manual)

A vast statewide law (called Chapter 53) mandating assessment of all new students for possible handicapping or gifted conditions was instituted in 1980. Thus another vast bureaucracy started testing five- and six-year olds. Finding the results of the first assessment unpalatable (30 percent were found "handicapped" and 2 percent "gifted") Macchiarola allegedly asked for new scoring norms. The result was that children entering kindergarten now had a better chance of scoring "gifted" (30 percent) and very little chance of being labeled "handicapped." Not a bad strategy, since we have few resources available to do anything about handicapped kindergarteners (a child has to be two years behind in reading to qualify for special education monies). Besides, everyone liked being called "gifted." The proliferation of "gifted" kindergarten classes was one result of this screening program. Meanwhile, a straightforward professionally administered hearing and vision exam for every entering student remains a utopian goal in our medically sophisticated city.

From the mid-1970s to the early 1980s, little happened except more window-dressing. A demoralized staff teaching larger classes on smaller paychecks gave the city its rising test scores. It did so both to "look good" and because the pressure on kids to get better scores increased.

Macchiarola's other innovation was the institution of two "gates" at fourth and seventh grades through which students scoring in the bottom 25th percentile could not pass. Inflated scores kept the number of holdovers to manageable proportions, but otherwise the only effect of these "gates" was to increase the number of students entering high school as adults—beyond the school-leaving age.

The good press Macchiarola's reforms received made their spread inevitable. Why not a citywide elementary science test? A social studies test? And by 1983 the N.Y. State Board of Regents got on the accountability bandwagon, instituting one of the most detailed and far-reaching top down educational packages in the nation. This new plan spelled out a statewide curriculum, complete with grade-by-grade testing mechanisms, from kindergarten through twelfth grade, for every accredited school—public, independent or parochial—in the state.

By a mere stroke of a pen, it solved the most complex educational issues. By regulation there was now a plan uniform for all, more "rigorous" and more detailed than former state guidelines and general graduation requirements. It promised equity and quality if students and teachers did their jobs as they were told.

Unlike the high schools, which the Regents curriculum had long controlled, the elementary schools had had room for considerable diversity. The Central Board for years had encouraged individualized instruction, matching curriculum to the child, and pedagogical innovation. Even though this rhetoric was not backed by structural support, at least it gave schools and teachers some elbow room. Some interesting high school innovations had also sprung up, offering alternate approaches to providing adolescents— particularly those most "at risk"— with academic skills. During Macchiarola's tenure as chancellor it was precisely this elbow room that had steadily been invaded. So while New York City's Board voiced opposition to the state mandates, it had, in fact, already begun to practice what the state was preaching.

All of this was occurring at a time when the employment prospects for New York's "at risk" students—always grim—had reached new lows. A social and political climate hardly friendly to poor minority families left these vulnerable young people with little hope. Even a high school diploma began to seem an unlikely dream. Still, there was no protest.

The union did voice objections, but it had limited clout. Its 1960s militancy had depended on the capacity to strike. Since most of those directly hurt by a strike were constituents of little political importance, and state penalties on strikers severe, the UFT had abandoned its old style of militancy. New York City's students were no longer a cross-section of its voting population. In 1964 over half the students were white. Twenty years later only 23 percent were white and 60 percent were poor enough to qualify for federal food subsidies. The union now depended on its members' electoral muscle, and on alliances with other powerful groups. It had to worry, also, about its public image. Gradually the union's leadership began to address issues with an eye to that broader public. This made it more flexible about traditional union issues, but it was now in a bind about exposing those deteriorating working conditions that it had no effective way of dealing with. It was now dependent on what "others" thought, not just on what teachers found credible. And these "others" were often corporations, business coalitions, and powerful public figures. Many of these "others" appreciated the union's new statesmanship, but they also wanted quick and measurable "results"—something to show for their support of public education.

Overworked teachers and principals, who never had much authorized autonomy anyway, were too overwhelmed with new city and state regulations to find the heart and energy to fight them off. They ignored some, followed others, were cynical about most. Macchiarola had provided a more friendly press; there was a kind of peace between the union and the world, and the state would now tell us what to do. At least we couldn't be blamed if it went wrong.

Then, for a brief moment in the spring of 1984, there was a flowering of hope and possibility. The mayor and the Board of Education had been forced to select a most unlikely successor to the retiring Macchiarola.

Mayor Koch's choice was Robert Wagner, a respected insider's politician. Wagner is, of course, white. Two minority candidates were also included in the final list of nominees: Tom Minter, a well-credentialed black educator then working at the Central Board, and Anthony Alvarado, superintendent of East Harlem's District 4. The three ran a lively public campaign. Although Alvarado captured interest everywhere, it seemed a foregone conclusion that Wagner would get the job. But the state commissioner, Gordon Amsbach, vetoed Wagner on the technical grounds that he had insufficient teaching experience. Consternation! Disbelief! What to do next? There was talk of starting a new search. But as a *New York Times* editorial noted in response to black and Hispanic outrage, doing so would expose the previous search as a charade. Alvarado was appointed chancellor of the public schools.

Alvarado, who rose from teacher to principal to district superintendent before he was 30, was now positioned to make history in American education. A sense of excitement stirred parent groups and the teachers' union. Within eight months, however, his promising career was tangled in an investigation of possible corruption and misuse of funds. Most of the charges were minor and some merely exposed standard system practices, but the very number of them seemed suspicious. His responses were evasive; media and public alarm grew; Alvarado resigned. The only educational legacy of his brief tenure was the creation of all-day kindergartens.

The board then selected Nathan Quinones as chancellor. Formerly head of the high school division (the only part of the system incontrovertibly still under Central control), he had the additional advantage of being Hispanic, thus averting any accusations that Alvarado's fall might have had racial implications. Quinones was a safe choice. (Ed. note: As we went to press Quinones had just announced that he was taking early retirement.)

The agenda stemming from the chancellor's office has slowed. Neither bottom-up nor bold top-down initiatives were Quinones's style. Nor did he enjoy the public/media "stature" of either Macchiarola or Alvarado. Reducing dropouts, truancy, and absenteeism were his stated major goals—a little each year. These are also the latest federal and state targets. New reports, time lines, and task forces are in place. The state and city have set up teams to "help" schools write plans for how they will improve—higher test scores and lower absentee figures. Lower class size in the early grades is probably Quinones's most important initiative. A subtle campaign to recentralize the city's schools is probably the most dangerous, although it's not clear who is initiating this one.

As I stare at the piles of memos and forms that confront me as a school principal, the job appears somewhere between a joke and an impossibility. The staff and I are directed instantly to implement new programs to resolve current social crises, to use the latest research on teaching, to tighten supervision, increase consultation, and to report back in detail on all the above. There are pages of new rules and regulations to study: the Regents plan alone would take a few months to make sense of. Responding to it would take a lifetime. Meanwhile, finding the funds to buy paper, repair our single rented typewriter, fix a computer, or tune the piano requires most of my time and imagination.

It's even harder this year. Money to run our school is always tight—an adventure in ingenuity and making do. Now an innovative UFT-sponsored plan to create workplace democracy has created instead schoolwide chaos. Previously principals received a lump sum (approximately $10–15 per student for the school year) to spend on all non-textbook needs. This year, the Central Board directed that teachers receive $200 each to order their own supplies. Sounds good! They were given an abbreviated catalogue, two weeks to complete their orders and no time for schoolwide consultation. Nor was anyone told that the $200 was not in addition to, but largely in place of, routinely available funds. The result: classrooms have gained some well-deserved extras but we have all lost the critical basics: paper, pencils, duplicating fluid, stamps, etc. Once again, a centrally imposed solution defeats an essentially sound idea.

Meanwhile the building in which we work is falling apart. Radiators leak, toilets back up, doors have no locks, windows are broken, fluorescent lights don't work because they need ballasts (which I am not allowed to go out and buy), desks are gouged with graffiti, and because we have too few chairs we have to carry them from classroom to classroom. The payroll secretary has more power over teachers than I do—she can dock their salaries and generally harass them if they are late, or forget to punch out, or are sick without a doctor's note. The custodial engineer is the boss of the building, and can prohibit teachers from coming in early or staying late, or dropping by on off days.

Any halfway decent camp sets aside more time for collective planning for a two-month summer recreation program than teachers are provided to plan a ten-month educational program. We are ordered to stick to "cognitive" (academic) goals, but our students still come to us with the exponential weight of unsolved economic and social family crises. We are ordered to give every child an hour's homework nightly—exact numbers of minutes per child per grade are centrally dictated—

and expected to also read, assess, and comment on each. All in one twenty-four hour day. We spend more time and energy making sure that no one who doesn't deserve it gets a free or reduced price school lunch than we do on making the lunchroom a decent place. In a system that refers to the midday meal as a "feeding program" (in England, it is called "dinner"), it is clear that the people doing the "feeding" and those being "fed" are not valued too highly.

Prestigious commissions—like Carnegie and Holmes—speak, at last, of the need to improve the status of teaching, of giving the people who must implement programs the power to design them. And they are right. But they often miss the significance of the details that stand in our way. The struggle is not only over weighty academic rights, but also these seemingly small and petty ones. Reform must address both. But it won't until teachers get more actively involved in the reform movement.

One pioneering county in Florida is planning to rename teachers "executives." But the teachers I know do not object to being called "teachers"; it is teaching that they want to get back to! They resent the time spent "managing," scrounging, making do, not the time spent "teaching." Serious, rooted change cannot happen unless the knowledge of those who do the job is tapped. To make this possible requires support, time—and patience. Patience above all. Mandates only seem efficient because they can at least make claim to "quick cures," in time for the next election. But when we speak of educating for democratic citizenship, rather than job training, patience is at the heart. Perseverance, reflection, flexibility, intelligence . . . but also patience. Schools will not become educationally successful by deadlines and mandates. The only kind of mandates that could help would be of quite a different order. Can mandates be designed that support school-based initiative, inquiry, and decision making? Could we mandate that schools provide teachers with time to talk and plan together? Or that schools be required to make their beliefs and practices public? For a starter maybe we could mandate that employers give parents time off to visit school.

School people don't insist on working in a vacuum, "doing their own thing." They want to be "exposed." The more "exposure" the better—so that schooling becomes visible in many ways, not just through numbers and statistics. Formal schooling, after all, occupies at least a dozen of our most impressionable years, and we are involved again as parents when our children go to school. Nearly half a lifetime; years that have enormous influence on public habits, values, and competencies. Hardly an insignificant topic for public discussion. This kind of attention might produce lots of criticism, not just applause. But while teachers (including me) might not always like informed criticism, we would acknowledge more of it, and it could thus lead to real discourse. Strangling schools with red tape and system-wide mandates—big ones or little ones—is what is truly inefficient. Until those who make decisions, including "the public," can see the specific local connections between policy and practice, we will not make the breakthroughs that our rhetoric demands. There just isn't a faster route.

—1987

why the sandinistas lost
PAUL BERMAN

A few days before the Somoza dictatorship was overthrown in 1979, Anastasio Somoza Debayle called a demonstration for himself in central Managua. A vast crowd descended on the rally grounds. A Nicaraguan journalist tells me that, looking at the immensity and enthusiasm of the crowd, one would never have guessed that most Nicaraguans hated Somoza and that even some of the cheering multitude secretly detested the man and his government.

Why did people who felt that way come to demonstrate for him? Because for anyone who depended on state contracts or employment or needed some sort of favor, attending Somocista rallies was the soul of common sense. Not to mention that, should you ever tilt into opposition, the Somocista government was likely to organize a Liberal party mob to keep you in line—tough characters drawn from the jails and the underworld who could be called out to march in the streets and assault anyone thought to oppose the regime. There was the additional intimidating fact that Somoza maintained a ruthless army of eight thousand men.

When General Somoza asked you to come to a demonstration and cheer at his name, you had good reason, therefore, to give that invitation serious thought. You stood in the sun and chanted, "Viva Somoza!" And when the opportunity arose—you overthrew the bastard.

A few days before the Nicaraguan elections last February, the Sandinista Front for National Liberation held a mammoth campaign rally in the big Managua plaza. There were at least two hundred thousand people, or, by the most common estimate, three hundred fifty thousand (meaning ten percent of the entire country), or possibly more than four hundred thousand. It was the biggest election rally in Nicaraguan history and widely regarded as a sure indication of impending Sandinista victory.

Yet four days later, when the people voted in what was guaranteed to be a secret ballot, only five hundred eighty thousand persons from the entire country put their mark in the Sandinista column. A large percentage of the crowd that chanted the Sandinista slogans must have entered the polling booth and voted for the person who had been vilified for years as the antipatriotic representative of the oligarchs and Yankee imperialists, Violeta Barrios de Chamorro—whose own crowds never exceeded fifty thousand.

A similar incongruity cropped up in the famously disastrous pre-election polls. When Ted Koppel said on *Nightline* two days before the election, "Almost certainly, the Sandinistas will win," he was relying on scientific polling data. People who told the pollsters they were going to vote Sandinista must have behaved precisely like the mammoth assemblage in Managua—public Sandinistas who privately got rid of the Sandinistas at the first possible moment.

Why did Nicaraguans behave in those mysterious ways? It was not because Sandinista Nicaragua ever became an out-and-out totalitarian state. But as the Somozas showed years ago, out-and-out totalitarianism is not necessary for getting crowds of unhappy Nicaraguans to chant praise of the government. A degree of freedom for a paper like *La Prensa* and for a multiparty parliament—dozens of parties! hundreds!—is perfectly compatible with a reasonably effective system for coercing the population, so long as the opposition press and political groups have no power.

The Sandinista Front is a vertical, centralized, military-style structure that, during its ten years in power, incorporated political coercion into its activity, including the best of its features: its revolutionary reforms in land distribution, health services, and education. To advance in school, for instance, to get grade points, it was a good idea to cooperate with the draft and to march in the Sandinista parades.

A little more than a year before the 1990 election I attended a national day parade in the town of Masaya and watched hundreds of schoolchildren bearing red-and-black Sandinista banners march in formation down the muddy avenue to the cathedral plaza. It was the sort of scene that struck naive visitors as a sign of Sandinista popularity. In reality the town of Masaya was the most radical place in Nicaragua, a Kronstadt of the tropics that had long since come to oppose the Sandinistas, as anyone could tell from private conversations (and indeed the town and especially its proletarian barrio voted strongly against the Sandinistas in the election). Yet the children carried the red-and-black, while on the sidewalks, the proud parents—or perhaps humiliated parents—cheered.

Violence, terror, and absolute power weren't required to get those children to carry Sandinista flags. Control over the schools was sufficient. Or in the case of getting neighborhoods to collaborate, control over rice and bean rations. Or in the case of artisans or farmers, control over raw materials.

The Sandinistas could, if necessary, call on violence, too. The Sandinista People's Army, eight times larger than Somoza's National Guard, exercised political control merely through selective use of the draft, plus the political indoctrination that accompanied military training. The Ministry of the Interior fielded a small army of its own along with a secret police whose training (from East Germany's fraternal Ministry of the Interior) was strictly the best. Plus the Sandinistas, too, maintained government mobs—though, this time, the mobs didn't come from the criminal class but from the 19th of July Sandinista Youth and the government employees.

An important means of social control was the threat of expropriation. A dispossessed rural and urban labor force has been growing in Nicaragua ever since the coffee boom of the 1880s; yet the country as a whole has never taken on a proletarian quality. Large numbers of families, poor as they are, have never lost their claim to a tiny plot of farmland, or a part-time or full-time artisan business, or rights over a stall at the market. These families were vulnerable in the extreme to Sandinista threats of expropriation (just as, under Somoza, they were vulnerable to the identical threat, though in different forms).

When the Sandinistas asked you to carry a banner through the streets or to cheer Daniel Ortega, you might have any number of reasons, then, to cooperate. When pollsters came around to ask you questions, you might have greater wariness over East German security techniques than the pollsters seemed to recognize (even if, in the political "opening" of the last three years, fear of the Ministry of Interior police tended to diminish). Possibly the Sandinistas offered you a T-shirt and a cap with Sandinista emblems. You might put them on. The shirt and cap were very likely the newest, cleanest clothes you owned.

You might not even be entirely certain of the true state of your own feelings—given that almost everyone authentically loved the Sandinistas as the beginning of the revolution. Still, as the years wore on, your feelings sorted themselves out. And when two thousand election ob-servers from around the world had tramped across every plaza in Nic-aragua and everyone had a chance to see these observers in the flesh, when at last you came to suspect that the February 1990 ballot was going to be secret, and when you have meditated sufficiently on Cardinal Obando y Bravo's repeated admonition that a dignified person does not sell his vote—well! In that case you entered the polling booth, and you put your faith in God and Jimmy Carter.

Serious reporters and commentators on Nicaraguan politics were badly misled about last February's election by the polls and the immen-sity of the Sandinista demonstrations because these observers seemed to think that, what with the antigovernment newspapers and radio sta-tions and opposition parties, the average Nicaraguan must have felt sufficiently free to express true opinions. But in Nicaragua pluralism and authoritarianism have coexisted through two social systems.

To what degree is the United States responsible for turning people against the Sandinista Front? The blocking of financial credits begin-ning early in the 1980s, the U.S. embargo that began in 1985, above all the contra war that was financed and for several years directed by Ameri-can agents—these policies were never justified, morally or politically, and have had terrible effects. Yet imperial destructiveness can explain only so much.

One of the main goals of the Nicaraguan revolution was to eliminate dependence on the United States, to diversify the foreign market and sources of capital. The Sandinistas were not wholly unsuccessful in these efforts. U.S. customers disappeared by White House executive order; yet customers from other countries largely took their place, some-times by order of the Kremlin.

The Soviet Union in recent years sent Nicaragua, according to a Soviet acknowledgement early in 1990, almost a million dollars a day of civilian aid in credits and goods—possibly more in earlier years. The East Germans, Cubans, and others sent additional aid and technical advice. Military aid reached equivalent levels, making altogether, according to the usual estimate, a billion dollars a year of East Bloc aid during most of the 1980s. Western Europe sent a hundred million dollars or more a year. In the early years, Mexico and Venezuela sent oil, and in recent years emigrant remittances may have reached as high as (roughly estimating) a hundred million.

Capital mostly flowed out of Latin America in the last decade, because of the debt crisis and other disasters. However, in Nicaragua's case, as the economist José Luis Medal has pointed out, net capital flowed in. Nicaragua's national debt multiplied many times. U.S. policy was intended to strangle Nicaragua; yet the actual effect was merely to prevent capital from flowing at a higher rate than it did.

Trying to tally up economic consequences of a war can seem a little revolting. Almost 1 percent of the entire population, an extraordinary figure, was killed in the contra fighting. Obviously the economic consequences were profound. But is it possible to define these consequences without appearing to minimize the horror of what has occurred?

The war damaged the economy in three main ways. It required the Sandinistas to divert probably more than 50 percent of the government budget to defense. Yet the remainder, because of the aid pouring in from around the world, still surpassed what the Somoza government ever had. The effect of the defense budget was to limit what was nonetheless a growth in funds at the government's disposal.

The war displaced part of the labor force into the army, which was another bad blow to the economy. Still, the work force in Nicaragua, owing to overall population growth, did not diminish during the last ten years. It increased by four hundred thousand persons. If previously productive lands sometimes went untilled under Sandinista rule, that was not because the army swallowed the work force. At the end of the Sandinista period, unemployment reached 30 percent, in spite of army enlistment. Labor displacement to the army, harmful though it was, cannot by itself explain the economic collapse.

Finally, the contra war wreaked physical damage to the coffee harvest, to livestock, and to mining. Most of the physical damage occurred, however, in the regions where the contras were strongest—the remotest, poorest, least developed sections of the country, which have never been central to the economy. The heart of the economy, in the rich agricultural departments on the Pacific coast, was pretty much untouched by the fighting.

Then came the Arias plan and the 1987 ceasefire, and though sporadic fighting continued ever after, the remote coffee fincas, livestock ranches, and mines in the contra zones were in most cases physically able to revive production. Yet it was only then, in 1988 and 1989, that the economy finally tumbled down the stairs. Production fell 1 or 2 percent a year during the period when the war was at full steam, with inflation at 1,800 percent. But with the ceasefire more or less in place, production fell by 7 or 8 percent a year. Inflation in 1988 reached 36,000 percent.

The period after the ceasefire was when industrial workers in Managua finally sank to an incredible 10 percent of what they had enjoyed under the last Somoza. The mass scrounging in garbage dumps, the widespread signs of a hunger that modern Nicaragua had never previously known, the reduction to two and even one meal a day for masses of the poor—these horrible phenomena, which had been visible in earlier years but were usually denied by Sandinista supporters, now became undeniable. The war was a crucial element in that calamity. Still, if other aspects of Nicaraguan life had been going well, neither the war nor hostility from the United States would have sufficed to sink the economy.

Was a corrupt and privileged bureaucratic "new class" an additional factor of major proportions, as some people say? The rise of a Sandinista bureaucracy did generate the kind of extreme class division that is characteristic of communist regimes—the system, above all, of special stores with American products for the elite *nomenklatura*. Some spectacular examples of high living have turned up: the private fleets of cars, the expropriated beach houses. But the Sandinista elite in Nicaragua never exceeded some 5,000 persons. The privileges had a bad effect on morale and on Sandinista popularity and led to a couple of celebrated party resignations. Sandinista privileges could not have had much effect on the economy.

Or, as other people say, was "mismanagement" the main problem? The Sandinistas relied partly on Bulgarian advisers for the economy, and it may be that, yes, the Bulgarians proved less than brilliant. The grotesqueries of Sandinista pricing have become clichés. Everyone in Nicaragua recalls the time when a tractor tire cost more than a tractor, a glass of ice water more than a gallon of gasoline. Big industrial Investments—a deepwater port on the Atlantic coast, a milk refinery—were ill conceived. On top of which came Hurricane Joan in 1988, followed the next year by droughts, then by excessive rains. What hasn't happened to poor Nicaragua!

Even so, I think the gravest of the problems was political, in its origin ideological. The Sandinistas came to power at an auspicious moment. The United States, still with the administration of Jimmy Carter, sent more aid than the Somozas had seen in years. The Soviet Union was supportive. Of the countries in the region, Venezuela, one of the richest, and Costa Rica, the nearest, were enthusiastically pro-Sandinista.

The original revolutionary junta included both the Sandinistas and Mrs. Chamorro and was supported by an overwhelming and ardent majority. Merely by expropriating the Somoza properties and the estates of Somoza's cronies, the revolutionary government controlled 20 percent of the national wealth, plus the national banking system, which ought to have sufficed for instituting a thoroughgoing social reform.

A sentiment for some sort of democratic socialism was so widespread that even the traditional Catholic hierarchy pronounced in favor of the word "socialism," though most people seemed to mean by that something like what existed in Costa Rica. And why not? Costa Rica was and remains a living proof that, in spite of every reactionary instinct of the State Department's Latin American desk, Central America need not dwell forever under the shadow of oligarchic feudalism and political terror.

The social democratic party in Costa Rica—Oscar Arias's National Liberation party—staged a revolution of its own at the end of the 1940s and was able during the next years to institute magnificent reforms. Costa Rica is a poor country with drug problems, a bad press law, a vulnerability to foreign meddling, and every sort of difficulty. Yet schooling grew to be as democratically available as in France or Norway. Infant mortality sank to as low as any place in Latin America. Life expectancy rose as high as in the United States. The army was abolished. Labor won rights. Somehow the Costa Ricans managed not to fall into a state of hostility with Washington, D.C. Central Americans flee *to* Costa Rica, not *from* it. There are no political exiles.

The Sandinistas, when they seized power in 1979, likewise employed a social democratic vocabulary and spoke of nonalignment. In reality the original Sandinista idea was Cuban, with some significant democratic modifications. When Sandinistas used the word socialism, they meant a party-state system characterized by centralized administration and state ownership—state farms, for instance, as in Cuba. Accordingly the Sandinistas nationalized foreign commerce and, as much as possible, internal commerce, too, so that almost everyone who wanted to buy or sell was supposed to conduct business through the Sandinista ministries.

The Sandinistas set out to absorb every possible institution into either the new state system or into the Sandinista Front, to incorporate all the existing workers' organizations, cooperatives, trade unions, and political parties into a pyramidal "people's democracy" of mass participation under Sandinista control. They tried to establish an ideological orientation toward Cuban-like ideals (for instance, by using Cuban teachers and East German materials in the grand literacy program of the early years, while rejecting Costa Rican teachers who were eager to participate). They tried to impose their own church faction, the so-called Popular Church of the Poor, over the orthodox Catholic mainstream—all of this through methods of popular enthusiasm, honest persuasion, state coercion, mob control, defamation campaigns, and outright repression.

The result was a short period of stunned confusion on the part of everyone who had expected something more democratic from the overthrow of the Somozas. Then the Sandinistas discovered that one sector after another was no longer cooperating with the revolutionary junta. Of the five original junta members, Mrs. Chamorro and two guerrilla heroes went into opposition, leaving only Daniel Ortega and his eventual vice president, Sergio Ramírez.

In normal democratic circumstances, the discovery by the government that its program was less than wildly popular should not have provoked still graver problems. But in the case of the Sandinistas, one other crucial element played a role. As Tomás Borge, the Minister of the Interior, repeated early this year, "Sandinismo is Marxism applied to the reality of Nicaragua"—by which he meant, of course, the Marxism of Lenin and Fidel. Sandinismo is the kind of doctrine that Václav Havel had in mind when he wrote of the inability of Marxists to understand the "mechanisms of their own political influence, thus paradoxically making them precisely what they, as Marxists, so often suspect others of being—victims of 'false consciousness.'"

The Sandinistas, when they look in the mirror, have always seen the vanguard of the people, the highest expression of the workers and the campesinos; and when they look at their opponents, they have always seen the enemies of the people and the representatives of the oligarchic past. In accord with their pluralist commitments from 1979, the Sandinistas steadfastly specified that opposition groups would retain the right to exist in a Sandinista Nicaragua. Yet they never granted these groups a moral legitimacy. The groups could exist, thanks to Sandinista forbearance, but they were never supposed to mount a serious opposition.

Anytime that non-Sandinista movements or institutions threatened to become sufficiently active to influence events, the Sandinistas' first instinct was to denounce them as foes of the revolution. The Miskito Indians of the east coast who rejected centralization, the northern campesinos who rejected state agriculture, the Catholic hierarchy with their following among the poor who rejected the Sandinista-dominated church faction, the right-wing and left-wing trade unionists who struggled for trade union autonomy, the small right-wing and left-wing political parties that declined to merge with the Sandinista Front, the market women who carried canastas of nonstate tangerines into hungry Managua, the staff at *La Prensa* who published the country's most popular newspaper— all found themselves beyond the pale of Sandinista acceptability. And the vanguard of the people never noticed that the list of "CIA agents," oligarchic elements," "Somocista National Guards," and "agents of imperialism" gradually came to resemble an entity that could only be described, except by the Sandinistas, as "the people."

Why didn't the Sandinistas back off and re-create at least some aspect of the original revolutionary coalition? They tried. But their backing off was always partial and begrudging. How could it not be, when the Sandinistas honestly imagined themselves to be the leaders of the vast Nicaraguan majority? In this last election, the prospect that Sandinismo might end up winning less than a majority seems never to have crossed their minds. Most of the top commandantes didn't even bother to run for the National Assembly, so certain were they of maintaining their government portfolios (or party posts in a party-state).

The result was the biggest incongruity of all. The Sandinistas dominated Nicaragua for ten years, but the more they dominated, the less they controlled. The Sandinistas pointed in the direction of state modernization and a proletarianized party-led egalitarianism, and the people silently trudged the other way, as if determined to undermine every scheme, even the commendable schemes, that emanated from the Ministry of Planning. The black market grew. The professional and managerial class (followed by poorer people) fled to Costa Rica and the United States. The workday quietly diminished. Perhaps if the Sandinistas had cracked down a lot harder, things would have gone a little smoother. But the Sandinistas never had a Stalinist vocation, and in any case, every time they did crack down, which was often enough, the effects went from bad to worse.

The grimmest consequences of all occurred among the primitive campesinos of certain areas in the north, Jinotega, Chontales, and Boaco. The Sandinistas ordered the campesinos to buy and sell through the state at disastrous prices and to join the Sandinista militia and other institutions, and a portion of the campesinos not only refused but ran away to the mountains to join the contras. The Sandinistas called the contras a tiny mercenary force of U.S. agents, enemies of the people. But in these remote hill regions, the contras, misled and deceived and exploited though they were by the CIA, did not take up arms for mercenary reasons. They were, as Sergio Ramírez has recognized, a Nicaraguan Vendée, though in some cases they weren't even right-wing. It's a little-known fact, but some of the first contras had originally been Sandinista guerrillas themselves. The local legitimacy of these contras can now be seen from the election results in rustic towns like Siuna and La Rosita, which voted anti-Sandinista in spite of having been the sites of grisly contra atrocities.

The Sandinistas let themselves be carried away by their own grand

and colorful mythology—and a myth, as Cyrano de Bergerac says, is a sort of a truth that is also a sort of a lie. In Sandinista myth making, the lies ultimately got the upper hand. When the commandantes walked to the mike to address the chanting multitude, they said: At least we have forged a national independence! Which was sort of a truth but mostly sort of a lie, given that the people who sweltered in the sun listening to the fiery speeches did not feel so independent.

Observers who failed to notice the steady decline in Sandinista popularity have tended to say in the aftermath of last February's election that Nicaraguans voted their stomachs, not their hearts. Or else that people voted for Chamorro—but never intended for her to win. Or voted for Chamorro in a mad whim that instantly they regretted. Those explanations are, in my view, further examples of "false consciousness."

There are of course people who still love the Sandinistas—people who honestly agree with them, the families of leaders, the people who are loyal to the Sandinista cult of the martyrs, people who have undergone too much in the name of Sandinismo to give it up now. Some of the campesinos who have won land titles will remain loyal. The Sandinista small farmers and ranchers' association is well regarded. Naturally the Front has a strong base among the more privileged managers and administrators in the state sector or the state-dependent sector and among army officers (though a shocking percentage at some of the army bases voted for Chamorro's coalition). The Sandinistas have a quality of relative modernity that none of the opposition groups can claim and that exercises an attraction for the more forward-thinking and secular university students, who always did make up the core of Sandinista support. The intelligentsia is Sandinista.

All in all the Sandinista vote reached 40.8 percent—though that figure surely overstates the reality. During the 1989 Polish elections, emigrés were allowed to vote from abroad. Nicaragua's emigrés of the last ten years account for between 15 and 20 percent of the entire population, who, if they had enjoyed a similar right, would have lowered the Sandinista percentage to the middle thirties (the overwhelming emigré opinion detests the Sandinistas).

The campaign was accompanied by a steady drizzle of Sandinista threats and pressures. Sandinista mobs played an active role in the early months. After the invasion of Panama, General Humberto Ortega said that, in case of a similar invasion of Nicaragua, treasonable "elements" would be executed. Everyone knew that the elements in question were, of course, the supporters of UNO. Local death threats against UNO supporters were a constant. There were threats of expropriation—even a threat from Daniel Ortega to expropriate Violeta Chamorro's home after the election, which ordinary people must have taken as a threat to them as well. None of these threats became severe enough to produce an international outcry, but neither did they let up. They may have dissuaded many people from voting for Chamorro.

Will the Sandinistas be able to mobilize their significant remaining social base for progressive goals in the future? Will they support the useful projects that the Chamorro government may undertake, or will they continue to regard any force but their own as illegitimate? Will the Sandinistas abandon their military-like vertical organization and the idea of bringing all of society into it, as some of the East Bloc communists have done? Will they have public conventions and publicly acknowledged factions? Will the rank and file be given the chance to elect party leaders? That has never occurred in the history of the Sandinista Front.

Undoubtedly the external pressures to go in democratic directions are considerable right now, and undoubtedly many Sandinistas agree. Democratic instincts have never been absent from the Front. One sign of that during the election, virtually unnoticed in the American press, was the distant but notable third-place finish of a left-wing splinter candidate, Moisés Hassán, one of the guerrilla heroes who served in the original revolutionary junta and who was for several years the mayor of Managua. Hassán has offered articulate criticisms of Sandinista self-deception.

His splinter movement is unlikely to grow into a powerful party, but the fact of finishing third must mean that significant numbers of Sandinista supporters who would never consider voting for Violeta Chamorro nonetheless wanted to protest the orientation of the Front. And what will happen to the Front when large numbers of Sandinista stalwarts who have been studying in the Soviet Union and Eastern Europe return to Nicaragua? These young people may bring back a different sort of education than they were intended to receive. Democratic instincts among the Sandinistas may end up being reinforced.

Does the turn against Sandinismo meanwhile signal the end or the defeat of the Nicaraguan revolution? If the revolution is defined along the lines of Third World Marxist national liberation, defeat appears to be at hand. But the Nicaraguan revolution has all along followed another course, hidden beneath the political struggles of the different parties. Ever since the overthrow of Somoza, the poor have undertaken what can be described as large-scale programs of their own—above all, a mass seizure of property.

From the start of the revolution, campesinos set out to take land. They did this at first by occupying the Somocista haciendas, even without Sandinista backing. When the Sandinistas organized state farms and seminationalized cooperatives, the campesinos struggled against these new rulers, too—sometimes by protesting from within the Sandinista system (supported by the small farmers and ranchers' association), sometimes by going over to the contras. Later still, when the Front made a well-advised turn away from state agriculture, the campesinos continued to struggle for land, this time with the blessings of the Front.

Some of the landowners who for good or bad reasons have lost property to Sandinista expropriations will now try to get their lands returned, which will lead to nasty fights. But whatever the fate of these disputes under Chamorro's government, a massive agrarian reform, the largest in Latin America, remains a stubborn fact, unlikely to disappear. The countryside in Nicaragua has changed shape.

A similar grass-roots democratization of property has been going on in the cities, though in ways that tend to be economically unproductive. The growth of shanty towns combined with the rise of the black market (which the Sandinistas first tried to suppress, then were forced to legalize or at least tolerate) has meant the development of thousands of new tiny businesses—wretched peddler-sized enterprises, which by themselves will never generate wealth. Yet these enterprises of the so-called marginal sector do represent a further distribution of economic power. As the economist Medal has observed, a humble class of traders has been emerging from the unofficial peddler stalls and the backroom dealings of the black market—people who may not be so poor as they seem and who may, in fact, be taking the first steps toward a modest accumulation of capital.

It is tragic that Sandinista policies ended up in bitter conflict with these movements of very poor people. The campesinos, artisans, and traders have always needed cooperative institutions and a friendly government to make their tiny enterprises efficient. The possibility of endowing at least some of these movements with a socialist ethic, which was undeniable at the start of the revolution, has been lost in large measure; the word "socialism" itself, which people esteemed ten years ago, has taken on some of the odor that the Somozas managed to give to the word "capitalism."

Even so, the energy that led impoverished campesinos to seize their own farms or to come to the city and go into some sort of tiny business, the dynamism that led other people to flee to Costa Rica and the United States and to send back hundreds of millions of dollars—this energy remains. February's election is a dramatic instance. To vote against the Sandinista Front in spite of every threat, to sustain a belief in opposition groups that had been made to appear for ten years as impotent foolish agents of an enemy country, to hold on to a sense of a non-Sandinista Nicaraguan reality that even most foreign reporters were unable to perceive—all this reveals a considerable ability to resist domination from above.

The election of a government whose top figures are committed to democratic rights is in itself a step forward for the real revolution, the revolution of the poor. How that new government will perform, whether it will favor capital at the expense of everything else, whether it will control corruption, whether it will be able to cope with dangerous contra bands in the remote districts and with a Sandinista bureaucracy—all that is impossible to predict. The circle around Chamorro contains some high-minded individuals with an orientation to the democratic left, but also some parties and figures from the anti-Somocista right. Chamorro herself is not a powerful individual, or even a healthy one. The Chamorro family (prominent among the Sandinistas, too) does not exactly represent a break from Nicaraguan tradition.

The central point nonetheless remains that masses of poor people have somehow not yet lost their own initiative. In the aftermath of the election, a writer for the *L.A. Weekly*, Anthony Palazzo, reporting from a small Atlantic coast town, asked the innkeeper about Chamorro, and the innkeeper replied: "We Nicaraguans love to fight. We fought to get Somoza out and we fought to get the Sandinistas out. And if we don't like her, we'll push her out too." That has a Nicaraguan timbre to it.

The revolution in that country is an authentic social revolution, not merely a political one. The revolution is no longer young. But neither is it over.

—1990

the feminization of poverty
BARBARA EHRENREICH AND
FRANCES FOX PIVEN

Despite the widespread misperception that women are achieving economic equality, their economic status has deteriorated sharply since the late 1960s. Today women—and children—are the primary beneficiaries of social welfare programs for the poor. Between the mid-'60s and mid-'70s, the number of poor adult males declined, while the number of the poor in households headed by women swelled by 100,000 a year. By 1980, America's poor were predominantly female; two out of three adults whose incomes fell below the official federal poverty line were women, and more than half the families who were poor were headed by women. This trend prompted the National Advisory Council on Economic Opportunity (since then disbanded by the Reagan administration) to observe that "All other things being equal, if the proportion of poor in female-headed households were to continue to increase at the same rate as it did from 1967 to 1978, the poverty population would be composed solely of women and their children before the year 2000." Poverty in the United States has always been disproportionately concentrated among minorities, but the convergence of gender and class is unprecedented in American history.

The causes for the feminization of poverty are rooted in profound changes in American society. Like most industrialized capitalist countries, we have long presumed a "family-wage" system. The achievement of a family wage for men, meaning earnings sufficient to support a wife and children, was an important victory of the late 19th- and early 20th-century labor struggles. But this achievement by unionized male workers helped to thwart women's aspirations for higher wages, particularly in typically female occupations. Of course, not all men and certainly not all black men earned enough to support families, nor were all women supported by men. Nevertheless, the assumption that women entered the work force only as secondary workers reinforced the segregation of women into low-paying occupations and legitimized systematic wage discrimination against women. For those women who could depend on the earnings of a male breadwinner, however, the system did offer economic security, if not the dignity of economic independence.

In the course of only two decades, the family-wage system has ceased to provide economic security for women and their children. Increasingly, women must depend on their own earnings, and even when they do not, they can't count as they once did on the earnings of men. Yet the assumption of the family-wage system remains firmly embedded in a wage structure that offers women, hour for hour, only 59 percent of the average male wage. What is usually called "the breakdown of the family" occurred without equalizing changes in the labor market, and this accounts for the disproportionate impoverishment of women.

For many women, poverty begins when their marriage ends. Half of the marriages in the United States now end in divorce, and in 80 percent of these divorces the children remain with their mothers. Child-support payments are a negligible source of income for most of these families. Forty percent of divorced fathers contribute nothing, and those who do contribute pay on the average less than $2,100 a year. Many other women are poor before they become mothers and, for them, having the sole responsibility for children is only another barrier to achieving economic self-sufficiency in the labor market.

Women who both raise and support their children need, of course, to earn a "family wage," just as many married women also need to earn a substantial portion of their families' income.

Yet the average annual income for working women now is $11,000 a year, and less than $8,000 for black single mothers. According to the Bureau of Labor Statistics, a family of four now requires $25,000 a year to maintain an "intermediate" standard of living. The primary reason for the low earnings of women is occupational segregation. The overwhelming majority (80 percent) of jobs held by women are concentrated in only 20 of 420 occupations listed by the Department of Labor. These occupations are mainly in retail sales, clerical work, light assembly, the catch-all category of "service work," and they are characteristically low paid and dead ended. In fact, real earnings have been declining in the sectors of the work force where women are concentrated. Between 1973 and 1979 average hourly earnings in services, measured in 1972 dollars, fell from $3.16 to $3.08; earnings in retail trade fell

from $2.70 to $2.61. In the same period, earnings in largely male manufacturing jobs increased.

As a result of the combined effects of changes in family patterns and
occupational segregation, the fastest growing group among the female
poor are single mothers with young children. By 1981, the Census reported 9.4 million female heads of families. (Meanwhile, the media's
fancy notwithstanding, the number of men raising children on their
own showed no significant increase in the decade of the '70s.) The
increase in households headed by women is most striking among blacks.
Some 45 percent of black families are now headed by women, as compared to 14 percent of white families. But despite the stereotype of the
"black welfare mother," poor female-headed households are increasing
more rapidly among whites than among blacks.

What are the chances for progress out of the occupational ghetto of
"women's work"? Some trends are encouraging. Where only 4 percent of
the nation's lawyers and judges were women in 1971, women accounted
for 14 percent in 1981. In the same period the percentage of the nation's
female physicians rose from 9 to 22 percent, the percentage of female
engineers increased four-fold (from 1 percent to 4 percent), and the
number of women holding skilled blue-collar jobs also increased. But
despite these gains by a narrow stratum of better-prepared women,
average female earnings relative to men actually declined slightly, from
over 60 percent in the 1950s to 59 percent today. The stability of this
ratio—despite the striking gains made by some women, particularly in
the professions—is depressing evidence of the deterioration of the economic status of the majority of women workers.

Long-term structural trends within the U.S. economy offer little
hope that market forces will produce an upturn in women's occupational prospects. And it's not because the the number of jobs available to
women is declining. In fact, low-paid "women's work" is expanding,
because of two important trends in the labor market.

One is the long-term sectoral shift away from manufacturing and
toward service and clerical jobs. In the 1970s this shift accelerated as a
result of both expansion in the service and retail sectors and a rapid
decline in manufacturing, especially in the highly unionized and well-
paid steel, automobile, and rubber industries. According to Emma

Rothschild, 70 percent of all new private-sector jobs created between 1973 and 1980 were stereotypically women's jobs in such areas as fast foods, data processing and other business services, and health care. The result is a marked feminization of the work force, but in jobs that are "badly paid, unchanging, and economically unproductive."

A second trend affecting both the gender composition of the work force and women's economic status is the reorganization of work associated with increasing automation. In his classic 1974 study, *Labor and Monopoly Capital,* Harry Braverman showed that the pressure to maximize profits leads employers to replace well-paid, skilled jobs with badly paid, unskilled jobs that are likely to be defined as "women's work." Automation, and most spectacularly the automation made possible by new microelectronic technology, accelerates this trend toward what Braverman calls "the degradation of labor." Skilled jobs for men become less skilled jobs for women; and skilled work for women is replaced by less skilled work: the machinist is replaced by an unskilled operator, the department-store buyer by the clerk who tends a computerized inventory system, the secretary by the word-processor operator.

In short, the occupational ghetto of "women's work" has grown larger, and opportunities for both men and women outside this ghetto have shrunk. One obvious consequence is that fewer men will be able to earn a family wage—a fact that renders the anti-feminist vision of a restored family with the father the breadwinner and the mother the housewife utterly hollow. More and more women, married or not, will have no choice but to be wage earners. Another consequence is that many women will be poor and remain poor, whether or not they are employed.

Women and Social-Welfare Programs

In a hostile economy, women —and not only poor women—have come to rely more and more on government social-welfare programs for their economic security. In part this results from women's greater longevity, which enables them to benefit disproportionately from programs where eligibility is determined mainly by age. Thus women receive 54 percent of all Social Security benefits, despite the fact that the average benefit paid to women is almost one-third lower than that paid to men ($215.80

a month compared to $308.70). Similarly, almost 60 percent of those covered by Medicare are women. Flawed though these programs may be, they are critical to the survival of a majority of older women who would otherwise be desperately poor.

Other programs are not age-tested, but "means-tested"; eligibility is conditional on poverty. The reliance of women on these programs has risen apace with the increase of poverty among women. In particular, female-headed families have come to rely heavily on government social-welfare programs. In 1979, according to the Census Bureau, over 3.3 million of these families, or 34.6 percent of the total number of female-headed families, received AFDC; an almost equal number were covered by Medicaid; 2.6 million were enrolled in the Food Stamp program; and 2.3 were enrolled in the school lunch program. Thus government social-welfare benefits have reduced some of the income gap suffered by the families headed by women who can no longer rely on a male wage. In other words, the breakdown of a system of intrafamily income transfers from husband to wife has been partially offset by the expansion of a system of public income transfers.

A second group of women who benefit from government social-welfare programs are those in the expanding low-wage service and cleri-cal sectors of the work force. For these women, social-welfare programs provide some protection against employer abuses, whether low wages, unpaid overtime work, speed-ups, or personal and sexual harassment. It is easier for a woman to resist unfair demands, and risk being fired, when she knows the result will not be starvation for herself and her children. Furthermore, because social-welfare benefits reduce despera-tion among the unemployed, they are less likely to undercut the wages and working conditions of those who do have jobs. By reducing eco-nomic insecurity, the social programs thus enhance the workplace power of millions of low-wage working women.

The third group of women whose livelihood depends on social-welfare programs are those who are employed by them. In 1980, fully 70 percent of the 17.3 million social-service jobs on all levels of government (including education) were held by women. These jobs accounted for fully a quarter of all female employment, according to Lisa Peattie and Martin Rein of MIT, and for about half of all professional jobs held by women. As the Reagan administration presses for a shift of funds from social welfare to military spending, a good many of these jobs will be lost, without compensatory employment gains for women. Only 0.5 percent of the entire female work force is engaged in work on military contracts. A study by Employment Research Associates estimates that with each $1 billion increase in the military budget, 9,500 jobs are lost to women in social welfare or the private sector.

Accomplishments and Failures

The achievements of America's federally sponsored welfare programs are obvious, especially for women, but not only for women. Social Security provides some guarantees against the terrors of a poverty-stricken old age for the millions of Americans who have no private pensions, or whose pensions fall woefully short of a subsistence income. Medicaid and Medicare make it possible for more millions of both the elderly and the poor—who are, of course, the groups most likely to suffer from chronic disease and disabilities—to receive the medical attention previously largely unavailable to them. Unemployment insurance reduces some of the fear of joblessness for most of the middle class as well as the poor, and helps tide over those who are out of work through the dislocations caused by cyclical downturns and shifting patterns of investment. Federal disability programs make the fate of the ill and the crippled less miserable. Nutritional programs, particularly Food Stamps and supplements for women and infants, are credited with significantly reducing hunger and the most common forms of malnutrition. And Aid to Families with Dependent Children (AFDC) provides at least a meager subsistence for millions of the most desperately impoverished mothers and their children. All told, an estimated one-third of Americans now depend to some degree on government social welfare programs.

In addition to easing the economic insecurity of millions of Americans, federally funded social-welfare programs often made possible innovative services and new opportunities for citizen participation. In a number of the Great Society programs of the 1960s, the federal government effectively bypassed entrenched local political hierarchies and called for "maximum feasible participation" of the communities served. People who never before had a role in public decision-making gained positions on the federally mandated community advisory boards of health, mental health, and multiservice centers, giving the recipients of services, for the first time, a voice in determining what their needs were and how they might best be met. Similarly, federal funding for rape crisis centers and battered women's refuges bypassed local male politicians and gave women, many of them feminist activists, a chance to create client-centered services sensitive to women's needs. Republican hostility to these programs stems, in no small part, from their role in the political empowerment of women, minorities, and the poor.

There is no question, however, that the social-welfare programs established in response to the upheavals of the 1930s and 1960s are flawed and imperfect. Their loudest critics today are on the Republican right. For nearly two decades, however, groups that depended on the programs had been sharply critical, including client groups and their advocates, women's organizations, and labor unions. On the surface, it may therefore seem that no one, neither on the right nor the left, supports the social-welfare programs, and this helps account for the timid response that has been made to the Reagan administration cuts.

In fact, however, very different sorts of criticisms are at issue. The right attacks the programs for their high cost and their presumably corrosive effect on the incentive to work. By contrast, the left criticizes the programs for bureaucratic indifference to clients; for the low level of benefits or services; for the punitive terms often exacted as a condition for receiving benefits or services; and for profiteering by businesses involved in the provision of services. Not only is this a different critique than that made by the right; it is in fact an opposing critique, and it stems from an opposite assessment of the responsibility of government.

Effects of Political & Business Pressures

In the most important sense, the shortcomings of American social welfare result from the complex political forces that shaped the programs and continue to shape them over time. Demands by the unemployed or the poor or the aged were resisted by employer interests fearing that if government provided subsistence to large numbers of people, labor markets would be weakened. As a result, the benefit levels of the key income-maintenance programs, including unemployment insurance and AFDC, have always been very low. Other programs, particularly those that provided "in-kind" benefits in the form of food subsidies or housing, or those that provided such services as medical care, easily became the target of lobbyists who stood to profit from the provision of benefits or services.

Business pressures also explain why a number of the most important programs were left to state (and sometimes local) governments to administer. For reasons that are hardly mysterious, business interests have always exerted great influence on state and local programs. When businessmen demand low taxes and restrictive social programs at the state or local level, they wield the threat of relocation. Moreover, because business interests can successfully resist state and local taxes, the revenues to fund programs at the state and local level must be extracted from regressive taxes on working people. This pattern in turn generates a climate of resentment and hostility toward locally financed programs for the poor. As a consequence, benefit levels set by the states have been kept well below the lowest local wage rates. In addition, programs have been thoroughly encased in an elaborate bureaucratic apparatus of procedures and conditions so that as little aid as possible would be given to as few as possible. Finally, the degrading treatment of those who survived the bureaucratic run-arounds ensured that few would choose the dole who could otherwise survive.

The AFDC and Medicaid programs illustrate the deforming effects of private business interests on American social welfare. AFDC is notorious for its humiliating treatment of clients and the inadequacy of the benefits it provides. Monthly payments to a family of three averaged slightly under $300 in 1980, and only nine states provide more than $400 a month. In no state is the combination of AFDC and Food Stamps sufficient to raise a family up to the official poverty line. AFDC originated as a program of cash benefits to impoverished mothers raising children without a male breadwinner, and it reflected the recognition that such women could not be expected to support their children by their own efforts. However, that recognition has always been at war with another, usually unstated, imperative—that government must not provide benefits competing with low-wage work. Thus, although it is the only program that attempts to meet the daily needs of poor children,

AFDC is pegged far below the poverty level in order, ultimately, to avoid any challenge to the determination of wages by market forces.

The gratuitous humiliation inflicted upon clients by welfare bureaucracies reinforces this effect, for it works to ensure that few will choose welfare over work, no matter what the terms. Of course, abysmal poverty and degrading treatment have other effects—depressing the expectations of poor women and their children, destroying their morale, and ensuring that they do not come to believe they have legitimate rights, even to a subsistence income. In this way, AFDC helps create the very caricature of the demoralized and dependent recipient, which is then used to justify the harshness of the program.

The Medicaid program illustrates different flaws resulting from the influence of different market interests. For decades before Medicaid and Medicare were legislated, private interests in the health sector, particularly the American Medical Association and the insurance industry, had fiercely and successfully resisted any major program of government health insurance. Medicaid and Medicare were passed over the bitter resistance of the AMA, and then only in a form ensuring that the new government financing mechanisms would not affect private control of the organization and delivery of medical care. From the inception of these programs in 1966, health reformers criticized them as inadequate and patchwork substitutes for a national health service that would guarantee the actual delivery of high-quality care. Even so, reform groups expected that Medicaid would make health care financially accessible to many of the nation's "medically indigent" (people who while not classified as poor, nevertheless cannot afford medical care).

While Medicaid helped many of the nation's poor to gain access to medical attention, the program had other, unexpectedly perverse effects. Medicaid, combined with Medicare, contributed to the rapid and still escalating costs of medical care. Conservative critics argue this is the result of excessive consumption of health services by the poor and elderly, and that prices have risen with increased demand. However, the healthy system is notoriously impervious to ordinary laws of supply and demand. It is mainly doctors who determine the demand for health services; only they can decide whether a problem will be dealt with in one visit or through extensive diagnostic and treatment procedures.

Moreover, provider groups such as the American Medical Association and the American Hospital Association have lobbied hard, and largely successfully, to minimize government control of the prices of their services. As a consequence, these programs have turned out to be a bonanza for the medical industry. For everyone else, especially the over 30 million people who presently lack coverage of any kind, it has meant spiraling medical costs.

Like AFDC, Medicaid is administered and partly financed by the states, and benefits and eligibility have been largely left to the discretion of the states. The states have set eligibility levels so that most of the people the program was originally intended to serve have been excluded. In fact, in almost all states, Medicaid eligibility was tied to welfare eligibility. Strained state budgets, combined with the identification of Medicaid as a "welfare program," made it an easy target for budget-cutters. Consequently, as medical inflation encouraged by some features of the program drove costs up, Medicaid coverage shrank, providing fewer services to proportionately fewer of the people who need care.

None of these failures is the result of the inevitable bumbling of "Big Government." Rather, they were the result of a federal government so weak it ceded administrative control over many of the programs to states and localities where they were cannibalized by hostile interests, so weak it could not establish decent benefit levels, and so weak it could not curb the distortions forced on it by private market interests. A weak government has produced weak programs, and weak programs are indeed difficult to defend.

The welfare state's critics on the right pointed a clear direction for the contraction of the programs that the Reagan administration has attempted to implement. Underlying each of its major initiatives was an effort, not only to slash benefits and services, but to increase the power of business interests and reduce the power of beneficiary groups. This was the significance of the Administration's "New Federalism" proposals, which would entirely have abdicated the federal role in the AFDC or the Food Stamp program in favor of state and local government. The Administration's persistent efforts to eliminate the legal-services program and to rewrite the regulations of a number of the programs so as to weaken procedural safeguards are similarly an effort to shift power relations by expunging the legal rights of program beneficiaries.

Some Guidelines from the Left

If the welfare state's critics on the right have pointed a direction for concrete changes, so does the critique developed by left and liberal reformers. In fact, the specific elements of an expanded and reformed social-welfare policy have been outlined before, both by the Welfare Rights movement in the 1960s and by the feminist movement in the 1970s. Our agenda should begin, very simply, with the demand for higher levels of benefits. Nothing could be more critical to the well-being of poor women and children than an immediate increase in the benefit levels of the AFDC program, for example, which, at a minimum, should support families at a level above what is officially defined as "poverty."

Beyond this obvious short-term goal, we should begin to work for organizational reforms that will strengthen the influence of the beneficiaries of income-maintenance programs and reduce the influence of business. Three basic principles can guide us.

First, responsibility for social-welfare programs should be firmly fixed at the federal level. Influence from the right works for decentralization to the state level, in order to increase the power of business interests over the income-maintenance programs that bear most directly on labor markets. For just this reason we should fight for the outright nationalization of financing and policy-making responsibility for such programs as AFDC, unemployment insurance, and Medicaid. Benefits and eligibility standards should be uniform across the nation, and their financing should not be subject to the whims of state legislators.

Second, bureaucratic discretion in the determination of eligibility and benefits should be reduced. Notwithstanding its avowed hostility to "government interference," the right has worked to increase bureaucratic discretion and to strip beneficiaries of procedural protections. Arbitrary and variable decisions can be shattering to recipients and reinforce the notion that social-welfare programs are a form of charity. It follows that we should work for the elimination of elaborate conditions for determining eligibility—conditions that inevitably will increase bureaucratic discretion and intimidate applicants. In their stead, we should promote broad and easily determined criteria that reduce the need for invasive investigation and give benefits and services the status of *legal rights*.

Third, over the longer term, we should work toward the consolidation of programs so as to promote common stakes and stronger alliances among the many segments of the American population that have come to rely upon the welfare state. The present system separates means-tested programs such as Medicaid from universal programs such as Medicare and Social Security, thus breeding competition and animosity among recipient groups. Worse, within these broad categories, an incredible array of disparate programs applies differently to people depending on their age, their sex, on the specifics of former employment, on marital status, or even on the value of their home furnishings. The right has capitalized on this fragmentation of social-welfare programs and their recipients. It follows that we would work for a unified system that, through the breadth and strength of its constituency, would not be vulnerable to attack by a business-oriented president or Congress.

An adequate and unified system of income maintenance would go a long way toward easing the economic insecurity of low-paid working women and toward improving the lives of women now living in poverty. But an income-support program cannot provide goods and services if these are not available in the market at affordable prices. Private business has not found it profitable to operate child-care centers or clinics offering primary and preventive health care in low-income areas, much less centers for rape victims or refuges for battered women. Market-priced housing and health services too will remain beyond the reach of most women, even if the income programs are improved.

Of all these services, perhaps none is more critical to women than child-care provisions. It seems obvious that without affordable and reliable child-care options, mothers of young children should not be expected to enter the labor market or job-training programs. Yet now many women are forced to do exactly this, leaving an estimated 6 to 7 million young children without any preschool or after-school care, and millions more with informal and often substandard child-care arrangements. Equally important, for teen-agers as well as adult women, is access to a full range of reproductive health services, from contraception to abortion to prenatal care. In the past three years, access to these services has been steadily reduced. Yet for women, these services mean the "right to control our own bodies," and they are preconditions for economic security.

In the face of the harsh assault from the right, we need to renew the long-standing feminist commitment to government-funded social services. For the short term, the first priority is to reverse the cutbacks in government spending for low-income housing, day-care centers, refuges (which have depended heavily on federal grants), and other services. In the long term we need to build up these services, not as stop-gap measures but as a vital part of our social infrastructure, which must meet the critical needs of a vast sector of the population. Services that have heretofore been limited by narrowly defined eligibility criteria (such as subsidized day care) should be expanded because they are necessary, and because expansion will ensure a broad constituency of support and public involvement. Finally, services that have been offered as "commodities" to more or less passive "consumers" (like most medical care) should be redesigned to increase client participation and influence. There is a wealth of experience to draw on: health centers and refuges run by women and child-care centers run by community groups are only some of the examples of services organized to involve and empower clients. The democratic spirit that infuses such "alternative" service institutions, combined with government responsibility for sustained and adequate national funding, points an important direction for the reform of the American welfare state.

The Meaning of the "Gender Gap"

Political expediency is clearly a factor in the assault on the social-welfare programs. The Reagan administration does not depend on the poor for votes, and their lack of organizational resources makes effective resistance at the national level difficult. Further, the fragmentation of the American social-welfare programs has taken its toll in fragmentation and division among beneficiaries. But this overlooks a politically critical fact: the American poor are disproportionately women. With the revival of feminism in the late 1960s, women have developed a considerable organizational capacity, and a consciousness of common interests that cuts across class lines. As a result, the Reagan administration's policies are galvanizing a broad movement that joins together middle-class, working-class, and poor women.

The women's movement of the last two decades, like that of the late 19th century, has looked to government as the guarantor of women's rights, as in the intense mobilization for the ERA; it has also looked to government as a guarantor of economic security. As early as 1967, the "bill of rights" adopted at the first national conference of NOW called for government action to alleviate poverty, to enforce laws against sex discrimination in employment, and to improve the circumstances of older women through changes in the Social Security system. Ten years later, when thousands of women gathered at Houston for the First National Women's Conference, they passed a far-ranging series of resolutions calling for, among other things, a major federal role in the provision of child-care services, a federal program of national health insurance, a federal policy of full employment, and increases in federal funding for AFDC and other income-support programs to "provide an adequate standard of living." Taken as a whole, the Houston resolutions amount to a demand, not only for greater federal intervention against sex discrimination, but for the creation of an adequate social-welfare system for all Americans.

In the years that have passed since the Houston conference, the need for expanded and reliable social-welfare programs has become even more acute. For one thing, the experience of the '70s shows that employment is not a solution to women's poverty: in what are typically "women's jobs," full-time and year-round work does not necessarily bring one over the poverty level. Despite the ups and downs of the business cycle, the expansion of low-paid "women's work" continues, and this points to the continued need for public income supports and services for women, whether they are employed or not. Furthermore, a growing proportion of poor women are mothers of young children. Even with a vast expansion of child-care services, some women may prefer to remain at home with their small children rather than do double duty as full-time employees and full-time homemakers. Poor women, and especially single mothers, should have this option, just as the wives of the affluent do, and social-welfare programs should make the choice possible.

These are the reasons, then, that women, and especially feminists, now lead the way in resisting the attempt to destroy the welfare state. They are no small force. Moreover, they are not alone in this effort. The Reagan administration still waves the banner of laissez-faire, but the banner is tattered and unconvincing. The public economy exists, in reality and in the understanding of most Americans. The central political question that has emerged is not whether government shall play a large role in American life, but who will pay for and who will gain from what government does. The significance of the steady stream of poll data showing women's strong disapproval of the Reagan policies is that women have been the first to recognize the question, and the first to offer the answer of resounding support for government policies promoting economic security and equality.

—1984

NINETIES

A paradigmatic text in this regard is the television series "Gilligan's Island," whose seventy-two episodes constitute a master-narrative of imprisonment, escape, and reimprisonment which eerily encodes a Lacanian construct of compulsive reenactment within a Foucaultian scenario of a panoptic social order in which resistance to power is merely one of the forms assumed by power itself. . . . The key figure of "Gilligan" enacts a dialectic of absence and presence. In his relations with the Skipper, the Millionaire, and the Professor, Gilligan is the repressed, the excluded, The Other. . . . But the binarism of this duality is deconstructed by Gilligan's relations with Ginger, the movie star. Here Gilligan himself is the oppressor: under the male gaze of Gilligan, Ginger becomes the Feminine-as-Other.

Brian Morton, "How Not to Write for Dissent," 1990

foreword

JOANNE BARKAN

Every decade adds images to the indelible collection we carry around in our minds. For the nineties, most of us can conjure up Nelson Mandela striding out of a South African prison in February 1990; Norman Schwartzkopf, with maps and pointer, briefing the press during the first Gulf War in February 1991; the beseeching eyes of starved Muslim men pressed against a concentration camp fence during the 1992–95 Bosnian war; Yitzhak Rabin and Yasir Arafat shaking hands on the White House lawn in September 1993 to affirm the Oslo Peace Accord; the Federal Building in Oklahoma City with its exterior walls blown off in April 1995; Bill Clinton glaring into TV cameras in August 1998, claiming, "I did not have sexual relations with that woman"; and, finally, the crystal ball in Times Square dropping at the stroke of midnight to mark the end of the decade, century, millennium, and Y2K nonevent.

Articles in *Dissent* considered these and a wide range of other topics in the nineties, but we also had our obsessions—specifically, four big questions that we worried about endlessly.

The first emerged from Communism's collapse, which, of course, *Dissent* saw as a great good. We speculated about a more inclusive, multilateral world order and new dangers in a world dominated by one superpower. But most often we worried about prospects for the democratic left in a post-Communist world. Resolute optimists—typically found outside *Dissent*—saw the end of Communism as a grand opening for democratic socialism, or at least Swedish-style social democracy: the good folks would no longer be confused with the totalitarian left. *Dissent*ers, however, thought it more likely that the ideological triumph of the "free market" would undermine the entire left, making it harder to defend the welfare state, let alone more radical forms of social justice. We were correct. Conservatives effectively shaped the collapse of Communism into proof that only privatization and unregulated capitalism remained viable options.

No one worried more about this unqualified celebration of the free market and its effect on left politics than *Dissent*'s founding editor, Irving Howe, a democratic socialist since the age of fourteen. He continued to

243

explore the possible mechanisms of a socialist society and solicited articles for an ongoing series on market socialism (collected in a volume called *Why Market Socialism? Voices from* Dissent). "Will the socialist ideal survive?" was what he wanted to talk about over dinner one evening at the end of April 1993. When I said I thought it would reemerge in some form at some point, he immediately asked, "But will I be around to see it?" Irving died a week later, leaving his *Dissent* comrades bereft and his *Dissent* readers with one last article on the importance of utopian vision (see "Two Cheers for Utopia").

Our second major concern in the nineties was the eruption of rabid nationalism and ethnic violence on a scale not seen in decades. Genocidal slaughter, rape, and torture used systematically as weapons of war—who had responsibility for stopping these in places such as Bosnia, Rwanda, Kosovo, and East Timor? *Dissent* pressed hard for a "politics of rescue"; we insisted that ending the horrors as quickly as possible took precedence over certifying the foreign policy record of the rescuers. This put *Dissent* at odds with many American and European leftists who saw any U.S. rescue effort as an unacceptable imperialist ploy. In a renewed debate on nationalism, we published articles that challenged traditional Marxist thinking and reconsidered "tamed nationalisms" that could accommodate autonomous cultures and plural loyalties (see Mitchell Cohen's "Rooted Cosmopolitanism"). No democracy without pluralism—the nineties made that clear.

Dissent also devoted hundreds of pages to "globalization"—the third major issue. Everyone was talking about it, but did it exist? Some of our writers argued that the American economy had been equally integrated into a world market a century earlier; the notion of globalization at the end of the twentieth century, with its threat of jobs moving overseas, served as an excuse for employers to hold down wages and weaken labor unions. We examined the near-global deregulation of financial markets (initiated by the United States in the 1970s), floating exchange rates, and massive capital flows at cyber-speed. These, many of us argued, undermined what remained of the growth-oriented world order that John Maynard Keynes envisioned at the close of the Second World War (see my "The Old Welfare State in the New Age of Competition"). We analyzed feasible reforms to stabilize global finance, but we argued that the barriers to reform were political, not technical or economic.

Those political barriers were *Dissent*'s fourth big worry. The Reagan era ended in 1992, but why did it usher in such a weak alternative, namely the Clinton presidency? Candidate Clinton, several of our writers maintained, had run the most left-wing presidential campaign since the mid-1930s. But he governed like a hapless centrist with no power to resist corporate interests. For the rest of the decade, *Dissenters* debated why this was so. Was Clinton spineless? Was he constrained by or in step with a moderate electorate? Did hypersensitive markets ("Wall Street reacted badly this morning . . .") exert serious pressure? Did a Republican Congress stymie him after 1994? The answers implied political choices for the left and electoral strategies beyond the Clinton years.

Clinton got sole credit for wrecking his second term with a sex scandal. Yet, for a brief moment, it looked as though some good might come out of the mess. A majority of Americans never believed that Clinton's asinine personal behavior amounted to an impeachable offense. The Republicans' failure to oust him divided their party; the Democrats emerged more united (see Sean Wilentz's "Bankruptcy and Zeal"). But hope was illusory. The scandal and breakdown of the Clinton-Gore partnership contributed to Al Gore's near miss in the electoral college in 2000.

It's often said that the U.S. left makes progress during a Democratic administration because not all its resources are drained away in defensive battles. The nineties didn't work that way. The left was no bigger and not at all invigorated at the decade's end. What to do about it? The question never goes away. *Dissent* has always kept up a broad search for answers—in politics, civil society, economic reform, and critical culture (see Marshall Berman's "Jaytalking"). And the socialist ideal?

By the end of the nineties, we were devoting fewer pages to definitions of democratic socialism and sketches of its possible institutions. As one of the *Dissenters* who wrote some about market socialism, I didn't object. The differences between successful left-wing social democracy and feasible democratic socialism intrigued me, but they didn't feel high-priority. Maybe that was, in part, a mistake. Maybe we needed more utopian thinking—not necessarily about the mechanisms of socialism but about an ideal attractive enough to remind us of where we wanted to go and why it has been worth the effort.

two cheers for utopia
IRVING HOWE

We live in a time of diminished expectations. It's not exactly a time of conservative dominance, although the dominant politics in some countries is an unenthusiastic conservatism. Nor is it a time of liberal dominance, although in the United States the Clinton administration has given rise to some liberal hopes, by no means certain of realization. And it's certainly not a time of leftist domination, even though moderate social democratic parties hold office in some European countries.

It's tempting to compare this post–cold war moment to the postrevolutionary decades of early nineteenth-century England. But the comparison is of slight value, since what we are experiencing might better be called a postcounterrevolutionary moment. Idealistic visions, utopian hopes, desires for social renovation are all out of fashion—indeed, are regarded as dangerous illusions that set off memories of totalitarian disasters. Leftist bashing, in both newspaper editorials and learned books, is very much in. The current catchword is sobriety, which sometimes looks like a cover for depression.

This is true of the intellectual world, with the exception of a few mavericks like Günter Grass. It is also true for what remains of the European left—either solid, decent social democrats with barely a touch of fire left in them or unrepentant communists masquerading as socialists in Eastern Europe.

There are, of course, many reasons for this mood indigo, only a few years after the enthusiasm raised by the "velvet revolution" in Czechoslovakia and the Gorbachev reforms in the former Soviet Union. But in this comment I want to focus on only one reason: the aftermath, or perhaps more accurately, the aftertaste of the collapse of communism.

Some years ago Theodore Draper made a remark in conversation that has stuck in my mind: the central experience of the twentieth century, he said, was communism, like it or hate it. To be sure, there was fascism and the end of colonialism, but fascism could be seen as essentially a ghastly reaction to the rise of radicalism and the end of colonialism as an all-but-inevitable cluster of events. In its years of influence and

247

power, communism seized upon the imagination of millions of people throughout the world. Communist parties were powerful in most of the major European countries; a bit later, they appropriated the heritage of anticolonialism in Asian and African countries; and even in the United States, where the Communist party was never a major force, it has been reliably estimated that nearly a million people passed through the Stalinist milieu (not the party) between, say, 1920 and 1950.

Declaring itself the legatee of humanism and the bearer of good news, communism inspired thousands—no, hundreds of thousands—of workers, students, intellectuals, to feats of devotion and, sometimes, heroism. Seldom have so many good people sacrificed themselves for so bad a cause. There were of course careerists, hacks and thugs in the communist movement; but for many ordinary people "the movement" burned with flames of hope. Those of us who were long-time anti-Stalinists, enclosed in our little groups and sects, found it hard to acknowledge the idealism—twisted, distorted, corrupted yet idealism nonetheless—that went into the communist movement. To be sure, in the East European countries the communist dictatorships attracted a large share of careerists (the kinds of people who in the United States might have been Republican officeholders). But there, too, the communists gained the support of decent, misguided followers. When the anti-Stalinist groups won over a handful of people from the Communist parties, it was almost always people who were intellectually and psychologically exhausted, their fanaticism burned out and their intellectual energies diminished.

The communist movement destroyed entire generations. The sheer waste of human resources, of the energies that might have been available for social renovation, is incalculable. With many rank-and-file militants, the sequel has been silence. With a good many former communist leaders, the sequel has been an ugly form of nationalism—as in Yugoslavia, where the leaders of both Serbia and Croatia are former prominent communists.

The results of this great historical disaster are staggering. Even those of us in the United States, insulated by our native mythologies, who were never tempted by Communism, are experiencing the consequences. New generations, new energies do not arrive overnight. There has first to be an interval of weariness, disillusionment, "pragmatism"—and diminished expectations.

You can see the signs of this exhaustion if you pick up any of the leading intellectual journals. Some are sour (usually edited by ex-radicals) and others are timid (usually edited by quasiliberals). Some subsist by mocking the hopes of their youth. Others avoid any long-range expectations or desires. Still others narrow their focus of concern to the daily routines of politics, sometimes saying useful things, though not much more.

What I've been saying here holds, I'm afraid, for large segments of the European social democracy. Let me be clear: if I lived in any of the major European countries, I would belong to or support the social democratic party. I might be critical, I might tilt a little toward whatever left wing it had. But I would be part of it.

Yet the truth is that, except in one or two countries, social democracy today has become a decent and honorable party that (rhetoric apart—and that even less and less) does not really aspire to move beyond the status quo. Little of the spirit of socialism remains in these parties. That much said, it's only fair to add that this isn't entirely their fault. For one thing, the constituencies of these parties, the people who vote for them, also share in their spiritual hesitation, their intellectual skepticism and bewilderment. It's not as if "the masses" are pressing the social democrats for a more radical outlook. Nor is it as if there were a clear socialist idea or vision that the parties reject. For the truth—as every *Dissent* reader learns from every issue we publish, perhaps to excess—is that the socialist idea is as precarious as the ideas of the conservatives and liberals, though the latter have the advantage of being at ease with the existing social and political order, while the social democrats presumably desire some change. The difficulty of formulating an attractive program is far more serious for the social democrats than for their opponents. Devoted to decency and democracy—no small matters—the social democrats cannot evoke the idealism and selflessness of the socialist yesterday. The memories of yesterday grow dimmer; one of the last to embody these was Willy Brandt, and now he is gone.

So there really is no point in the old-style leftist denunciation of social democracy. What we can and should criticize the social democrats for is not that they have failed to come up with the "answers"; it is for having largely abandoned the questions.

Well, we *Dissent*ers, the handful of us, try to hold fast to the vision of social transformation, even as we have dropped many of the traditional proposals for how to reach it. Some of us call this belief socialism, out of a wish for historical continuity or for lack of a better label. It's not that we're smarter than most European social democrats; not at all. Our advantage, if that's what it is, consists in the fact that we are distant from power and therefore able or, indeed, driven to think in terms of long-range possibilities, the revival of the democratic left in what may turn out to be the not-very-near future. Of course we also respond to immediate issues, so that *Dissent* carries articles about taxes, health care, budget crises, and so on. But even if, at a given moment, the immediate issues loom large, at least some of us want to think in terms of long-range options. We want, that is, to avoid the provincialism of the immediate.

That's why in almost every issue of *Dissent* you'll find one or two articles about "market socialism" or allied topics. Some of our readers, I suspect, quietly skip past these articles. That's OK, as long as they see why we print them. Often enough, these articles are provisional, a little abstract, and inclined to disagreements with one another. They don't necessarily paint a picture of an actual future—who can? But they are efforts to indicate possibilities of renewal. They provide materials for developments some of us will never live to see. They are, if you please, sketches of utopia.

That word "utopia" has come into disrepute. In much intellectual discussion it tends to be used as a term of dismissal. And, of course, there are versions of utopia—based on force or terror or the will of a self-appointed "vanguard"—that are abhorrent. We have had enough of these.

But there are other utopias. There is the democratic utopianism that runs like a bright thread through American intellectual life—call it Emersonianism, call it republicanism, call it whatever you like. There is the utopia of community and egalitarianism.

In an essay Lewis Coser and I wrote some forty years ago in the second issue of *Dissent,* we quoted a passage from Ernst Cassirer that still speaks to our condition:

> A Utopia is not a portrait of the real world, of the actual political or social order. It exists at no moment of time and at no point in space; it is a "nowhere." But just such a conception of a nowhere has stood the test and proved its strength in the development of the modern world. It follows from the nature and character of ethical thought that it can never condescend to the "given." The ethical world is never given; it is forever in the making.

In the sense that Cassirer speaks of it, utopianism is a necessity of the moral imagination. It doesn't necessarily entail a particular politics; it doesn't ensure wisdom about current affairs. What it does provide is a guiding perspective, a belief or hope for the future, an understanding that nothing is more mistaken than the common notion that what exists today will continue to exist tomorrow. This kind of utopianism is really another way of appreciating the variety and surprise that history makes possible—possible, nothing more. It is a testimony to the resourcefulness that humanity now and then displays (together with other, far less attractive characteristics). It is a claim for the value of desire, the practicality of yearning—as against the deadliness of acquiescing in the "given" simply because it is here.

With all due modesty, I think this version of utopianism speaks for us. So, to friend and foe, at a moment when the embers of utopianism seem very low, I'd say: You want to call us utopians? That's fine with me.

—1993

rooted cosmopolitanism

MITCHELL COHEN

The resurgence of nationalism after the collapse of communism startled many observers in the West. What could have been more stark than the contrast between Western and Eastern Europe? As the European Community sought new modes of integration, nationalist virulence asserted itself in more than one of the previously communist lands. The bloody unraveling of Yugoslavia has been the most potent example, and the fear remains that the former Soviet Union could become Yugoslavia writ large. Evidently, Leninist and Stalinist dominion led neither to a withering away nor to the successful repression of national sentiments. (At the same time, Western European integration has proven to be a complicated matter, resisted in some quarters and accompanied by xenophobic outbursts in others.)

It is gradually becoming clear that nationalist aspirations were sometimes mistaken for democratic ambitions by Western observers of the momentous events between 1989 and 1991. Earlier, during the cold war, both theorists of totalitarianism and Stalinists, each for their own reasons, tried to convince us that ideology was redesigning in its own image every nook and cranny of—and brain cell in—Soviet-style societies. It is now evident how wrong they were, how much more complicated history has been. Much seems not to have been remade, but frozen or stunted or integrated and used by these regimes. National sentiment is one example, and it is a particularly thorny problem for the left.

The left, historically, never came adequately to grips with nationalism, and was often confounded by its intransigence. Consequently, its reemergence poses old quandaries anew. Marx's famous quip about modernity, that "all that's solid melts into air," would seem an appropriate metaphor for the last two years, save for one aspect of the modern world: national consciousness. Apart from circumstances in which nationalism served anti-imperialist purposes, the left has tended to wishful anticipation of the dissipation of nations. For example, Eric Hobsbawm, one of the finest Marxist historians, wrote as recently as 1990: "The owl of Minerva, which brings wisdom, said Hegel, flies out at dusk. It is a good sign that it is now circling around nations and nationalism."

The left, habitually, advanced two linked assertions about nations: that they are products of history and not embodiments of timeless collective essences; and they should be regarded as epiphenomena, that is, as secondary (if often bothersome) matters. I generally agree with the first point but think the second misconceived. Considerable contemporary scholarship—not only of the left—addresses precisely these issues. Anthony Smith, in his thoughtful book *The Ethnic Origins of Nations* (1987), elucidates them neatly by means of a (Greek) ontological twist. He reminds us that Parmenides, the ancient Eleatic, proposed that "what is, is." He meant that change, "becoming," is illusion. A "Parmenidean" approach discerns in nations something inherent in human existence, something primordial that makes historical reappearances in varied guises yet that is in some way essential. The assumption is like that of Herder: nature creates nations. In contrast to Parmenides, Heraclitus of Epheus held that "all things are in a state of flux." A Heraclitian perspective on nations would emphasize their historicity. Nations, on this account, are a distinct product of modernity. They could not have come into being in earlier conditions, and will likely be transcended in the future. Thus Ernest Gellner, for instance, argues with characteristic erudition, in *Nations and Nationalism* (1983), that nations come of the transition from "agro-literate" to industrial societies, and Benedict Anderson, in *Imagined Communities* (1983), contends that however subjectively ancient nationalists perceive their nations to be, they are objectively modern.

Smith seeks a middle ground between Parmenides and Heraclitus. He accepts the modernity of nations but traces their origins as far back as antiquity in what he calls *ethnie*, at whose core is a complex of myths and symbols tied to "the characteristic forms or styles and genres of certain historical configurations of peoples." All of them generate ethnocentrism, a sense of collective uniqueness and exclusivity that can be found, for example, in the oppositions between Greek and *barbaroi*, between Jews and pagan idolaters, in the self-conception of the Chinese as the Middle Kingdom, and in the Arab-Moslem notion of *Dar al-Islam*. In the West, an array of economic, political, and cultural transformations produced nations out of *ethnie*. So, rather than a break between pre-modernity and modernity, Smith perceives a political transformation leading from *ethnie* towards notions of common citizenship.

The "collective uniqueness" of a social entity is a problematic notion for Marxism, which ascribed the most salient features of human reality to social class and conceived the future to be embodied in a *universal* class whose interests represented those of humanity as a whole. The proletariat's victory was to give birth to a classless society—the first truly universal society. Nations and nationalism had to be viewed as epiphenomena. In the socialist future, with human "prehistory" left behind, there would be a new social individual dwelling amid socialist humanity. Nothing would mediate between the individual and the human community writ large.

Marx was radically Heraclitian. However, one can find in his writings on nationalism at least two paradigms, as Shlomo Avineri notes. Before 1848 Marx believed that because of the universalizing tendencies of the capitalist market "national differences and antagonisms between peoples are daily more and more vanishing" (*The Communist Manifesto*). National cultural distinctions among workers were, objectively, secondary matters—at best. As Marx wrote in his unfinished critique of Friedrich List (1845), "The nationality of the worker is neither French, nor English, nor German, it is *labor, free slavery, self-huckstering*. His government is neither French nor English nor German, it is *capital*. His native air is neither French nor German nor English, it is factory air."

In Marx's post-1848 paradigm, nationalism tends to be a superstructural device employed by the bourgeoisie in its pursuit of expanding markets abroad and domestic mastery. In the first paradigm, the natural course of capitalist development ought to lead to the withering away of nationalism; in the second paradigm, nationalism is sustained by capitalists, distracting proletarians from their class interests and leading to the intensification of conflicts among nations.

Despite their divergences, the two paradigms are linked by Marx's insistence that "workers have no country." In both, nations and national cultures are viewed as historically created but, finally, as epiphenomena; Marx's ultimate vision is of a universal culture. It couldn't be otherwise if

workers are the universal class, have no country, and breathe only fac
tory air as their native air.

The difficulty is that this universal culture is something quite abstract. Here we may discern in Marx a problematic inheritance of Enlightenment rationalism. Now, few have been more incisive than Marx
in criticizing bourgeois forms of abstract universalism, particularly concepts of the individual. He contrasted the Robinson Crusoe individual
imagined by many capitalist ideologists with his own notion of "social
individuals." In a trenchant passage in the *Grundrisse* he wrote:

> The more deeply we go back into history, the more does the indi-
> vidual appear as dependent, as belonging to a greater whole. . . . The
> human being is in the most literal sense a *zoon politikon* [political
> animal], not merely a gregarious animal, but an animal which can
> individuate itself only in the midst of society. Production by an
> isolated individual outside society . . . is as much of an absurdity as is
> the development of language without individuals living *together*
> and talking to each other.

In short, the self-created rugged individualist is an ideological fiction.

But Marx did not go far enough, and he thereby encouraged an
abstract proletarian internationalism in place of abstract bourgeois universalism. Among other things he should have said that individuals
belong to greater wholes, not to a greater whole. Just as an individual is
not an abstract entity, neither are the social realities through which one
individuates oneself. The worker's native air may be factory air, and not
French or German or English, but when the worker demands rights, it
will be in French or German or English. By making a parallel between
the producing and the speaking individual Marx—unintentionally—
implies the essential point. Societies are differentiated not only through
productive relations but through language and culture, particularly national languages and cultures in the modern era. The most fruitful
Marxist analyses of nationalism recognized just this. In *Die National-
itätenfrage und die Sozialdemokratie* (1907) Otto Bauer argued that a
nation is constituted by "common history as the effective cause, common culture and common descent as the means by which it produces its

effects, a common language as the mediator of common culture, both its product and producer." Instead of proposing a classless society that would negate or homogenize national cultures, he advocated a federal socialist state that would provide national minorities with cultural autonomy on a "personal" (that is, nonterritorial) basis. Consequently, Bauer avoided the class reductionism that leads to an esperanto vision of socialist culture—a vision no less one-sided than that of nationalists who cannot see beyond their own tongues.

However, it is not true that all nationalists have had chauvinist views of the world and that all expressions of national sentiment represent particularist evil. For one example, a central current within the history of French socialism has been quite nationalist "when the nation in question represented the universal values of justice and progress" and anti-nationalist when "*la nation*" meant chauvinism and clericalism. When Jean Jaurès rallied to the cause of the Dreyfusards, he refused to allow the right wing to be identified with "*la nation,*" and concurrently demanded of the left that it make the French republic together with universal human values its cause. Any assault on human rights had to be its charge, not solely proletarian interests narrowly defined.

Nationalists, like nationalisms, play different roles in different situations. As Avineri points out, in Marx's own day at least one socialist, Moses Hess, argued that nations should be conceived as mediators between the person and humanity. Hess, in response to Jew-hatred, espoused a socialist Jewish state as one link in an international chain of national redemptions. The title of his 1862 tract—*Rom und Jerusalem*—was not incidental, for Mazzini had made essentially the same arguments, though with republicanism in the place of Hess's socialism. Morever, the apostle of Italian nationalism did not preach devotion to the nation alone but told his followers: "You are *men* before you are *citizens.*" Like his Jewish counterpart, he saw the nation as a mediator between the individual and humanity; Mazzini and Hess both proposed their peoples' independence as sparks for universal liberation and not solely as particularist enterprises. The agenda was not just a flag but a pacific world of free nations. One may oppose their programs, find them bleary eyed, ill-conceived, or historically deluded, but they cannot be classified as belligerent exclusivists. It is true that neither Hess nor

Mazzini elaborated their ideas with the trenchancy of the author of *Capital*, Yet they grasped something that the more formidable mind did not.

To recognize the modernity of nations and to discard the notion that they incarnate timeless collective essences should not be translated simplistically into the proposition that nations and nationalism are nothing more than epiphenomena. Although it is incorrect to speak of "nations" before, roughly, the fifteenth and sixteenth centuries, and nationalism before the French revolution, national cultures and national consciousness take on an autonomy beyond their origins. It is as historically spurious as it is politically hazardous to homogenize nationalist movements and sentiments.

Let's take a contemporary example. I think it incumbent upon the left—and everyone else—to speak out forcefully on behalf of the Kurds. Not just forcefully, but honestly, which is impossible apart from advancing Kurdish national aspirations. Kurds sometimes define their aspirations as autonomy (within Iraq or Turkey), sometimes as independence; social democracy is not their priority. Shall we tell them that Westerners will support them so that in a future era they can embody Western leftist ideas of universal humanity (whatever those are nowadays)? It is difficult to imagine a more condescending posture. And what should Kurds make of the part of the left that, preoccupied singularly by anti-imperialist indignation, draws attention to the Kurdish tragedy solely to indict American policy in the Gulf (as if Saddam Hussein would otherwise have been benevolent)? My point is simple: this is an oppressed nationality. Kurds are oppressed as Kurds and not as members of generalized categories. Their problem must be addressed in its specificity. Their national sentiments are legitimate, both intrinsically and as a response to oppression.

I do not mean to underestimate the murderous catastrophes wrought by nationalist fanaticism, especially in our century. (The Kurds themselves do not have entirely clean historical hands; should an independent Kurdistan arise, one would demand of it the same respect of minority rights Kurds should have been afforded in Iraq or Turkey.) Rather, I want to argue against conceiving nationalism as an either/or proposition: either all its forms to be condemned or all its expressions to be sanctioned. Both possibilities are inherently perilous. Michael Walzer has suggested what seems to me to be a sagacious alternative, that of domesticating nationalism's more dangerous impulses, seeking to integrate and counterbalance them within broader pluralistic frameworks. A useful historical model, as he notes, is religion, which, once a primary source of slaughter throughout Europe, was domesticated after its battered apostles reconciled themselves to multireligious societies and, consequently, to tolerance. I would add that this ultimately meant resigning themselves to an important principle, one that is key to such domestication and to which I will presently return, that of the legitimacy of plural loyalties and therefore difference.

I employ the word "difference" with some hesitation, because it is now encumbered by faddish, often vacuous, usages. This baggage aside, "difference" is a vital historical and contemporary question in American and European societies. It has also been a longstanding problem for the left, rooted in that troublesome dimension of the left's Enlightenment heritage to which I alluded when discussing Marx. The friar tells Lessing's "Nathan the Wise": "You're a Christian soul! By God, a better Christian never lived." Nathan replies, "And well for us! For what makes me for you a Christian, makes yourself for me a Jew." A universal quality—reason—makes this identity of Christian and Jew possible. The tolerance suggested is based on equivalence, not acceptance of difference: the play is entitled "Nathan the Wise," not "Nathan the Jew." In later left-wing versions, membership in the universal class became the solvent of differences, on the way to a universal, classless society.

Yet, there are and will be "differences" not assimilable to sweeping universalist prescriptions. Although much of the left conceived the classless society as the melting pot of humanity, a striking alternative was formulated by an American radical not long before the U.S. entered World War I. It was a moment in which nativist prejudices against immigrants intensified considerably in this country. Many of these newcomers were stirred by European events, often asserting bonds to their "old countries." This begot huffy indignation, especially on the part of American Brahmins: why, these immigrants simply weren't becoming proper "Americans."

In his July 1916 essay, "Trans-national America," a young WASP named Randolph Bourne fashioned a remarkable retort. "As the unpleasant truth has come upon us that assimilation in this country was proceeding on lines very different from those we had marked out for it," he wrote, "we found ourselves inclined to blame those who were thwarting our prophecies. The truth became culpable." What was at stake was the relation between culture and democracy. "We act"—Bourne's "we" was dominant Anglo-America—"as if we want Americanization to take place only on our own terms, and not by the consent of the governed." Against the "thinly disguised panic which calls itself 'patriotism,'" he proposed celebrating as culturally invigorating the hyphen in Polish-American, Irish-American, Jewish-American, German-American, and so on. He went so far as to propose referring also to "English-Americans."

Instead of a melting pot, Bourne envisioned "trans-nationality." This was "a weaving back and forth with other lands, of many threads of all sizes and colors. Any movement which attempts to thwart the weaving, or to dye the fabric any one color or disentangle the threads of the strands, is false to this cosmopolitan vision." In a subsequent essay, Bourne argued that this thinking pointed toward "new concepts of the state, of nationality, of citizenship, of allegiance." Here we find a multidimensional conception of political society and human relations, one that implies an important democratic principle: the legitimacy of plural loyalties.

Perhaps I am not stretching the Austro-Marxists' purposes too far if I suggest that they too accepted this principle by championing a class politics aimed at fashioning a federal socialist republic in which there would be systems of both territorial representation and national linguistic cultural—personal—autonomy. This was at odds with the radical universalism of Marx or Luxemburg (and with the expectation that the state would wither away).

The Austro-Marxist position was expounded in a specific context: a debate inside a socialist movement within a multinational empire. One can also find a notion of plural loyalty articulated by the left within a national movement, with the use, notably, of metaphors like Bourne's—threads and cloth. In the late 1920s and early 1930s the growing dominance of the Labor-left within the Zionist movement was threatened by the right-wing "Revisionists" led by Vladimir Jabotinsky. The latter proclaimed himself a "pure" nationalist and denounced his adversaries as "*shaatnez,*" a mixture of wool and cotton proscribed in Jewish garments by religious orthodoxy. The national raiment, in his formulation, had to be unsullied by foreign admixtures and universalistic notions such as socialism. David Ben-Gurion, then Labor's leader and later the first premier of Israel, proclaimed the very concept of *shaatnez* to be a deceit. A national movement without social conceptions was an abstraction, and Zionism, like any national movement, could be good or bad depending on the society it fashioned. He declared—changing the metaphor—that unlike the right, the Zionist left stood not in one circle (that of nationalism) but in many circles, and "when we stand in two circles it isn't a question of standing in two separate areas, one moment in one and the next in another, but rather in what is common territory to both of them." He continued:

> In reality we don't stand within two circles alone, but within many circles—as citizens of Palestine we stand in the circle of the Land of Israel, as Jews we stand in the circle of a nation that aspires to its homeland, as workers we stand in the circle of the working class, as sons of our generation we stand in the circle of modern history; our women comrades stand in the circle of the working women's movement in its struggle for liberation.

To stand in many circles is to accept the principle of plural loyalties. It must be readily conceded that ascribing to such a principle and practicing it are two different things. But for my purposes here, it is the theoretical point that is most salient, together with the fact that it has direct implications for concepts of citizenship. This was articulated with acuity by one of Ben-Gurion's colleagues, the American Labor Zionist thinker Hayim Greenberg, in his 1948 essay, "Patriotism and Plural Loyalties." Greenberg took the example of an Italian-speaking Swiss citizen. "He hardly knows himself how many different loyalties he harbors in various degrees." As a Swiss he owes fidelity to Switzerland; he is also a patriot of his canton. Whatever his "race," he feels a cultural and linguistic kinship to Italians in Italy. If he is Catholic he feels ties to Catholics around the world and in various regards accepts the "sovereignty" of the vatican. Poor man should he become a UN official. And we should add: if he is a she, she may well have keen allegiances to the women's movement.

How shall we regard this individual? As a bundle of prospective betrayals? Or ought we to accept, indeed value, the legitimacy of "pluralist-social relationships, attachments, sentiments and loyalties"? The true democrat, maintained Greenberg, will seek not to destroy but to harmonize such differences.

Which doesn't mean that they are easily harmonized. Plural dimensions of human identity often don't rest easily with each other, and sometimes not at all. Such discontents are the hobgoblins of what I'd call "unidevotionalists," those vigilant and anxious beings who are endlessly obsessed with litmus tests of absolute loyalty. Alas, their questions and answers, always so earnest, are ever easy. For them it is unimaginable that an individual might actually face moral dilemmas, might confront legitimate conflicts of fealty, might have to inquire of the rights and wrongs of contesting demands, might be compelled to assess the consequences of embracing this or that position. Unidevotionalists have their flag; they salute it; they legitimate only particularisms, usually just their own. Such one-sidedness—no less than that of abstract universalism—frustrates democratic pluralism, which demands refusal of singular answers (to borrow again from Walzer).

It might seem that among today's advocates of multiculturalism a left has emerged that recognizes the problems I've been raising. Certainly, parallels to earlier discussions of national identity and culture can be found in the debates on multiculturalism. Yet I fear that too many votaries of multiculturalism have become unreflective celebrants of particularism, now that the working class has not fulfilled its universalizing mission. Missing is adequate meditation on the grounds of cultural diversity within a democratic society. Too often, the word "difference" is intoned indignantly without consideration of the "trans" of "transnationality," of the intersection of the hyphens Bourne—rightly—celebrated.

Bourne spoke of a cloth of many threads, but he still spoke of a cloth. If one asserts differences without conceptualizing the territory of multicultural exchange, one may reinvent just those particularist perils dreaded in nationalism by the historical left. In a world of resurgent nationalisms, and in an America debating multiculturalism, what is needed is the fashioning of a dialectical concept of root*ed* cosmopolitanism, which accepts a multiplicity of roots and branches and that rests on the legitimacy of plural loyalties, of standing in many circles, but with common ground.

—1992

the old welfare state in the new age of competition

JOANNE BARKAN

In 1944, John Maynard Keynes suffered a heart attack as he ran up a flight of stairs on his way to yet another committee meeting in the New Hampshire resort called Bretton Woods. Meetings, especially those deciding the economic fate of the world, take their toll. In addition to battling health problems, Keynes wrangled over postwar international monetary, employment, and spending policies. He won only some of the disputes at the Bretton Woods conference. Less than two years later, he died without realizing that he had secured enough to pave the way for a growth-oriented world order and, on the national level, the Keynesian welfare state.

In the largely tragic sweep of human history, the postwar period stands out as a high point— seriously flawed, yes, but still a high point— of economic development, redistribution, and social justice in parts of the world. It's over now, undermined by conditions that Keynes predicted and hoped to avoid. The title of this article turns out to be an antinomy—the old welfare state has no place in the new age of competition.

Leftists generally agree on what went right for twenty-five years after the war. Briefly, the story goes like this: Keynes advocated liberalized international trade, but he opposed (even more vigorously, some say) an open financial order. Without controls on the movement of capital and a stable system of pegged exchange rates, Keynes believed national governments would not have enough autonomy to pursue full employment and welfare-state policies. Deregulate capital and allow exchange rates to float, Keynes warned, and the consequences for the welfare state would be grim.

Governments wouldn't be able to set the interest rates they needed; money would be shipped abroad to avoid taxes; economic elites would use the threat of a capital strike to manipulate legislation; speculators would destabilize entire economies by shifting vast amounts of capital from one country to another in search of high interest rates and appreciating currencies. (The only thing Keynes couldn't predict was how fast computer-aided capital flows could be.)

The Bretton Woods accords did a fair job of limiting the problems. The agreements incorporated fixed exchange rates pegged to the dollar and some capital controls. To varying degrees, the industrialized nations devised fiscal and monetary policies aimed at full employment. As world creditor, the United States underwrote the development of the West European welfare states. Workers joined unions. U.S. hegemony provided stability in a way that served Keynesianism more than Lord Keynes had expected—and more than conservative elites wanted.

The result in many countries was a virtuous cycle that funded the welfare state: greater employment, rising wages, and market competition spurred investments to increase productivity; as productivity rose, workers in a tight labor market won still higher wages; better wages boosted aggregate demand that in turn sustained employment. Social critics, of course, pointed to real problems: consumerism, alienation, vacuous mass culture, environmental degradation, persistent North/South inequality, neocolonialism, and U.S. imperialism. Yet within the successful Keynesian economies, workers shared the benefits of rising productivity, and citizens gained fundamental security through the welfare state.

Things fall apart. Most commentators agree on the list of factors that pulled the system down: export rivalry from newly industrialized nations where labor unions were weak or outlawed; inflation exported around the world by the United States as it tried to pay for the Vietnam War; slackened commitment to full employment because of that inflation; weakening of the U.S. dollar and, consequently, of the U.S. hegemonic role as world creditor.

Instead of carrying out a Keynesian mission to facilitate growth, the World Bank and International Monetary Fund became the international debt police. They squeezed second and third world economies, constricting global demand. In 1973, the Nixon administration threw out the fixed exchange rates of Bretton Woods. Over the next decade or so, the United States pressured other countries to decontrol their financial systems. U.S. elites believed that given complete freedom in international finance, they could reestablish their hegemony. Instead they made instability a key characteristic of the period.

Everything Keynes warned would happen did happen. The virtuous cycle that funded the welfare state has been replaced by a downward spiral: falling wages reduce aggregate demand, production slows down, unemployment rises; this increases the need for government transfer payments but shrinks the tax base; welfare state expenditures and government investments are cut; demand falls further. As growth slows around the world, international competition intensifies; wages are held down everywhere, and in second and third world countries, wages don't reflect productivity gains; demand falters; high unemployment becomes chronic; markets are glutted; trade barriers go up. In a globalized economy, labor standards converge, but now they converge downward. The welfare state comes under permanent siege.

Given this most un-Keynesian context—call it global Thatcherism—progressives in elected office usually fail to upgrade or even protect the welfare state. Their embittered radical supporters inevitably scream bad faith, cowardice, collusion with economic elites, and incompetence. No doubt, these play a role in many cases, but to ignore the slender autonomy of an individual national government in today's global market is to deny reality.

A few years ago, many leftists thought regional markets governed by social charters would solve the autonomy problem. If, for example, the European Union (EU) set high standards for welfare provision and labor relations, it would create the equivalent of a strong welfare state in a market large enough to sustain autonomous policies for growth. A regional social charter sounded like a good idea; it *is* a good idea. But alone it can't save the welfare state.

At present, the EU provides modest subsidies to support its weakest members. But suppose the Union set up a rigorous charter that required all members to meet fairly high welfare and labor standards. Weak nations—for example, Portugal—would need much more help. The aid would have to come from wealthier members—let's say, Germany. The German government could either cut back its own welfare state to help pay for Portugal's or it could raise taxes on its own citizens. The German electorate would almost certainly reject either solution.

Suppose instead that the EU adopted a social charter with standards as low as those of the weakest member or a charter with fine principles and no teeth (the latter pretty well describes the actual social policy of the EU). Capital might move to Portugal to take advantage of lower wages and taxes. In the best-case scenario, those investments would translate into jobs; workers would organize and win higher wages; tax revenues would increase to pay for a better welfare state; and then . . . investments would seek out lower wages in, say, South Korea. If workers there managed to organize and win more, the capital would move to Malaysia. The point is simple: in a global market where capital is hyper-mobile, regional charters without capital controls aren't sufficient to protect the welfare state.

Some prominent European theorists believe the left should abandon the welfare state once and for all and escape the "logic of capital." Their alternative is a *welfare society* that breaks the link between work and income. The scheme looks like this: the government would guarantee everyone an income; some people would do traditional jobs, others would be busy with alternative activities; some would work full time, others part time; some would work for a few months or years, others would take over for them. Sufficient income for society would come from some highly productive sectors that competed successfully in the global market. The definition of work would change, as would people's attitude toward it.

The remarkable thing about this proposal is that it defies good sense in so many domains—economics, politics, psychology, ethics, history. To start, what are these hyperproductive sectors that will generate wealth for an entire society? If they existed, one assumes hard-pressed governments would already be using them to shore up the welfare state. What makes the technology or skills required so exclusive and non-exportable that a society could count on keeping the jobs? U.S.-based transnational corporations now ship sophisticated software design jobs to India and Poland. Weren't those the jobs supposedly reserved for the first world?

The welfare society has as little political feasibility as economic po-tential. Few people in income-producing sectors would vote for a pro-gram requiring them to support "able-bodied" men and women who didn't work in the traditional sense or who put in less time or less ef-fort. The project presupposes humans with radically different priorities, values, and psychological capacities for solidarity. Parts of the left have always built their models on "the new man and woman." It's an un-sound foundation.

The welfare society raises the same questions as older, discredited propositions. Without any income incentive, why would a sufficient number of people (or anyone, for that matter) scrub hotel bathrooms, resurface highways, or sell towels at Macy's—especially while others wrote poetry, painted landscapes, and picked up a regular paycheck? Would everyone take turns doing the grubby but essential jobs? Who would decide what's essential? Suppose someone refused essential work. Would society coerce that individual? Would everyone receive the same income? If not, who would decide income levels? On what basis? What would insulate the decisions from political manipulation?

As markets shifted, the welfare society would need new income-producing sectors. But who would select and develop them if income weren't linked to work? The welfare society seems to require extensive planning of the kind that has already been a historic flop. The model conjures up a vision not of greater freedom but of bureaucracy, stagnation, and state intrusion.

This unpromising scheme grows out of legitimate and pressing concerns. Europeans face structural unemployment of 10 percent or more in the most prosperous countries of the West; young people can't find jobs. The East European nations have even greater reserves of unemployed people, and they will work for less, driving down wages in the West. Seeing no solution to the problem, some radicals have given up on the traditional left goal of full employment. They've pushed economic measures such as the reduced work week and work sharing (today used as partial or stopgap responses to unemployment) to their logical limit. Their welfare society is actually an immense expansion of the welfare state. The effort is understandable but unconvincing.

Over the last decade or so, left support has grown for a more coherent idea: a Keynesian world order designed to fit the current globalized economy. This means reestablishing a virtuous cycle of high employment, rising wages, economic growth, and welfare-state development in the context of liberalized world trade. (A word about growth: leftists usually recognize that growth must be "ecologically sensitive," that is, economic activity must integrate both repairing and protecting the environment. As many experts point out, the process is likely to generate new technology and jobs.)

This position is so sensible, so persuasive, so obvious, even, that one feels compelled to ferret out the difficulties. A new global Keynesianism will require at least a loose consensus among the economically powerful nations (the United States, Japan, and Germany) in favor of expansionary policies. We've heard good rhetoric on the subject. For example, presidential candidate Clinton's conception of a new world order sounded nicely Keynesian. In reality, however, individual national governments bend to the will of financial markets. These latter now function as autocrats in a peculiarly anthropomorphized way ("the markets are jittery . . . the markets reacted badly . . . the markets want to see . . ."). Unfortunately, the markets loathe Keynes. Somehow—no one knows how—consensus for full employment and sustaining aggregate demand must grow strong enough to buck the markets.

Global Keynesianism will also require either new international institutions or revised mandates for the International Monetary Fund and the World Bank. In addition to providing resources for growth, they would have to slow down and shrink capital flows, which means getting the largest of the genies back in the bottle. Adequate instruments exist in the abstract—transaction taxes, stiffer banking regulations, fixed currency exchange rates—but not much can happen until the major economies act in concert.

Labor movements are another problem. In the past, workers benefited from rising productivity by organizing unions to win higher wages. As a result, a growing economy generated revenue for the welfare state, while labor applied political pressure to win reforms. Thus unions figured prominently in the Keynesian equation. What characterizes the current period is not so much the conservative assault on unions (that's happened before), but the lack of interest, even hostility, of many working people and progressives.

In Sweden, unions once stood high in public opinion; citizens believed that the labor movement acted in society's general interest. Now many Swedes believe unions represent less constructive, narrow interests. Since about 85 percent of the work force belongs to unions, the criticism comes in part from members. In Italy, unions have not only lost membership, they've become more fragmented as independent local organizations draw employees away from the established confederations. Narrow interests often do prevail, and public support for labor has declined. More than before, attitudes all across Europe are tinged with the apathy and antagonism that are an old story in the United States.

The typical relationship between labor and the so-called new social movements (the feminist, environmental, gay rights, and cultural identity movements) has been neither consistently close nor highly productive. There's no news here. More noteworthy is the growing distance since the early 1980s between unions in many countries and the left-of-center political parties that built the welfare state (consider Britain, the United States, Italy, and even Sweden). In office or trying to get there, the parties have less to offer labor; as they look for ways to cut spending or placate the markets, they frequently oppose union demands.

Since labor unions have been powerful advocates of the welfare state, the spreading antagonism toward them undermines the welfare state's prospects. In addition, a new Keynesian order will require wages to rise significantly in the second and third worlds where labor unions are often unfree or suppressed. This places another burden on first world unions: they must hold themselves together and at the same time direct attention and resources to developing countries.

Global Thatcherism gave the right a new angle on demonizing the welfare state: not only do government handouts suck the energy out of a nation and eat away its moral fiber, they cripple its performance in the world market. The left can't defend the welfare state by arguing *only* that it produces social justice that, in turn, makes democracy meaningful.

The welfare state also has to be defended as a structural mechanism promoting economic growth. It sustains aggregate demand and, more useful in argument, increases productivity. For example, public education, worker retraining, and apprenticeship programs improve skills; child care and home care for the elderly allow more women to enter the labor market; health care reduces the waste of human resources.

Another argument for the welfare state is the link between equality and growth. Recent studies of the Asian economic "miracles" show that reducing the gap between rich and poor produces faster per capita income growth nationwide. The poor use additional resources to better themselves and their children economically, and this benefits society as a whole. The studies happily contradict the standard doctrine that growth in developing nations and rising inequality were linked. By redistributing wealth in the direction of greater equality, the welfare state can promote growth.

So much for the less problematic arguments. More difficult questions revolve around an issue that makes many leftists uncomfortable: efficiency. Michael Harrington often pointed out that the generation of Danes who fought for and won sick pay used the benefit only when they were sick; the next generation began to abuse the system. Then there's the well-worn example of skyrocketing absentee rates in workplaces all over Europe on the Mondays after big soccer games.

Swedish industrialists claim they open new plants abroad because absentee rates in Sweden are too high; they can't maintain quality because they don't know who will show up for work. Perhaps this is just "boss talk" to intimidate workers; perhaps it's only a cover for an embarrassing lack of economic patriotism. Yet absentee rates in a Volvo plant in Goteborg dropped from 15 percent a few years ago to less than 5 percent after the sick-pay system was adjusted (*New York Times,* October 4, 1994). The reform, passed by a conservative government in December 1992, delayed the start of sick pay until the second day of missed work.

According to Assar Lindbeck, Sweden's most prominent mainstream economist, welfare-state insurance programs need deductibles of some kind to deal with abuse and inefficiency. Some leftists (this writer included) would agree as long as deductibles remain small enough for lower-income people to manage without hardship. But other leftists see any reduction of benefits as a class-biased attack on welfare-state redistribution. This makes it easy to stake out a position, but it won't protect the welfare state for long.

Cost and efficiency can turn into impossible political dilemmas for responsible left parties. Lindbeck recounted an incident of the September 1994 Swedish election campaign: The polls showed the Social Democratic party (SAP) at about 50 percent and headed for a big victory that would put them back into government. To deal with a gargantuan budget deficit accumulated during the recession (under the conservative government), the SAP proposed a benefits adjustment. Working parents, who get sixty days sick-child leave per child each year with compensation, would not be paid for the first day missed. The response was outrage. The SAP fell to 45 percent in one week and withdrew the proposal.

The composition of welfare-state expenditures poses another problem. In theory, it makes sense to spend on labor market policies (worker education, skills training, job placement, relocation) that raise employment levels and productivity, rather than transfer payments (unemployment compensation, public assistance for the poor). But in a world organized around the cost-cutting principle, good jobs aren't waiting for newly trained workers. Courses and programs often become holding pens for the long-term unemployed. Although they are still preferable to the misery of inadequate transfer payments, labor market policies can't function effectively unless there is enough economic growth to generate jobs.

John Maynard Keynes, living in 1995 and speaking on *MacNeil/ Lehrer,* would propose nothing less than turning global Thatcherism upside down. Conservatives would holler that he meant to overthrow the economic laws of the universe. He might well reply that he wanted only this: to translate need into demand. A new virtuous cycle of economic growth, full employment, and rising wages would permit people who needed apartments, milk, overcoats, penicillin, math courses, child care, and refrigerators to make acquisitions in the market and fund the welfare state. The virtuous cycle wouldn't require an elaborate economic apparatus. Indeed, a stable system of pegged exchange rates, institutions to regulate international capital flows and curb risky banking practices, mechanisms to lighten the debt burden of third world nations, and democratic labor unions might suffice.

Since global Thatcherism makes the rich richer, they need everyone else to believe that the system, like hurricane season, is beyond human control. But political choices, not economic inevitability, produced the current mess. Reckless currency speculation, for example, would stop tomorrow morning if governments restabilized exchange rates. In general, Keynes could have his way if the U.S., Japanese, and German governments committed themselves to worldwide growth while jostling other governments to do the same.

A Keynesian world order, if it ever came about, would be a loose, unevenly realized affair—an agreement among economic leaders, resting on a few assumptions, a few regulations, and a couple of refurbished institutions. It's not too much to hope for, and yet a sober assessment must conclude that everything right now is moving in the opposite direction: the predatory search for markets, fierce competition, beggar-thy-neighbor policies, social strife within nations, restrictive trade practices, risky banking practices, and uncontrolled speculation.

For many observers, this period bears a worrisome resemblance to the years after the First World War. If there is a pattern here, perhaps a Keynesian world order lies *somewhere* up ahead. Of course, it took cataclysmic events—the Great Depression and the Second World War—to create an opening for Lord Keynes. Carrying out another round of reforms without economic collapse or global conflagration would count as progress of a revolutionary kind.

—1995

bankruptcy and zeal

SEAN WILENTZ

Now that the dust has started to settle, it's time to assess why the congressional Republicans, in the face of overwhelmingly hostile public opinion, pursued the impeachment of President Clinton to the bitter end. Overwrought idealism was partly responsible, as was the intimidation of more moderate members by the hard-line party leadership, as were the whims of fortune. But one of the dirty secrets of impeachment may be that the Republicans had nothing better to do. By setting their sights on removing an already besmirched Bill Clinton, Republicans unwittingly exposed their party's intellectual bankruptcy, especially at the national level. And by pursuing impeachment as zealously as they did, they compounded that bankruptcy by alienating millions of voters.

The turnabout is astonishing. For nearly two decades, Republicans and their allied think tanks and policy packaging firms had seemingly swept aside most traces of oppositional thinking. Dependable liberal battle cries—for state-stimulated full employment, advancing racial integration, and more—grew fainter by the year. The very idea of activist government, outside the realm of foreign affairs, became fatal to the touch. Republican panaceas, from the supply-side Laffer curve to the "just-say-no" anti-drug policy, did not exactly work their magic, but neither did their failure seem to discredit the Republicans' working assumptions, fiercely libertarian with respect to economic policy and fiercely moralistic with respect to social policy. "We've largely won the battle of ideas," Kate O'Beirne, formerly of the Heritage Foundation, recently boasted. "We are in the implementation stage right now." Indeed, some commentators claim that that Republican thinking infected the Democrats as well, especially inside the Clinton White House—though this reasoning makes it difficult to understand why so many Republicans, and virtually all hard-line conservatives, hate Clinton so deeply. Yet today, poll after poll shows that the public is fed up with the right-wing moralizers, has no particular interest in tax cuts, and fears that the Republicans will undermine popular universal entitlements.

The Republicans' intellectual crisis cannot be blamed on complacency. Indeed, faith in what Irving Kristol once referred to as the inverted Gramscianism of the modern GOP—that is, control the prevailing view of reality and you control politics—has only deepened during the Clinton years. According to a recent report by the left-liberal National Committee for Responsive Philanthropy (NCRP), the nation's twenty leading conservative policy institutions have more than doubled their combined budgets since 1992, spending $158 million in 1996 alone—$20 million more than the Republican Party raised and spent during that election year in soft-money contributions.

The five best-known institutions on the NCRP's list (the Heritage Foundation, Hoover Institution, Center for Strategic and International Studies, American Enterprise Institute, and Free Congress Research and Education Foundation) accounted for about half of the total in 1996; the rest was lavished on smaller, tightly focused groups, each dedicated to advancing core elements of the conservative agenda. By attracting increased contributions from the corporate sector, and by tightening their connections with political operatives (in Washington and the states) as well as with grassroots activists, this conglomeration of organizations has turned policy advocacy on the right into something like a permanent, well-coordinated, national political campaign.

Yet in the immediate aftermath of the impeachment struggle, it looked as if the GOP's research-and-promotion efforts had succumbed to the law of diminishing returns. The prospects were especially grim for the party's social-conservative wing. Since 1978, when the activist Paul Weyrich and his allies invented the Moral Majority, Republicans had built an invaluable new base among politicized conservative evangelicals. Even when public displeasure at the GOP televangelists mounted late in the Reagan years, and even after the Moral Majority disbanded, a more secular version of moral majoritarianism gained vast exposure and considerable momentum, thanks to publicists like William Bennett and operations like the Free Congress Foundation. In this version, America's chief problems were moral, not economic or political; they stemmed from the cultural relativism and permissiveness imposed by a relatively small but powerful 1960s left; and they could be measured by the breakdown of fundamental social institutions, above all the family.

This is not the occasion to ponder how the twists and turns of liberal politics gave intellectual hostages to the right-wing cultural warriors. What is plain is that, although Bennett's books and others' may still soar to the top of the bestseller lists, there is now despair on the cultural right, not just about their political strategy but about their very conception of the nation. After all their efforts, abortion remains legal and the National Endowment for the Arts exists. During the presidency of the despised baby-boomer Clinton, the right wing's key statistical markers of the nation's cultural breakdown—violent crime, out-of-wedlock births, divorce, drunk driving, expanding welfare rolls—not only failed to worsen; they actually improved.

Despite Clinton's gross stupidity with Monica Lewinsky and his attempts to deceive—which many right-wing commentators reasonably considered political manna from heaven—a rock-solid majority of the public remained in the president's corner against his accusers. And when push came to shove in the impeachment trial, the cultural right, although capable of overawing the House Republican caucus, could not make a convincing constitutional argument that Clinton's misdeeds warranted his removal from office.

Some veterans of the lost cause have put on a brave face and vowed to soldier on. The Reverend Pat Robertson made headlines late in the impeachment drama when he conceded tactical defeat—prematurely, in the eyes of some of his followers. Yet Robertson still insists that if religious voters would rally to elect "an evangelical, born again president" and a like-minded Congress, "we could roll back many of the bad things that have been done in government." The Reverend Jerry Falwell agrees, as do the Republican presidential hopeful Gary Bauer (who is running against what he calls "the virtue deficit") and James Dobson of Focus on the Family. ("Never give in," Dobson has proclaimed, waxing Churchillian; "never, never, never.")

Other influential conservatives, however, have admitted to their confusion after impeachment and have called for, at the very least, a reappraisal of their culture war assumptions. "A lot of people are angry that [Clinton] got off," Phyllis Schlafly, head of the Eagle Forum, remarked last February. "They just don't understand it. They're shaking their heads: what is the problem?" Schlafly still believes that a majority of Americans share her ultraconservative moral values, but criticizes the Republican Congress for being too "defensive" in vindicating those values—a most ungrateful complaint, it would seem, coming after Monicagate.

William Bennett, who reads the polls as closely as he says he reads his Aquinas, is much less confident of public backing. Shocked at what he has called, with his characteristic modesty, the first divergence ever between his own point of view and that of the American majority, Bennett now demands a tragic consideration of what he has labeled "the death of outrage." Other cultural warriors have suggested that it may be too late even for that. In his last-ditch arguments during the Senate impeachment trial, Representative Henry Hyde sounded an apocalyptic chord: "I wonder if, after this culture war is over that we are engaged in," Hyde declared, "an America will survive that will be worth fighting to defend." With Clinton acquitted, presumably, the end is ever more nigh.

Overtaken by failure, some generals in the GOP cultural army have even called for a dignified surrender, an Appomattox. "I no longer believe that there is a moral majority," Paul Weyrich, now head of the Free Congress Foundation, told his fellow conservative leaders after the impeachment trial. In place of political action, he counseled "separation" from society by promoting home schooling, the formation of private courts of justice, and removing televisions from decent homes. Shortly thereafter, Cal Thomas (the syndicated columnist and former Moral Majority spokesman) and the Reverend Ed Dobson (a former Falwell aide) went even further, claiming in a new book, *Blinded by Might,* that the Moral Majority, indeed the entire effort to elevate moralism through politics, had been wrongheaded from the start.

For Thomas, the problems besetting the religious right have, in part, to do with their own cultural style. Conservatives, he has remarked, are "an upset people. We don't like being happy. We're always looking for an enemy—just as the left is—to play on people's fears, which increases cynicism." More to the point, he and Dobson contend that politics was never their proper arena. "Religious conservatives, no matter how well organized, can't save America," they write. "Only God can." And so, they conclude, conservative Christians should go back to their churches and convert the world the old-fashioned way, one sinner at a time.

Insofar as Weyrich, Thomas, and Dobson (Ed, not James) reflect religious conservative opinion in general—which is not self-evident—their abdication may mark a resurgence of the antipolitical stance that had traditionally dominated conservative American evangelicalism. (In the 1980s, among the harshest critics of the so-called religious right were the fundamentalist leaders of institutions such as Bob Jones University, who insisted that involvement in politics would do far more damage to the word of God than the word of God could ever do to redeem politics.) But what is truly striking is how, along with their more secular and more hopeful erstwhile allies, the cultural warriors gaze with utter horror on how most Americans think and live.

For Weyrich, the "ever-wider sewer" that is America is "caught up in a collapse of historic proportions, a collapse so great that it simply overwhelms politics." Likewise for the journalist P. J. O'Rourke, who is more of a dandy than a doomsday man, the mere sight of ordinary Americans is nauseating: "masses waddling into airports, business offices and churches dressed in drooping sweats or fuschia warm-up suits or mainsail-sized Bermuda shorts, each with a mobile phone in one ear and a Walkman in the other and sucking Diet Pepsi through a straw." Add to that the conceit, heard everywhere in the mainstream as well as the conservative press during the impeachment hearings, that the booming economy has corrupted our collective sense of moral virtue, and you have the sort of condemnation of America that one has gotten used to hearing mainly from young suburban malcontents and Left Bank leftists. Ronald Reagan's sunny "It's Morning in America" has given way to fear and loathing on the right.

The spitefulness of the cultural right is matched by the increasingly far-fetched ideas proffered by the other major wing of the Republican party, the economic conservatives. With American capitalism booming, the Dow bouncing well above 10,000, unemployment down, the federal budget in surplus, and the welfare bogeyman seemingly scotched—all under a Democratic administration—it is hard for the economic conservatives to gain much political traction. About all they are left with, in the realm of ideas, are proposals for tax cuts. These ideas, however, are far less attractive than they once were, given the public perception of looming crises in Social Security and Medicare. And the proposals themselves, although neatly packaged as economic lifesavers for the average American, are more obviously than ever windfalls for the rich.

Part of the economic conservatives' packaging involves overstating the federal tax burden currently borne by middle-class families. In her response to the president's State of the Union address last January, for example, Congresswoman Jennifer Dunn stated that a typical two-earner household pays nearly 40 percent of its income in taxes, a figure extrapolated from computations that more than 25 percent of that income goes to federal taxes—"the highest percentage of income ever paid in taxes by American families." Yet as Iris J. Lav has reported for the Center on Budget and Policy Priorities, these findings are based on arbitrary statistical methods that, among other things, set median two-earner family income at nearly $55,000—far above the Congressional Budget Office's median figure of $39,000. Using the CBO's methods, the actual average family federal tax burden comes to 18.9 percent in 1999, substantially less than Congresswoman Dunn suggests.

Dunn's inflated figures, however, served a larger purpose, which was to win support for congressional Republican leaders' first grand new proposal of the post-impeachment era—an across-the-board 10 percent cut in tax rates. By referring to the plan simply as a 10 percent tax cut (an elision dutifully repeated in the press), Republicans made it sound as if all Americans would benefit equally. But it took little economic expertise to see that, under our system, a cut in tax rates is far more regressive than a simple cut in taxes. Soon after the Republicans announced their plan, Citizens for Tax Justice reported that more than 60 percent of the benefits would go to the ten percent of taxpayers with the highest incomes. On average, the tax reduction for the lower 60 percent of all taxpayers—those with incomes below $38,000—would amount to $99. A large portion of low- and moderate-income families would receive no cut at all. By contrast, the top 10 percent of the income distribution would get, on average, nearly $4,000 a year, while the top 1 percent would get, on average, more than $20,000 per year. The inequities were so blatant that the Democrats did not need to put up much of a fight: faced with grumbling from their moderate members, the Republican leaders shelved their grand new proposal shortly after they announced it.

The death of the GOP 10 percent plan did not, to be sure, mark the utter extinction of Republican thinking. Remarkably, though, what remains consists chiefly of ideologically charged reworkings of Democratic proposals or rehashes of familiar Republican ideas. The White House proposes to set aside $1.8 trillion over the next decade to strengthen Social Security, while investing a portion of the surplus in the stock market; the Republicans come up with their own plan, setting aside roughly the same amount of money but creating private investment accounts within the retirement system. The White House proposes to increase spending on defense and education; so do the Republicans, though they would channel much more to defense and much less to education.

If all else fails, the GOP still has some old chestnuts in its pantry, including tort reform, school vouchers, and renewed attacks on affirmative action. Yet although the Democrats may be vulnerable here and there on these matters, it is hard to believe that the Republicans can successfully jerry-build an entire electoral program out of them, as they did in 1994. And at least some of the old reliable Republican ideas—opposing gun control, for example—may now cost more political support than they gain.

Embittered about America, reduced to promoting regressive tax cuts as their big new idea, the Republicans are suffering from the political fragmentation that normally accompanies intellectual exhaustion. The fragmentation is nothing new. For some years, more moderate northeastern Republicans have been trying to distance themselves from the cultural die-hards. Shortly after the Senate acquitted Clinton, several of these moderates, most notably New York's governor George Pataki, tried to round up support around the country for taking the party in a less moralistic direction. But those efforts achieved little more than to show how the party divisions had deepened during the impeachment drive. The GOP's early lineup of presidential hopefuls is indicative of the party's plight. The cultural conservatives have fielded Gary Bauer and Alan Keyes; Congressman John Kasich has jumped in as an updated Reaganomist; Lamar Alexander has centered his campaign on the "character" issue; Dan Quayle is hoping his graying temples will lend his candidacy credibility; Pat Buchanan is once more agitating the "lock and load" constituency; and Steve Forbes, having learned a few lessons from his failed bid in 1996, has enthusiastically courted the religious right while pushing his own regressive economic panacea, the flat tax—thereby combining two streams of thought that have nearly dried up.

No wonder the Republican Establishment is looking elsewhere for a candidate—above all, to reliable members of the Establishment family who are unburdened with much intellectual baggage of any kind. It is a remarkable fact that in every presidential year save one since 1952, the Republican national ticket has included either a Nixon, a Dole, or a Bush. Looking to 2000, Republicans get to choose between yet another Bush and yet another Dole (and, quite possibly, get a Bush-Dole ticket)—a son and a wife, neither identified in the national mind with anything more profound than their congenial personalities and family crests.

All of which might point to deep and lasting trouble ahead for the GOP were the Democrats and their liberal allies in better intellectual shape than they are. To be sure, impeachment and its aftermath has created far more authentic solidarity in Democratic ranks than has been seen in many years. Vice President Al Gore will face no serious challenge from his left for his party's nomination, and unless he stumbles badly, or unless the Kosovo mess becomes an unmitigated political disaster, he ought to gain the nod over Bill Bradley with a minimum of the traditional Democratic blood-letting. Lingering fury at the Republicans over impeachment, and promises for a more focused campaign to take back the House, look like they will galvanize recently listless Democratic constituencies to donate heavily and get out the vote. Yet it remains far easier to say what the Democrats stand against than what they stand for. The much-lamented tendency of liberal and left philanthropies to spread their funding thin, along with the lack of anything resembling a robust and well-coordinated party intelligentsia, connected with the party's base, still places the Democrats at an enormous disadvantage when it comes to shaping public perceptions. Efforts in that direction, under the broad heading of "the Third Way," have been sporadic and ambiguous, sometimes registering with the public as old-fashioned moderate Republicanism, sometimes as revamped social democracy, and sometimes as a renunciation of any ideas or goals beyond small-bore policy initiatives. The hostility of much of the news media, including the blatantly, even cheerily, right-wing Fox network, makes the job still tougher.

The worst thing that the Democrats could decide, under these circumstances, is that ideas don't really matter in politics. All that has happened in national affairs over the last thirty years proves just the opposite. The Republicans may be exhausted—but until now their inverted Gramscianism has proven enormously effective in shaping the terms of public debate. Bill Clinton has outmaneuvered them— but Democrats in general cannot count on fancy political footwork and co-optation to fulfill the function of a political creed. If the Republicans are intellectually bankrupt, the Democrats have barely begun to invest in their intellectual and political future, even though they have managed to gain a popular majority in a national election only once in the last thirty-five years. Unless the Democrats start making those investments, the Republicans' current intellectual breakdown will prove a squandered opportunity.

—1999

jaytalking

MARSHALL BERMAN

Considering the mass murder and Nazi-style brutality that engulf so much of the world in the 1990s, it takes *chutzpah* for an American to say that our collective life contains any trouble at all. Our economy is thriving. It wasn't so long ago that there was nothing out there for kids coming out of school and college; today, kids are getting jobs. After years of rising homicide rates, people are killing each other less. People are still getting AIDS, but more of them are staying alive. American society is more open and inclusive than ever; it's not just what you see on the Madison Square Garden station or MTV—though that itself is something—it's all the interracial families and their marvelously colored children out shopping any Saturday afternoon at your local mall. So we should lighten up and enjoy the good news, right?

We at *Dissent* crave joy as ardently as anybody. But it's not easy for us to lighten up. Most of us are in or near middle age, and we worry about what will be there for our children and their children. Here's something that troubles our minds: There seems to be no *critical culture* in America today. A critical culture is one that struggles actively over how human beings should live and what our life means. Most of us can remember living in the critical culture of the sixties—a few of us can even remember the critical culture of the thirties—and we can feel the difference. When a critical culture breaks down or wears out or fades away, sources of joy dry up. What makes this happen? Why has it happened now? Is the loss permanent? Or are there traces, fragments, intimations of a new critical culture just around the corner? Where might it come from? How can it come together? Is there anything people like us can do to help it come?

One symptom of the lack of a critical culture today is our fetishism of "order." Giuliani-type politicians have convinced many people, including those who control the mass media, not only that they personally have made the homicide rate go down, but that they have done something even more profound: "restored order." New York mayor Rudolph Giuliani's idea of order seems to require freeing the streets not only from beggars and homeless people, but also from newsstands, food vendors, and wandering artists. His 1997 re-election campaign featured born-again testimonies from people said to be lifelong Democrats and liberals who had come to love him, because, like Moses parting the waters, "The mayor has stopped the violence." During the campaign, he proclaimed that, now that he had ended the violence, the police were going to start arresting people for jaywalking. At that point, the great Jules Feiffer published a cartoon (on the *New York Times* op-ed page) depicting a man making nasty remarks about the mayor's priorities and his sense of civic life. In the last panel, a police officer arrests him. For what? he asks. For *jaytalking*. Feiffer's image gets it just right, not just about the mayor, but about the culture of the nineties, and its amazing lack of jaytalking. The most endearing quality of the sixties was the way it taught us to jaytalk: to talk back; to talk against the lights; to talk outside the designated lines; to talk like our great American blue jays (there they are in Audubon's *Birds of America*, Number 282), small birds who emit loud and raucous cries that no one can ignore.

How does a culture of jaytalking come into being? It requires three things: (1) powerful and provocative ideas; (2) smart and imaginative people working in various sectors of life, often wholly unaware of each other's existence; and (3) "experimental neighborhoods," places where people and ideas can bump into each other, and where young people, with little experience but boundless energy, along with middle-aged people longing to escape from "uptown" or "the boroughs" or "suburbia," can find or imagine new ways to put the ideas together, and to act out their new syntheses.

The critical culture of the sixties came from very diverse sources. There were our universities, enlarged and intellectually enriched in the cold war boom. C. Wright Mills, Irving Howe, Herbert Marcuse, Noam Chomsky, David Riesman, Norman O. Brown, were all "tenured radicals" who developed their dangerous ideas within the classiest academic crosswalks. (Many of the creators of Students for a Democratic Society were their students.) Mike Harrington and Jane Jacobs worked as journalists and editors. Grace Paley taught, did secretarial work, brought up kids, and organized demos (at first quite small) as she wrote. William H. Whyte, Norman Mailer, James Baldwin, Susan Sontag,

Walt Kelly, Dr. Seuss, all got rich from their books, and used their money to say things that would have got them in trouble (or gone unheard) if they were poor. Paul Goodman, like many great artists of the "New York School" generation, was supported by his wife; Dwight Macdonald, one of very few radicals from the *echt* ruling class, by his trust fund. Harold Rosenberg taught us to see through the mass media, to which he made one spectacular contribution: he was the man who created Smokey the Bear. The 1950s theatre produced *Death of a Salesman,* one of the permanently great radical plays, but also the avant-garde experiments of the Living Theatre, and Joseph Papp's Public Theatre, which synthesized vanguard dramaturgy with popular front marketing.

What about experimental neighborhoods? The 1950s offered plenty of these. As an ironic result of the flight of capital from American cities after World War II, every city gained grungy low-rent neighborhoods that could incubate bookstores and art studios and modern dance groups, experimental theatres, venues for jazz and folk music and performance, and the sort of shabby clubs and coffee houses and music stores and cabarets that nourished Lenny Bruce and Nichols and May and Woody Allen and Bob Dylan. New York's Village (first West, then East) is what I knew, but there were neighborhoods like this all over America. Late in the 1950s, they started to fill up with kids from all over metropolitan areas who could read the little magazines and the Grove Press paperbacks in the bookstores, hang out in streets and play their guitars in parks, hear sounds of music that carried from clubs they couldn't afford to go to, find intense people like themselves to walk and talk with through the night, and maybe to grope and love. These people transformed old and often sleepy streets into vibrant public spaces that never seemed to sleep at all.

New kinds of public spaces were embodied in two important new mass media: alternate weekly newspapers and listener-supported radio. Once more, it happened all over. New York's version features the *Village Voice* and WBAI. Both rallied superb arrays of jaytalkers (including Feiffer), and formed intense bonds with their audiences. America turned out to be full of people who were ready to listen to every minute and read every line in media that they felt were *their own.* These media taught their readers and listeners not only how to grow up, but how to act like citizens, to go into the streets and make trouble. The earliest struggles were to protect their own neighborhoods (in New York, Washington Square). But as the sixties unfolded, the new media made spiritual leaps, expanded their horizons, and developed into genuine moral educators. They taught their readers and listeners to think of black people, poor people, Vietnamese people, and victimized people everywhere as part of their neighborhoods.

Where will our culture find resources like these again? Maybe it won't, and crews of Bounderbys and Panglosses and mixed megapirates will rule the world forever. Or maybe only violent economic collapse will shake Americans out of their narcolepsy. This would put the left in the creepy position (where it has been before) of longing for horrible catastrophe. On the other hand, it may be, as it was forty years ago, that the country's very prosperity will give us slack, that it will create imaginative space where people can begin to think about a better life than this.

What forms will critical thought take? Some people think there are no critical ideas left. My own feeling is that there is a superabundance of critical ideas in the air, if we can learn to inhale. Marxian and Freudian thought are both immensely provocative, capable of endlessly new syntheses, spin-offs, and hybridizations. No one has the authority to say definitively what these ideas mean. Not even the founders could close the floodgates they had opened. (They tried, in vain.) Maybe tomorrow's incarnations will be deepened by feminism, or by environmentalism, or biology, or cybernetics, or by any number of things that blacks and other "people of color" will have to say, or by other forms of thought I know nothing of. Regardless, we should recognize that, with Marx and Freud, we are all living on top of radical gold mines.

I confess (and it isn't hard to detect), I am guilty of nostalgia for the sixties, days of my youth. But I can see at least two big ways in which the horizon for radicalism is clearer today. Many leftists of my generation disdained the USSR, but still had a deep (sometimes desperate) need to identify with *some* idealized Other as a focus for their longings. Since 1989, the need for an ideal Other has abated, or at least radically slackened. It's a great leap forward that people today can criticize and denounce life in the West without having to genuflect toward a mythical East.

The other big problem about sixties radicalism was its lack of connection to a labor movement. The New Left is usually blamed for this. But in fact, the AFL-CIO of those days, dominated by George Meany and his crew, was not only aggressive in its chauvinist patriotism, but strident in its particularism and anti-intellectuality. Obsessed with smashing the commies, it was as rigid and dictatorial as any Communist Party. It fired its old, politically incorrect organizers, and made no moves to hire new ones: it was totally uninterested in organizing the unorganized. The weakness of today's labor movement follows directly from the stupidity of yesterday's strong one. But John Sweeney's AFL-CIO has looked beyond its own *apparat,* opened up its horizons, and started to imagine how big and powerful the working class might be. The unions have opened up an Organizing Institute, and a new generation of brilliant organizers has come up. Labor has started winning big strikes, not only in New York and Los Angeles, where you might expect it, but in Las Vegas and North Carolina. The labor movement's Union Summers have not only trained several thousand young adults in organizing skills—many are working as organizers now, many more are fellow-travelers—but generated a vision, a sense of mission, a human solidarity, as the civil rights movement did in its Freedom Summer days. We should listen for jaytalk here.

One big problem for any critical culture to come is, how will its concerns and its ideas be transmitted and shared? There is no way to reach multitudes of people except through media of mass communication. Many people think our mass media inevitably turn all ideas into banal slogans. My own feeling is that, although most of the contents of our mass media are banal (like most of the contents of our most esoteric refereed journals), the biggest problem may be the exact opposite: too many ideas, coming through too many channels. New media played crucial roles creating and developing the critical culture of the sixties. In the nineties, along with books, newspapers, magazines, movies, theater, recorded music, broadcasting, and the new media of yesterday, there are so many *new* "new media," from the many forms of cable television, desktop publishing, video, 'zines, to e-mail and all the metamorphoses of the Net, that it is harder than ever not to be flooded out. As communications technologies metastasize, it will be even harder not to be flooded out tomorrow.

Some people aren't worried about this because they don't think our new media have much to say. An epigram of the early computer culture was "Garbage in, garbage out." A decade ago, Bruce Springsteen had a hit, "57 Channels And Nothing On." But anyone today who tries to listen and look around is bound to find that there's more "on" in American popular culture than most of us have thought. In the summer, when I'm freer to sample, my last week's collection included *Daria,* on cable television, an animated intellectual nonconformist teenage girl's so-called life Salinger's Franny, *geworfen* into Orange County; *Psychoanalysis, What Is It?* and *Prince of Thieves;* albums by the rapper and producer Prince Paul; the 'zine *Processed World,* a cyberpunk incarnation of *Dissent.* All this material shows impressive brains and sensitivity and critical awareness. If only there were ways for these people and people like them—including people like us—to connect and interact!

How can the people and the ideas come together? How can they crystallize into something? In the cyberworld, ideas are channeled into "chat rooms," a multitude of demographically small, segmented spaces, and focused on limited but intense "niche" audiences. Most of their chats seem to be pretty dull, as most chats are; still it could be that some small rooms have nourished ideas and perspectives that might make big differences. If only we knew how to break open those rooms, we could build Greenwich Villages in cyberspace. In these new experimental neighborhoods, the critical culture of tomorrow could be born.

Or maybe not. Maybe it all will happen on paper in "old" media, or in "old" Greenwich Villages, in old streets and restaurants and cafes and parks, through old-fashioned face-to-face encounters, among people who have lived through everything new that the eighties and nineties offered, and who feel a need for more: for insight beyond any Web site, for a promised land beyond the Net, where blue jays sing.

—2000

TURN OF THE CENTURY

The left has mostly squandered the cultural capital of the mass feminist movement by not taking its insights seriously and not carrying them forward into current crises. For example, there's little conceptual space now for building a practical, hard-headed peace movement that actively confronts the great pressure being put on masculinity since September 11. The U.S. fear of seeming weak receives no adequate critique. . . . The enemy strongman looms to an irrational size, an unknowable bogeyman, while the U.S. strongman seems solid and necessary, a bulwark against humiliation.

Ann Snitow, "A Revitalized Peace Movement," 2003

foreword
NICOLAUS MILLS

For those of us at *Dissent,* as for most Americans, the new century began on September 11, 2001. During the twelve years between the fall of the Berlin Wall in 1989 and the attacks on the World Trade Center and Pentagon, we at *Dissent* had always felt uneasy about the role America had chosen to play in a world in which it had become the only superpower following the collapse of the Soviet Union. But we were as surprised as everyone else by September 11.

In New York, where so many of us who work at *Dissent* live, our personal reactions were as varied as those of the city itself. Some of us immediately went down to the scene of the disaster to see for ourselves what happened; others put in time with the volunteer agencies helping disaster victims; others wrote checks to the funds set up for the families who had lost a loved one.

In a special issue of *Dissent* devoted to the killing fields of Yugoslavia, Rwanda, and East Timor, Samantha Power saw September 11 as a catastrophe with the potential for making America a more compassionate nation. In her essay "Raising the Cost of Genocide," which would later become part of her Pulitzer Prize–winning book, *A Problem from Hell,* Power wrote, "To earn a death sentence, it was enough in the last century to be an Armenian, a Jew, or a Tutsi. On September 11, it was enough to be an American. Instead of causing Americans to retreat from global humanitarian engagement, the terrorist attacks could cause us to empathize with peoples victimized by genocide."

But when September 11 was followed by the invasion of Afghanistan and the invasion of Afghanistan was followed by the invasion of Iraq, America's role in the world at large became far more complicated for us at *Dissent* than when September 11 alone was our focus. Power called for humanitarian intervention in countries in which the civilian population was subjected to mass slaughter and unable to defend itself. After September 11, what concerned us at *Dissent* was not only the question of when humanitarian intervention is justified but when intervention in the name of self-defense cannot be justified.

We worried, as the essays in this concluding section of *50 Years of*

Dissent show, that when a nation as powerful as America feels threatened, it is easily tempted into replacing multilateral cooperation with unilateralism, conflating wars of choice with wars of last resort. The danger of America acting as a nation that assumes for itself the rights of a modern empire lies at the heart of two of the essays in this section. In "Acting Alone" the literary critic David Bromwich provides a close reading of the "The National Security Strategy of the United States of America," the September 2002 document that the Bush administration used to justify initiating unilateral action around the globe, and ends his essay by concluding that the document is contradictory as well as naïve. "Defensive, ambitious, and self-contradictory," Bromwich writes, "it is perhaps the most innocent statement of policy ever exhibited by a major power in the history of the world." In "Dissenting from the American Empire" James Rule goes even further, arguing that America has become such a danger to itself and others that the left cannot afford to confine itself to critiquing America's international successes and failures. It must put its energy into articulating its own vision of what a just, twenty-first-century world community would look like.

For Michael Walzer and Michael Kazin, being right about what has gone wrong with American foreign policy since September 11 is not, however, sufficient, especially when we are dealing with a president who plays fast and loose with the truth. In "Can There Be a Decent Left?" Walzer points up how with regard to Afghanistan many on the left set up standards of military engagement that were intended to make fighting al-Qaeda and the Taliban there impossible. He then goes on to argue that what we need these days is a realistic assessment of America's role in the world by a left that does not automatically blame America first for the world's ills but accepts an ambivalent relation to American power, acknowledging that the United States was, for example, wrong on Guatemala in 1954 and right on Kosovo in 1999. In "A Patriotic Left" Michael Kazin takes a similar line, asserting that a left critique of America need not be grounded in anti-Americanism. It can also be grounded in an intelligent patriotism that, in the tradition of such historically radical reformers as Jane Addams and Martin Luther King, makes love of country the starting point for social change.

In focusing so intently on global politics, we at *Dissent* have not succumbed to the notion that as we begin a new century, domestic politics have become irrelevant. From the civil rights abuses that the Patriot Act has made possible to the current crisis in health care, reflected in figures showing 43.6 million Americans without health insurance, we believe that America faces internal dangers that, if nothing is done about them, will only grow worse as our already massive budget deficits pile up. A politics of security must link well-being at home with well-being abroad, must protect Americans from terrorism but also from unemployment, poverty, and illness if it is to command broad support.

The key is to make sure such a politics of security has credibility: to acknowledge that nowadays the left cannot, any more than it could during the 1950s, when *Dissent* began and fears of nuclear war were rampant, expect to be heard on questions of social justice if it cannot provide answers for the understandable fears so many Americans have of being attacked on their own soil. In this regard we have come full circle from the start of the atomic age and the Eisenhower era, even if those who frighten us and those who currently lead our country seem so much smaller in stature than the men and women who dominated our lives a half-century ago.

raising the cost of genocide

SAMANTHA POWER

Raphael Lemkin, a Polish jurist who lost forty-nine members of his family in the Holocaust, invented the word "genocide" in 1944 because he believed that, in the aftermath of the Turkish "race murder" of the Armenians and Hitler's attempt to exterminate the Jews, the world's "civilized" powers needed to band together to outlaw crimes that were said to "shock the conscience." Prior to Lemkin's coinage, the systematic targeting of national, ethnic, or religious groups was known as "barbarity," a word that Lemkin believed failed to convey the unique horror of the crime. "Genocide," he hoped, would send shudders down the spines of those who heard it and oblige them to prevent, punish, and even suppress the carnage.

An amateur historian of mass slaughter from medieval times to the twentieth century, Lemkin knew that genocide would continue to occur with "biological regularity." Moreover, he knew from reviewing the recent past that if it were left to political leaders to decide how to respond, they would inevitably privilege their short-term interests over both the moral imperative of stopping genocide and the long-term consequences of ignoring it.

In 1948, largely on Lemkin's prodding, the UN General Assembly unanimously passed the United Nations' first-ever human rights treaty, the Genocide Convention, which required signatories "to undertake to prevent and punish" genocide. The Convention's language was vague on precisely how the UN member states would meet their obligations, making no mention of military intervention and trusting that domestic prosecution of future "genocidists" would deter massacres. Still, the lively debates over ratification that occurred in national legislatures testified to the seriousness with which delegates believed they were committing their country's resources and prestige to banning targeted slaughter.

More than a half century has passed since the Genocide Convention came into effect, and genocide has proceeded virtually unabated. Press coverage of the atrocities has generated outrage, but it has generally been insufficient to prompt outsiders to act. As the 1990s showed, particularly in the reactions of the United States and Europe to carnage in Yugoslavia and Rwanda (the scene, in 1994, of the fastest and most efficient genocidal campaign of the twentieth century), Western countries replicated the pattern established in their earlier responses to the rise and domination of Hitler—long after they had supposedly internalized the "lessons of the Holocaust."

In order to understand this pattern—and by extension, put an end to it—we must first confront the grim record of international responses to genocide in the twentieth century. In 1915, the Turkish minister of the interior, Talaat Pasha, and the other Young Turk leaders set out to solve Turkey's "Armenia problem" by murdering leading Armenian intellectuals and deporting the rest of the population into the desert, where many would be killed by local gendarmerie, by starvation, or by disease. Some one million Armenians died. Germany, which was aligned with Turkey in the war, actively covered up eyewitness reports of atrocities. Russia, Britain, and France, fighting against Turkey and Germany in the war, publicized ghastly massacre reports. The Allies also called upon the United States to use its leverage as a neutral power either to convince Turkey to mend its ways or to press Germany to squeeze its ally. Woodrow Wilson's administration carefully guarded its neutrality, which was strongly favored by the American people, and resisted these calls for diplomatic intervention. With the exception of the U.S. ambassador in Constantinople (now Istanbul) Henry Morgenthau, Sr., and other consular officials in the field, U.S. officials remained mute. A nongovernmental organization known as the Armenia Atrocities Committee drew wide public attention to the murder of fellow Christians and even managed to raise money for humanitarian aid. But the group drew the ire of former president Theodore Roosevelt because it simultaneously denounced the Turkish slaughter and argued against U.S. military intervention with pacifist appeals to "put safety first." In the end, despite heavy coverage of the Turkish horrors in *The New York Times* and elsewhere, Wilson took no measures that would have put U.S. neutrality in doubt. When the United States finally entered the war in 1917, it did not declare war on Turkey and did not join the Allies' postwar efforts to prosecute Turkish war criminals.

The Nazi genocide, which followed two decades later, left six million Jews and five million Poles, Roma, homosexuals, and political opponents dead. Before the Holocaust, neither U.S. nor European diplomats uttered much protest when Germany passed the Nuremberg Laws and began destroying Jewish businesses, synagogues, and homes. Britain and France went to war with Germany after Hitler invaded Poland in September 1939. But President Franklin Roosevelt, like Wilson, kept America neutral. Only after the Japanese attack on Pearl Harbor and after Adolf Hitler declared war on the United States did the United States join the European battle. Together, the Allies did nothing directly aimed at impeding the Nazis' extermination of the Jews. They feared that drawing attention to the murder of Jews or admitting additional refugees would undermine domestic public support for the war. Thus, they downplayed the numerous and graphic atrocity reports smuggled out of Nazi-occupied territory or intercepted by Allied intelligence officials. They took shelter in the utter inconceivability of what was being documented. To those who pressed for sterner measures, Western leaders argued that the Allies would achieve more by focusing their military resources on winning battlefield victories than on disrupting concentration camp traffic.

The Nuremberg and Tokyo trials prosecuted the leading perpetrators of crimes against humanity after the Second World War. This represented a major inroad into state sovereignty. But political leaders saw the real crime of the Axis powers as waging a "crime against peace." The wartime perpetrators were not prosecuted for crimes they committed before the Nazi invasion of Poland. The cardinal sin was not seen to be Hitler's "genocide" (a term hardly used at Nuremberg), but his cross-border aggression, which was a permanent threat to international stability and, by inference, the strategic interests of the world's leading powers.

By contrast, the 1948 Genocide Convention, which Raphael Lemkin helped draft, made political leaders liable for genocide committed during peace or wartime, inside a state or outside it. Still, in 1969, Britain maintained active support for the Nigerian government while it starved and murdered the Ibo people of Biafra. Eyeing potentially vast oil reserves in Iboland, the United States and the other European powers followed the British lead, opposing Biafran secession and insisting that food be delivered through Lagos, even though the Nigerian government openly used starvation as a weapon of war. Two years later, the Western powers did not protest when Pakistan responded to a Bengali autonomy movement in East Pakistan by sending in its army and murdering more than a million people. The Nixon administration backed Pakistan, which was its intermediary with the People's Republic of China, and when the U.S. consul-general in Dhaka dissented, the State Department recalled him from his post. In 1972, when the Tutsi government in Burundi killed some hundred thousand Hutu, the Western powers downplayed the atrocities, treating them as an "internal affair." In all three cases of genocide, the economic and strategic interests of the United States and its European allies caused them to side with the genocidal governments and to invoke "sovereignty" as an excuse for refraining even from complaint.

One might have expected a more spirited response to the Cambodian genocide that occurred from 1975 to 1979 because it was communist radicals (known as the Khmer Rouge, or Red Khmer) who murdered nearly two million of the country's seven million people. But in the aftermath of Vietnam, Western governments paid little heed to bloodshed committed in a part of the world they were anxious to leave behind. President Gerald Ford denounced the Khmer Rouge's massacres for a month, but then went completely silent. President Jimmy Carter, the first U.S. president to champion human rights, made no mention of Pol Pot's slaughter for the first two years of his presidency. Although the United States had recently renewed diplomatic ties with China, U.S. officials did not ask China to use its influence with the Khmer Rouge. Once the Vietnamese had overthrown the genocidal Khmer Rouge regime in January 1979, the Carter administration, Ronald Reagan's administration, and all of the European powers maintained recognition of Pol Pot's bloody government in order to prevent the Vietnamese-installed government from being seated at the United Nations or leave the UN seat empty. Khmer Rouge representatives occupied Cambodia's seat at the UN for another decade.

In 1987–1988, Iraqi dictator Saddam Hussein set out to wipe out the country's rural Kurdish population. Iraqi soldiers and police bulldozed several thousand villages, rounded up and executed men, women, and children who remained in homes that fell within Hussein's "prohibited zones," and turned chemical weapons against the Kurdish people, sending tens of thousands of civilians fleeing into neighboring Turkey and Iran. Several European states armed Hussein in this period, and the Reagan administration provided more than five hundred million dollars worth of annual agricultural and manufacturing credits. For the first year of the campaign, none of the Western powers condemned the atrocities, even privately. When Senators Claiborne Pell (D-R.I.) and Jesse Helms (R-N.C.) introduced sanctions legislation that would have suspended the generous U.S. credit program, the Reagan administration and the farm lobby helped block the sanctions, even though the human toll of Hussein's gas attacks had earned front-page news coverage. The White House took the position it did because it had decided to maintain friendly relations with its Gulf ally (and enemy of its enemy, Iran) and to advance the interests of U.S. farmers and manufacturers. Most lawmakers on Capitol Hill wholeheartedly supported the U.S. policy of aiding Iraq even after the assault against the Kurds.

With the end of the cold war and the apparent rebirth of the UN (aided by the obsolescence of the superpower veto), one might have expected a greater readiness to prevent genocide. But the pattern of nonintervention established in 1915 proved durable. In 1992, when Bosnian Serbs began systematically deporting and murdering Muslims and Croats in Bosnia, the United States and Europe decided not to intervene with air strikes to protect civilians. They also opted not to lift a UN arms embargo against the Muslims, even though they knew the measure froze in place a gross imbalance between the outgunned Muslims and their Serb foes, who had inherited the arsenal of the Yugoslav National Army. Britain, France, and the Netherlands responded to public pressure by contributing peacekeepers, but the United States refused to risk its troops to deliver food or protect people under siege. European and American political leaders were unanimous in their belief that they had "no dog" in the Balkan fight. When Bill Clinton assumed the Oval Office in 1993, he contested his predecessor's tendency to blame "all sides" for the violence, pointing out that the bulk of the atrocities were being committed by the Serbs. But he did not contest the killing itself. Fearing confrontation with his military, unsure of domestic political support, and determined to avoid "Americanizing" the war and endangering

U.S. soldiers, Clinton avoided meaningful action. Some two hundred thousand people were killed in a three-and-a-half-year war.

The genocide in Rwanda, which occurred in 1994, two years after the beginning of the Bosnian War, left some eight hundred thousand Tutsi and moderate Hutu murdered in one hundred days. France armed and diplomatically defended the genocidal government. Belgium, which contributed troops to a UN mission meant to help usher in Hutu-Tutsi power-sharing, yanked its troops out of Rwanda despite its detailed understanding of the pace and scope of the early massacres. The Clinton administration, burned by a UN mission gone bad in Somalia, kept U.S. troops far from the scene of the crime. But, more egregiously, despite knowing that Tutsi were being systematically murdered, the Clinton team demanded that the UN peacekeepers in Rwanda be withdrawn and then resisted U.S. involvement of even the mildest form. Senior U.S. officials wanted to reduce the likelihood of eventually being drawn into Africa, and they sought to show a U.S. Congress skeptical of the UN that they had toughened up their approach to peacekeeping and learned, in the president's words, "to say 'no.'" Just as they had done during the Bosnia war, U.S. and European officials went out of their way to avoid branding the carnage "genocide." This decision was made partly out of fear of triggering their obligations under the Genocide Convention, but mainly it was done to avoid the moral stigma associated with allowing what Lemkin described as "the ultimate crime."

In sum, the United States and its European allies have wholeheartedly endorsed the pledge of "never again," while tolerating unspeakable atrocities that have been committed in clear view. The personalities, ideologies, and geopolitical constraints have shifted with time, but the major powers have consistently refused to take risks to suppress genocide. Whatever the growth in public awareness of the Holocaust and the triumphalism about the ascent of liberal democratic values, the last decade of the twentieth century was one of the most deadly in the grimmest century on record.

Genocide occurred after the cold war, after the growth of human rights groups, after the explosion of instant communications, and after the erection of the Holocaust Museum in Washington, D.C. Perversely, public awareness of the Holocaust often seemed to set the bar for concern so high that citizens and statesmen were able to tell themselves that contemporary genocides were not measuring up. As the writer David Rieff noted, "never again" might best be defined as, "Never again would Germans kill Jews in Europe in the 1940s." Either by averting their eyes or attending to more pressing conventional strategic and political concerns, Western leaders have repeatedly denounced the Holocaust and allowed genocide.

What is most shocking about the reaction of what Lemkin called the "civilized world" to these twentieth-century genocides is not that the Western powers did not deploy their ground forces to combat the atrocities. What is most shocking is that they did virtually nothing along a continuum of intervention—from the merely rhetorical to the aggressively military—to deter the crime. Because their "vital national interests" were not considered imperiled by mere genocide, military intervention was rarely even considered. But because it was not considered, high-level officials in the United States and Europe often were not involved in debating alternate policy options. Instead of giving genocide the moral attention it warranted and at least vigilantly denouncing the perpetrators, Western governments repeatedly trusted in negotiation, clung to diplomatic niceties and neutrality, and shipped humanitarian aid. Genocide was met again and again with a policy of silence.

And the Western powers did not merely do nothing. On occasion, they directly or indirectly aided those committing genocide. Beginning in 1979 and continuing throughout the 1980s, the United States orchestrated the vote at the UN to favor maintaining recognition of the Khmer Rouge. The Western powers sided with and supplied credits, military intelligence, and arms to Iraq while Hussein was attempting to wipe out Kurds in northern Iraq. The major powers used their clout on the UN Security Council to mandate the withdrawal of UN peacekeepers from Rwanda and to block the deployment of reinforcements. They maintained an arms embargo against the Bosnian Muslims even after it was clear that the arms ban prevented the Muslims from defending themselves. And they made promises to the people of Srebrenica and Rwanda they did not intend to keep.

Nearly a century after the "race murder" of the Armenians and more than a half century after the liberation of the Nazi death camps, the crucial question is, why do decent men and women who firmly believe genocide should "never again" be permitted allow it to happen? The most typical response throughout the twentieth century was, "We didn't know." But this is simply untrue. To be sure, the information emanating from countries victimized by genocide was imperfect. Embassy personnel were withdrawn, intelligence assets on the ground were scarce, editors were typically reluctant to assign their reporters to places where neither Western interests nor Western readers were engaged, and journalists who attempted to report the atrocities were limited in their mobility. As a result, refugee claims were difficult to confirm and body counts notoriously hard to establish. Because genocide is usually veiled beneath the cover of war, when the killing began, some Western officials had genuine difficulty initially distinguishing genocide from conventional conflict.

But although Western governments did not know all there was to know about the nature and scale of the violence, they knew plenty. Well-connected ambassadors and junior intelligence analysts pumped a steady stream of information up the chain to senior decision makers—both early warnings ahead of genocide and vivid documentation during it. Much of the best intelligence appeared in the morning papers. Back in 1915, when communications were far more primitive, *The New York Times* managed 145 stories about the Turkish massacre of Armenians. During the Holocaust, though stories on the extermination of the Jews were not given anywhere near the prominence they warranted, they did regularly appear. In 1994, the *Times* reported just four days after the beginning of the Rwanda genocide that "tens of thousands" of Rwandans had already been murdered. It devoted more column inches to the horrors of Bosnia between 1992 and 1995 than it did to any other single foreign story.

With advances in technology and in the monitoring of human rights groups, Western leaders have begun relying on a second claim: "We didn't fully appreciate." This President Clinton said in an apology delivered in Rwanda four years after the genocide: "We did not fully appreciate the depth and the speed of the unimaginable terror which engulfed you." This claim, too, is misleading. It is true that the atrocities that were known remained abstract and remote, rarely acquiring the status of knee-buckling knowledge among ordinary citizens. Because the savagery of genocide so defied our everyday experience, many of us failed to comprehend what we had never experienced first-hand. Armenian, Jewish, Cambodian, Tutsi, Bosnian, and other survivors and witnesses had trouble making "the unbelievable believable." The bystanders were thus able to inhabit what one Protestant theologian in the Second World War called the "twilight between knowing and not knowing."

But we must take responsibility for our incredulity. The Holocaust is too present in Western schoolbooks and culture today for genocide to be "unimaginable." We should have learned far sooner to trust even those accounts that could not be independently verified. The stories that emerge from genocidal societies are, by definition, "incredible." Case after case of wishful thinking debunked should have led us to shift the burden of proof away from the harried refugees and to the doubting skeptics who should be required to offer persuasive reasons for disputing refugee claims. A bias toward belief would do less harm than a bias toward disbelief. Instead of aggressively hunting for knowledge or publicizing what was already known, Western officials took shelter in the fog of plausible deniability. In the face of genocide, the search for certainty frequently became an excuse for paralysis and postponement. In most cases of genocide, those who "did not know" or "did not appreciate" chose not to do so.

The second consoling response usually offered to the question of why the major powers did so little to stop genocide is that any intervention would have been futile. Each time states began slaughtering and deporting their citizens, Western officials claimed that the proposed measures would do little to stem the horrors, or that they would do more harm than good. Usually the officials cited this lack of capacity to ameliorate suffering as a central reason for staying uninvolved. If the hatreds were "age-old" and "two-sided," as was usually claimed, and if the "parties" had in fact been killing one another "for centuries," the implication was that they would kill one another for centuries more. Thus, there was little a well-meaning band of foreign do-gooders could achieve by meddling.

It is difficult, in retrospect, to ascertain what a determined diplomatic, economic, legal, or military intervention could have achieved or what it would have cost. All we do know is that the perpetrators of genocide were quick studies who were remarkably attuned both to the tactics of their genocidal predecessors and to the world's response. From their brutal forerunners, they picked up lessons in everything from dehumanizing their victims and deploying euphemisms to constructing concentration camps and covering their tracks. And from the outside world, they learned the lesson of impunity.

The Turkish minister of the interior, Talaat Pasha, was aware that Sultan Abdul Hamid II had gotten away with murdering Armenians in 1895. In 1939 Hitler was emboldened by the fact that absolutely nobody "remembered the Armenians." Saddam Hussein noted the international community's relaxed response to his chemical weapons attacks against Iran and his bulldozing of Kurdish villages. He rightly assumed he would not be punished for using poison gases against the Kurds. Rwandan gunmen deliberately targeted the Belgian peacekeepers at the start of their genocide because they knew from the U.S. reaction to the deaths of eighteen U.S. soldiers in Somalia that the murder of Western troops would likely precipitate their withdrawal. The Bosnian Serbs publicly celebrated the Mogadishu casualties, knowing that they would never have to do battle with U.S. ground forces. Slobodan Milosevic saw that he got away with the brutal suppression of independence movements in Slovenia and Croatia and reasoned he would pay no price for doing the same in Bosnia and Kosovo. Because so many individual perpetrators were killing for the first time and deciding daily how far they would go, the United States and its European allies missed critical opportunities to try to deter them. When they ignored genocide around the world, the Western powers were not intending to "green light" the perpetrators. But because the killers told themselves they were doing the world a favor by "cleansing" the "undesirables," some surely interpreted silence as consent or even support.

Although it is impossible to know the impact of steps never taken, the best testament to what the Western powers might have achieved is what they did achieve. For all the talk of the futility of foreign involvement, in the rare instances that the United States and its allies took even small steps, they appear to have saved lives. After Senator Pell's sanctions effort forced a reluctant Reagan White House to condemn Saddam Hussein's gas attacks, the Iraqi dictator did not again use chemical weapons against the Kurds. In 1991, after the appeals of Turkey and the personal encounter of U.S. Secretary of State James Baker with Kurdish refugees, the allies succeeded in creating a safe haven for the Kurds in northern Iraq, enabling more than a million Kurds to return to their homes. On a smaller scale, a Rwandan hotel owner credits the mere phone calls of a U.S. diplomat with deterring militias from attacking Tutsi inhabitants of his hotel during the genocide. The 503 UN peace-keepers who remained in Rwanda throughout the genocide protected some twenty-five thousand Rwandans. NATO bombing in Bosnia, when it finally came, rapidly brought that three-and-a-half-year war to a close. Although imperfect, the NATO bombing campaign in Kosovo in 1999 liberated 1.7 million Albanians from tyrannical Serb rule. And a handful of NATO arrests in the former Yugoslavia has caused dozens of suspected war criminals to turn themselves into the UN war crimes tribunal. One cannot assume that every measure proposed would have been effective, but there is no doubt that even these small and tardy steps saved hundreds of thousands of lives. If the Western powers had made genocide prevention a priority, they could have saved countless more. The real reason the United States and the European states did not do what they could and should have done to stop genocide was not a lack of knowledge or a lack of capacity, but a lack of will. Simply put, Western leaders did not act because they did not want to. They believed that genocide was wrong, but they were not prepared to invest the military, financial, diplomatic, or domestic political capital needed to stop it. The policies crafted in response to each of the major genocides of the twentieth century were not the accidental products of neglect. They were concrete choices made by the world's most influential deci-sion makers after implicit and explicit weighing of costs and benefits. One of the most important and reluctant conclusions one must reach is that the record of the "civilized" world is not one of failure. It is one of "success." The system worked.

To illuminate this point, let us look specifically at the goals of pol-icy makers in the United States. The European responses have either tended to be driven by similar motivations as those of U.S. decision makers or the European allies have directly followed the U.S. lead. From the Armenia genocide forward, U.S. policy makers in the executive branch (usually with the passive backing of most members of Congress) have had two objectives. First, they wanted to avoid engagement in conflicts that posed little threat to American interests, narrowly defined.

Second, they hoped to contain the political costs and avoid the moral stigma associated with allowing genocide. By and large, they achieved both aims. In order to contain the political fallout, U.S. officials over-emphasized the ambiguity of the facts. They played up the likely down-sides of any proposed intervention. They steadfastly avoided use of the word "genocide," which they believed carried with it legal and moral (and thus political) imperatives to act. And they took solace in the normal operations of the foreign-policy bureaucracy, which permitted an illusion of continual deliberation, complex activity, and intense concern.

To understand why the United States did not do more to stem genocide, of course, it is not enough to focus on the actions of American presidents or their foreign-policy teams. In a democracy, even an ad-ministration disinclined to act can be pressured into doing so. This pressure can come from inside and outside. Bureaucrats within the system who grasp the stakes can patiently lobby or brazenly agitate in the hope of forcing their bosses to entertain a full range of options. Unfortunately, while every genocide generated some activism within the U.S. foreign-policy establishment, U.S. civil and foreign servants typically heeded what they took to be presidential indifference and public apathy. They assumed U.S. policy was immutable, that their concerns were already understood by their bosses, and that speaking (or walking) out would only reduce their capacity to improve the policy.

But the main reason American leaders can persist in turning away is that genocide in distant lands has not captivated American senators, congressional caucuses, Washington lobbyists, elite opinion shapers, grassroots groups, and individual constituents. The battle to stop gen-ocide has thus been repeatedly lost in the realm of domestic politics. Although isolated voices have protested the atrocities, Americans out-side the executive branch were largely mute when it mattered. As a result of this society-wide silence, officials at all levels of government calculated that the political costs of getting involved in genocide preven-tion far exceeded the costs of remaining uninvolved.

Here, the exception that proved the rule was the NATO air cam-paign in Bosnia. Bosnia was the only genocide of the twentieth century that was eventually met with a military response. The domestic pressure was intense. The U.S. failure to stop the atrocities generated a wave of resignations from the U.S. government. The protests of American officials in the foreign service were legitimated daily by sustained public and press activism outside Foggy Bottom. But NATO only intervened in 1995 with a heavy barrage of bombing when its assessment of the costs of intervening was lowered by the Croatian Army's rout of Serb forces, and when its assessment of the costs of *not* intervening was raised by the U.S. Congress's vote to unilaterally lift the arms embargo against the Bosnian Muslims. The lifting of the embargo embarrassed Clinton at home because foreign policy was being made on Capital Hill by a future presidential challenger, Senate Majority Leader Bob Dole. It also made it likely that European governments were going to pull their peacekeepers out of the Balkans, which would have required U.S. troop participation in a potentially bloody and certainly humiliating rescue mission. This scenario was one that President Clinton wanted to avoid on the eve of his bid for reelection.

With foreign policy crises all over the world implicating more traditional U.S. interests, the slaughter of civilians will rarely secure top-level attention on its own merits. It takes political pressure to put genocide "on the map" in Washington or in any of the European capitals. When Alison des Forges of Human Rights Watch met with National Security Adviser Anthony Lake two weeks into the Rwanda genocide, he informed her that the phones were not ringing. "Make more noise!" he urged. Because so little noise has been made about genocide, U.S. officials have opposed American intervention, firmly convinced that they were doing all they could—and, most important, all they should—in light of competing American interests and a highly circumscribed understanding of what was domestically "possible."

Although U.S. officials have sometimes expressed remorse after genocide, none fear professional accountability for their sins of omission. In the 1970s, Senate hearings on Capitol Hill documented abuses committed by America and its cold war allies in Latin America, southeast Asia, and elsewhere. As a result of this public reckoning and some of the formal checks instituted in its wake, U.S. foreign policy decision makers now fear repercussions for their sins of commission—for decisions they make and policies they shape that go wrong. But while everyone within the U.S. government has the incentive to avoid "another Somalia" or "another Vietnam," few think twice about playing a role in allowing "another Rwanda."

Other countries and institutions whose personnel were actually present when genocide was committed have been forced to be more introspective. The Netherlands, France, and the UN have each staged inquiries into their responsibility for the fall of Srebrenica and the massacres that followed. The inquiries did not lead to any notable political reforms, but they at least "named names," which might affect the behavior of bureaucrats the next time around. The United States has not looked back. When the UN's Srebrenica investigators approached the U.S. mission in New York for assistance, their phone calls were not returned. In the end, the UN team was forbidden from making any independent contact with U.S. government employees. The investigators were granted access to a group of hand-picked junior and mid-level officials who knew or revealed next to nothing about what the United States knew during the Srebrenica slaughter.

The French, the Belgians, the UN, and the Organization for African Unity have undertaken investigations on the Rwanda genocide. But in the United States, when Cynthia McKinney and Donald Payne, two disgruntled members of the Congressional Black Caucus (which was itself quiet during the 1994 massacres), attempted to stage hearings on the U.S. role, they were rebuffed. Two officials in the Clinton administration, one at the National Security Council, the other at the State Department, conducted internal studies on the administration's response to the Rwanda genocide. But they examined only the paper trail and did not publicly disclose their findings. What is needed are congressional inquiries with the power to subpoena documents and U.S. officials of all ranks and roles in the executive and legislative branches. Without meaningful disclosure, public awareness, and official shame, it is hard to imagine the U.S. response improving the next time around.

The September 11, 2001, attacks on the United States may have permanently altered U.S. foreign policy. The hope is that the attacks will make Americans inside and outside government more capable of imagining evil committed against innocent civilians. The fanatics targeting America resemble the perpetrators of genocide in their espousal of collective responsibility of the most savage kind. They attack civilians not because of anything the unwitting targets do personally, but because of who they are. To earn a death sentence, it was enough in the last century to be an Armenian, a Jew, or a Tutsi. On September 11, it was enough to be an American. Instead of causing Americans to retreat from global humanitarian engagement, the terrorist attacks could cause us to empathize with peoples victimized by genocide. In 1994, Rwanda, a country of eight million, experienced the equivalent of more than two World Trade Center attacks every single day for a hundred days. This was the proportional equivalent of two hundred and thirty thousand Americans killed each day, or twenty-three million Americans murdered in three months. When, on September 12, 2001, the United States turned for help to its allies, Americans were gratified by the overwhelming response. When the Tutsi cried out, by contrast, every country in the world turned away.

The fear, after September 11, is that the United States will view genocide prevention as a luxury it cannot afford as it sets out to better protect Americans. Some are now arguing, understandably, that fighting terrorism requires husbanding America's resources and avoiding "social work" such as humanitarian intervention, which is said to harm U.S. "readiness." Many believe that NATO's 1999 intervention in Kosovo and the current trial of Serbian president Slobodan Milosevic, which were once thought to mark important precedents, will in fact represent high-water marks for genocide prevention and punishment.

Without U.S. leadership, the last century showed, others will be unwilling to step forward to act, and genocide will continue. If the United States treats the war on terrorism as a war that can be prosecuted in a vacuum, with no regard for *genocidal* terror, it will be making a colossal mistake. There are two main reasons that the United States and its European allies should stop genocide. The first and most convincing reason is moral. When innocent life is being taken on such a scale and the United States and its allies have the power to stop the killing at reasonable risk, they have a duty to act. It is this belief that motivates most of those who seek intervention. But foreign policy is not driven by morality; it is driven by interests, narrowly defined. And history has shown that the suffering of victims has rarely been sufficient to spark a Western intervention.

The second reason for acting is the threat genocide in fact poses to

Western interests. Allowing genocide undermines regional and international stability, creates militarized refugees, and signals dictators that hate and murder are permissible tools of statecraft. Because these dangers to national interests are long-term dangers and not immediately apparent, however, they have rarely convinced top Western policy makers. Genocide has undermined regional stability, but the regions it destabilized tended also to lie outside the U.S. and European spheres of concern. Refugees have been militarized, but they tended not to wash up on America's shores. A key reason European leaders were more engaged in the Balkans in the 1990s than their American counterparts was that Bosnian refugees did land in Britain, France, and Germany. But generally genocidal regimes recognized that if they limited the spillover costs locally, they could count on Western leaders to stay disengaged. Thus intervention only came about on the rare occasions when the shorter-term political interests of Western policy makers were triggered.

American leadership remains essential for mobilizing local, regional, and international responses to genocide. But if it was difficult before September 11 to get U.S. decision makers to see the long-term costs of allowing genocide, it will be even harder today when U.S. security needs are so acute. Nonetheless, the record shows that trying to build walls around genocidal societies almost guarantees trouble down the road. American security and security for Americans abroad is contingent on international stability, and there is perhaps no greater source of havoc than a group of well-armed extremists bent on wiping out a people on ethnic, national, or religious grounds.

States that murder and torment their own citizens almost inevitably target citizens elsewhere. Their appetites become insatiable. Hitler began by persecuting his own people and then expanded his campaign to the rest of Europe and, in time, the United States. Saddam Hussein wiped out rural Kurdish life and then turned on Kuwait, sending his genocidal henchman Ali Hassan al-Majid to govern the newly occupied country. The United States now has reason to fear that the poisonous potions Hussein tried out on the Kurds will be used next against Americans. Milosevic took his wars from Slovenia and Croatia to Bosnia and then Kosovo. The United States and its European allies are still paying for their earlier neglect of the Balkans by having to grapple with violence in Macedonia that continues to threaten the stability of south-eastern Europe.

Citizens victimized by genocide or abandoned by the international community do not make good neighbors, as their thirst for vengeance, their irredentism, and their acceptance of violence as a means of generating change can turn them into future threats. In Bosnia, where the United States and Europe maintained an arms embargo against the Muslims, extremist Islamic fighters and proselytizers eventually turned up to offer succor. Some secular Muslim citizens became radicalized by the partnership, and the failed state of Bosnia became a haven for Islamic terrorists shunned elsewhere in the world. It appears that one of the organizations that infiltrated Bosnia in its hour of need and used it as a training base was Osama bin Laden's al-Qaeda. And however high the number of Islamic radicals that were imported during or created by the Serb slaughter of Bosnia's Muslims, the figure would have been exponentially higher if the United States and its allies had allowed the killing to continue past 1995. The current Bosnian government, one legacy of the U.S.-brokered Dayton Peace Agreement, is far from perfect, but it is at least a strategic partner in the war against terrorism. Without the belated NATO bombing and U.S. diplomatic leadership, that same Bosnian government might today be an American foe.

For the foreseeable future, American leadership will be necessary to stop or punish genocide. Clearly, the United States does not have the resources to simultaneously defend itself from attack and deploy its troops to every trouble spot where the threat of ethnic violence lurks. It must be extremely cautious about deploying U.S. forces abroad. But U.S. policy options should not be framed in terms of doing nothing or sending in the Marines. There will be times when the magnitude of the moral harm will demand risking U.S. military force. There will also be times when, owing to America's past dealings in the region, U.S. intervention will be singularly inappropriate. There will be times when the risk to U.S. soldiers will outweigh the benefits a military intervention would likely bring to the victims. There will be times when even a good-faith presidential effort to convince the American people of the value of intervening will fail to create a political constituency for U.S. military action.

But in such circumstances, just because the United States might not deploy its troops, it does not mean that a U.S. leadership role is not required or that other forms of intervention should not be tried. U.S. officials must focus less on avoiding embarrassing the United States and more on accurately diagnosing and treating the atrocities underway. Deliberately calling genocide something it is not—"civil war" or "tribal violence"—in order to mute public pressure is not only dishonest; it is detrimental to sound policy. Handling atrocity as war has led to the deployment of conflict resolution experts, the misguided pursuit of cease-fires, and the spiraling investment in "peace processes" that too often become stalling devices that shield murder.

Instead of regarding intervention as an all-or-nothing proposition, the United States and its allies should respond to genocide by publicly identifying and threatening its perpetrators with prosecution, demanding the expulsion of representatives of genocidal regimes from international institutions such as the United Nations, closing the perpetrators' embassies in Western capitals, and calling upon countries aligned with the perpetrators to ask them to use their influence. Depending on the circumstances, Western powers might establish economic sanctions or freeze foreign assets, impose an arms embargo, or, if warranted, lift an arms embargo. They might use their technical resources to jam inflammatory radio or television broadcasts that are essential to stirring panic and hate. They might set up safe areas to house refugees and civilians, and enforce them with well-armed and robustly mandated peacekeepers, air power, or both.

Genocide prevention is an immense burden and one that must be shared. But even if U.S. troops stay home, American leadership will be indispensable in assembling "coalitions of the willing" to deploy ground troops, in encouraging U.S. allies to step up their capacities, and in strengthening regional and international institutions that might eventually carry more of the weight.

For most of the second half of the twentieth century, the existence of the Genocide Convention appeared to achieve little. The United States did not ratify the Convention for forty years. Those countries that did ratify it never invoked it to stop or punish genocide. And instead of making Western policy makers more inclined to stop genocide, ratification seemed only to make them more reluctant to use the "g-word."

Still, Lemkin's coinage has done more good than harm. The international war crimes tribunals for the former Yugoslavia and Rwanda and the permanent International Criminal Court would have likely not come into existence without the Convention's passage. The punishment that takes place at these courts will help deter genocide in the long term. But more fundamentally, without the existence of the Convention, or Lemkin's proselytizing around it, the word genocide would not carry the moral stigma it has acquired. Hope for enforcement of the Genocide Convention lies in the stigma associated with committing the crime of genocide. And paradoxically hope also lies in the lengths to which Western policy makers have gone to vow never again to allow genocide and the comparable lengths to which they have gone, while allowing it, to deny its occurrence.

Because it is unlikely that Western leaders will have the vision to recognize that they endanger their countries' long-term vital national interests by allowing genocide, the most realistic hope for combating it lies in the rest of us creating short-term political costs for those who do nothing.

—2002

can there be a decent left?

MICHAEL WALZER

Leftist opposition to the war in Afghanistan faded in November and December of last year, not only because of the success of the war but also because of the enthusiasm with which so many Afghans greeted that success. The pictures of women showing their smiling faces to the world, of men shaving their beards, of girls in school, of boys playing soccer: all this was no doubt a slap in the face to leftist theories of American imperialism, but also politically disarming. There was (and is) still a lot to worry about: refugees, hunger, minimal law and order. But it was suddenly clear, even to many opponents of the war, that the Taliban regime had been the biggest obstacle to any serious effort to address the looming humanitarian crisis, and it was the American war that removed the obstacle. It looked (almost) like a war of liberation, a humanitarian intervention.

But the war was primarily neither of these things; it was a preventive war, designed to make it impossible to train terrorists in Afghanistan and to plan and organize attacks like that of September 11. And that war was never really accepted, in wide sections of the left, as either just or necessary. Recall the standard arguments against it: that we should have turned to the United Nations; that we had to prove the guilt of al-Qaeda and the Taliban and then organize international trials; and that the war, if it was fought at all, had to be fought without endangering civilians. The last point was intended to make fighting impossible. I haven't come across any arguments that seriously tried to describe how this (or any) war could be fought without putting civilians at risk, or to ask what degree of risk might be permissible, or to specify the risks that American soldiers should accept in order to reduce the risk of civilian deaths. All these were legitimate issues in Afghanistan, as they were in the Kosovo and Gulf wars. But among last fall's antiwar demonstrators, "Stop the bombing" wasn't a slogan that summarized a coherent view of the bombing—or of the alternatives to it. The truth is that most leftists were not committed to having a coherent view about things like that; they were committed to opposing the war, and they were prepared to oppose it without regard to its causes or character and without any visible concern about preventing future terrorist attacks.

A few left academics have tried to figure out how many civilians actually died in Afghanistan, aiming at as high a figure as possible, on the assumption, apparently, that if the number is greater than the number of people killed in the attacks on the Twin Towers, the war is unjust. At the moment, most of the numbers are propaganda; there is no reliable accounting. But the claim that the numbers matter in just this way—that the 3,120th death determines the injustice of the war—is wrong. It denies one of the most basic and best understood moral distinctions: between premeditated murder and unintended killing. And the denial isn't accidental, as if the people making it just forgot about, or didn't know about, the everyday moral world. The denial is willful: unintended killing by Americans in Afghanistan counts as murder. This can't be true anywhere else, for anybody else.

The radical failure of the left's response to the events of last fall raises a disturbing question: can there be a decent left in a superpower? Or more accurately, in the only superpower? Maybe the guilt produced by living in such a country and enjoying its privileges makes it impossible to sustain a decent (intelligent, responsible, morally nuanced) politics. Maybe festering resentment, ingrown anger, and self-hate are the inevitable results of the long years spent in fruitless opposition to the global reach of American power. Certainly, all those emotions were plain to see in the left's reaction to September 11, in the failure to register the horror of the attack or to acknowledge the human pain it caused, in the *schadenfreude* of so many of the first responses, the barely concealed glee that the imperial state had finally gotten what it deserved. Many people on the left recovered their moral balance in the weeks that followed; there is at least the beginning of what should be a long process of self-examination. But many more have still not brought themselves to think about what really happened.

Is there any way of escaping the politics of guilt and resentment on the home ground of a superpower? We might begin to worry about this question by looking at oppositional politics in older imperial states. I can't do that in any sustained way (historians take note), only very sketchily. The Boer War is a good place to begin, because of the fierce opposition it aroused in England—which wasn't marked, despite the cruelty of the war, by the kind of self-hate that we have seen on the American left. Nor were the "little Englanders" hostile to English politics and culture; they managed to take a stand against the empire without alienating themselves from its home country. Indeed, they were more likely to regard England as the home country of liberalism and parliamentary democracy. After all, the values of parliamentarianism (self-government, free speech, the right of opposition) did not support imperial rule. George Orwell's defense of patriotism seems to me an actual description of the feelings of many English liberals and leftists before his time and after (even of the Marxists, some of the best of whom were historians, like E. P. Thompson, who wrote sympathetically, indeed romantically, about the English people). Later on, during Margaret Thatcher's terms, and particularly during the Falklands War, the tone of the opposition was more bitter, but by then there was no empire, only sour memories.

I think that the French story is similar. For most of the imperial years, French leftists were as proud of their Frenchness as were people on the right—and perhaps with more justification. For wasn't France the birthplace of enlightenment, universal values, and human rights? The Algerian war gave rise to a more familiar self-hatred, most clearly manifest in Jean-Paul Sartre's defense of National Liberation Front (FLN) terrorism (in his preface to Franz Fanon's *Wretched of the Earth*): "To shoot down a European is to kill two birds with one stone, to destroy an oppressor and the man he oppresses at the same time: there remains a dead man and a free man." This suggests that it is actually a good thing to kill Europeans (they were mostly French), but Sartre did not volunteer to go himself and be killed so that one more Algerian would be a free man. His was a generalized, not a personal, self-hatred.

Why shouldn't the American story be like these two, with long years of healthy oppositionist politics, and only episodic resentment? Wasn't America a beacon of light to the Old World, a city on a hill, an unprecedented experiment in democratic politics? I grew up with the Americanism of the popular front in the 1930s and 1940s; I look back on it now and think that the Communist Party's effort to create a leftist pop culture, in an instant, as the party line turned, was kitschy and manipulative—and also politically very smart. Paul Robeson's "Ballad for Americans," whatever the quality of the music, provides at least a sense of what an unalienated American radicalism might be like. The days after September 11 would not have been a bad time for a popular front. What had happened that made something like that unthinkable?

The cold war, imperial adventures in Central America, Vietnam above all, and then the experience of globalization under American leadership: all these, for good reasons and bad, produced a pervasive leftist view of the United States as global bully—rich, privileged, selfish, hedonistic, and corrupt beyond remedy. The sense of a civilizing mission, which must have sustained parts of the British and French left in a more fully imperial setting (read John Stuart Mill on British India), never got off the ground here. Foreign aid, the Peace Corps, and nation building never took on the dimensions of a "mission"; they were mostly sidelines of U.S. foreign policy: underfunded, frequently in the shade of military operations. Certainly, there has been much to criticize in the policies of every U.S. government since the Second World War (see almost any back issue of *Dissent*). And yet, the leftist critique—most clearly, I think, from the Vietnam years forward (from the time of "Amerika," Viet Cong flags, and breathless trips to North Vietnam)—has been stupid, overwrought, grossly inaccurate. It is the product of what Philip Roth, in his novel *I Married a Communist*, aptly described as "the combination of embitterment and not thinking." The left has lost its bearings. Why?

I will suggest four reasons, without claiming that this is an exhaustive list. It is nothing more than a rough argument, an attempt to begin a debate.

(1) Ideology: the lingering effects of the Marxist theory of imperialism and of the third worldist doctrines of the 1960s and 1970s. We may think that we live in a postideological age, and maybe most of us do, but the traces of old ideologies can be found everywhere in the discourse of the left. Perhaps the most striking consequence is the inability of leftists to recognize or acknowledge the power of religion in the modern world. Whenever writers on the left say that the "root cause" of terror is global inequality or human poverty, the assertion is in fact a denial that religious motives really count. Theology, on this view,

is just the temporary, colloquial idiom in which the legitimate rage of oppressed men and women is expressed.

A few brave leftists described the Taliban regime and the al-Qaeda movement as examples of "clerical fascism," which at least gets the adjective right. And maybe "fascist" is close enough, even if this new politics doesn't look like the product of late capitalist degeneration. It gives the left a reason for opposing Islamic terror, which is an important achievement. But it would be better to find a reason in the realities of terrorism itself, in the idea of a holy war against the infidels, which is not the same thing as a war against inferior races or alien nations. In fact, Islamic radicalism is not, as fascism is, a racist or ultranationalist doctrine. Something else is going on, which we need to understand.

But ideologically primed leftists were likely to think that they already understood whatever needed to be understood. Any group that attacks the imperial power must be a representative of the oppressed, and its agenda must be the agenda of the left. It isn't necessary to listen to its spokesmen. What else can they want except . . . the redistribution of resources across the globe, the withdrawal of American soldiers from wherever they are, the closing down of aid programs for repressive governments, the end of the blockade of Iraq, and the establishment of a Palestinian state alongside Israel? I don't doubt that there is some overlap between this program and the dreams of al-Qaeda leaders—though al-Qaeda is not an egalitarian movement, and the idea that it supports a two-state solution to the Israeli-Palestinian conflict is crazy. The overlap is circumstantial and convenient, nothing more. A holy war against infidels is not, even unintentionally, unconsciously, or "objectively," a left politics. But how many leftists can even imagine a holy war against infidels?

(2) Powerlessness and alienation: leftists have no power in the United States, and most of us don't expect to exercise power, ever. Many left intellectuals live in America like internal aliens, refusing to identify with their fellow citizens, regarding any hint of patriotic feeling as a surrender to jingoism. That's why they had such difficulty responding emotionally to the attacks of September 11 or joining in the expressions of solidarity that followed. Equally important, that's why their participation in the policy debate after the attacks was so odd; their proposals (turn to the UN, collect evidence against bin Laden, and so on)

seem to have been developed with no concern for effectiveness and no sense of urgency. They talked and wrote as if they could not imagine themselves responsible for the lives of their fellow citizens. That was someone else's business: the business of the left was . . . what? To oppose the authorities, whatever they did. The good result of this opposition was a spirited defense of civil liberties. But even this defense displayed a certain willful irresponsibility and ineffectiveness, because so many leftists rushed to the defense of civil liberties while refusing to acknowledge that the country faced real dangers—as if there were no need at all to balance security and freedom. Maybe the right balance will emerge spontaneously from the clash of right-wing authoritarianism and left-wing absolutism, but it would be better practice for the left to figure out the right balance for itself, on its own; the effort would suggest a responsible politics and a real desire to exercise power, some day.

But what really marks the left, or a large part of it, is the bitterness that comes with abandoning any such desire. The alienation is radical. How else can one understand the unwillingness of people who, after all, live here, and whose children and grandchildren live here, to join in a serious debate about how to protect the country against future terrorist attacks? There is a pathology in this unwillingness, and it has already done us great damage.

(3) The moral purism of blaming America first: many leftists seem to believe that this is like blaming oneself, taking responsibility for the crimes of the imperial state. In fact, when we blame America, we also lift ourselves above the blameworthy (other) Americans. The left sets itself apart. Whatever America is doing in the world *isn't* our doing. In some sense, of course, that is true. The defeat of fascism in the middle years of the twentieth century and of communism in the last years were not our doing. Some of us, at least, thought that these efforts merited our support—or our "critical support." But this is a complicated and difficult politics, and it doesn't allow for the favorite posture of many American leftists: standing as a righteous minority, brave and determined, among the timid, the corrupt, and the wicked. A posture like that ensures at once the moral superiority of the left and its political failure.

(4) The sense of not being entitled to criticize anyone else: how can we live in the United States, the richest, most powerful, and most privileged country in the world—and say anything critical about people

who are poorer and weaker than we are? This was a major issue in the 1960s, when the New Left seemed to have discovered "oppression" for the first time, and we all enlisted on the side of oppressed men and women and failed, again and again, to criticize the authoritarianism and brutality that often scar their politics. There is no deeper impulse in left politics than this enlistment; solidarity with people in trouble seems to me the most profound commitment that leftists make. But this solidarity includes, or should include, a readiness to tell these people when we think they are acting wrongly, violating the values we share. Even the oppressed have obligations, and surely the first among these is not to murder innocent people, not to make terrorism their politics. Leftists who cannot insist upon this point, even to people poorer and weaker than they are, have abandoned both politics and morality for something else. They are radical only in their abjection. That was Sartre's radicalism, face-to-face with FLN terror, and it has been imitated by thousands since, excusing and apologizing for acts that any decent left would begin by condemning.

What ought to be done? I have a modest agenda: *put decency first,* and then we will see. So, let's go back over my list of reasons for the current indecency.

Ideology: We certainly need something better than the rag-tag Marxism with which so much of the left operates today—a Marxism whose chief effect is to turn world politics into a cheap melodrama, with all the villains dressed to look the part and one villain larger than life. A tough materialist analysis would be fine, so long as it is sophisticated enough to acknowledge that material interests don't exhaust the possibilities of human motivation. The spectacle of European leftists straining to find some economic reason for the Kosovo War (oil in the Balkans? a possible pipeline? was NATO reaching for control of the Black Sea?) was entertaining at the time, but it doesn't bear repeating. For the moment we can make do with a little humility, an openness to heterodox ideas, a sharp eye for the real world, and a readiness to attend to moral as well as materialist arguments. This last point is especially important. The encounter with Islamic radicalism, and with other versions of politicized religion, should help us understand that high among our interests are our values: secular enlightenment, human rights, and democratic government. Left politics starts with the defense of these three.

Alienation and powerlessness: It is a common idea on the left that political responsibility is something like temperance, moderation, and cleanliness—good bourgeois values that are incompatible with radical politics or incisive social criticism. You have to be a little wild to be a radical. That isn't a crazy idea, and alienated intellectuals may well have, more than anyone else, the anger necessary to begin the critical project and the lust for intellectual combat that sustains it. But they don't necessarily get things right, and the angrier they are and the more they are locked into their combative posture, the more likely they are to get things wrong. What was necessary after September 11, and what is necessary now, is an engagement with our fellow citizens that recognizes the fellowship. We can be as critical as we like, but these are people whose fate we share; we are responsible for their safety as they are for ours, and our politics has to reflect that mutual responsibility. When they are attacked, so are we; and we should join willingly and constructively in debates about how to defend the country. Once again: we should act as if we won't always be powerless.

Blaming America first: Not everything that goes badly in the world goes badly because of us. The United States is not omnipotent, and its leaders should not be taken as co-conspirators in every human disaster. The left has little difficulty understanding the need for distributive justice with regard to resources, but we have been practically clueless about the just distribution of praise and blame. To take the obvious example: in the second half of the twentieth century, the United States fought both just and unjust wars, undertook both just and unjust interventions. It would be a useful exercise to work through the lists and test our capacity to make distinctions—to recognize, say, that the United States was wrong in Guatemala in 1954 and right in Kosovo in 1999. Why can't we accept an ambivalent relation to American power, acknowledging that it has had good and bad effects in the world? But shouldn't an internationalist left demand a more egalitarian distribution of power? Well, yes, in principle; but any actual redistribution will have to be judged by the quality of the states that would be empowered by it. Faced with states like, say, Saddam Hussein's Iraq, I don't think we have to support a global redistribution of political power.

Not blaming anyone else: The world (and this includes the third world) is too full of hatred, cruelty, and corruption for any left, even the American left, to suspend its judgment about what's going on. It's not the case that because we are privileged we should turn inward and focus our criticism only on ourselves. In fact, inwardness is one of our privileges; it is often a form of political self-indulgence. Yes, we are entitled to blame the others whenever they are blameworthy; in fact, it is only when we do that, when we denounce, say, the authoritarianism of third world governments, that we will find our true comrades—the local opponents of the maximal leaders and military juntas, who are often waiting for our recognition and support. If we value democracy, we have to be prepared to defend it, at home, of course, but not only there.

I would once have said that we were well along: the American left has an honorable history, and we have certainly gotten some things right, above all, our opposition to domestic and global inequalities. But what the aftermath of September 11 suggests is that we have not advanced very far—and not always in the right direction. The left needs to begin again.

—2002

a patriotic left

MICHAEL KAZIN

I love my country. I love its passionate and endlessly inventive culture, its remarkably diverse landscape, its agonizing and wonderful history. I particularly cherish its civic ideals—social equality, individual liberty, a populist democracy—and the unending struggle to put their laudable, if often contradictory, claims into practice. I realize that patriotism, like any powerful ideology, is a "construction" with multiple uses, some of which I abhor. But I persist in drawing stimulation and pride from my American identity.

Regrettably, this is not a popular sentiment on the contemporary left. Antiwar activists view patriotism as a smokescreen for U.S. hegemony, while radical academics mock the notion of "American exceptionalism" as a relic of the cold war, a triumphal myth we should quickly outgrow. All the rallying around the flag after September 11 increased the disdain many leftists feel for the sentiment that lies behind it. "The globe, not the flag, is the symbol that's wanted now," scolded Katha Pollitt in the *Nation*. Noam Chomsky described patriotic blather as simply the governing elite's way of telling its subjects, "You shut up and be obedient, and I'll relentlessly advance my own interests."

Both views betray an ignorance of American history, as well as a quixotic desire to leap from a distasteful present to a gauzy future liberated from the fetters of nationalism. Love of country was a demotic faith long before September 11, a fact that previous lefts understood and attempted to turn to their advantage. In the United States, Karl Marx's dictum that the workers have no country has been refuted time and again. It has been not wage earners but the upper classes—from New England gentry on the Grand Tour a century ago to globe-trotting executives and cybertech professionals today—who view America with an ambivalent shrug, reminiscent of Gertrude Stein's line, "America is my country, Paris is my hometown."

One can, like Pollitt and Chomsky, curse as jingoistic all those "United We Stand" and "God Bless America" signs and hope somehow to transcend patriotism in the name of global harmony. Or one can empathize with the communal spirit that animates them, embracing the ideals of the nation and learning from past efforts to put them into practice in the service of far-reaching reform.

An earlier version of American patriotism was a forerunner of the modern genre: pride in the first nation organized around a set of social beliefs rather than a shared geography and history. In its novelty, Americanism gave citizens of the new republic both a way to understand and to stand for purposes that transcended their self-interest. Of course, these purposes were not always noble ones. As historian Gary Gerstle points out in his recent book *American Crucible,* "racial nationalism" dominated much of American life through the nineteenth century and into the early decades of the twentieth. It led some white Americans to justify exterminating Indians, others to hold slaves, and still others to bar immigrants who did not possess "Anglo-Saxon" genes. But the tolerant alternative, which Gerstle calls "civic nationalism," also inspired many Americans in the modern era to help liberate Europe from fascism and Stalinism and to organize at home for social and economic justice.

For American leftists, patriotism was indispensable. It made their dissent and rebellion intelligible to their fellow citizens—and located them within the national narrative, fighting to shape a common future. Tom Paine praised his adopted homeland as an "asylum for mankind"—which gave him a forum to denounce regressive taxes and propose free public education. Elizabeth Cady Stanton issued a "Woman's Declaration of Rights" on the centennial of the Declaration of Independence and argued that denying the vote to women was a violation of the Fourteenth Amendment. Union activists in the Gilded Age such as Eugene Debs and Mother Jones accused employers of crushing the individuality and self-respect of workers. When Debs became a socialist, he described his new vision in the American idiom, as "the equal rights of all to manage and control" society. Half a century later, Martin Luther King, Jr., told his fellow bus boycotters, "If we are wrong—the Supreme Court of this nation is wrong" and proclaimed that "the great glory of American democracy is the right to protest for right."

One could easily list analogous statements from such pioneering reformers as Jane Addams and Betty Friedan, unionists Sidney Hillman and Cesar Chavez, and the gay liberationist Harvey Milk. Without

patriotic appeals, the great social movements that attacked inequalities of class, gender, and race in the United States—and spread their
messianic rhetoric around the world—would never have gotten off
the ground.

Even slavery couldn't extinguish the promise radicals found in the
American creed. On Independence Day, 1852, Frederick Douglass gave
an angry, eloquent address that asked, "What to the slave is the Fourth
of July?" Every account quotes the fugitive-turned-abolitionist speaking
truth to white power: "Your celebration is a sham; your boasted liberty,
an unholy license; your national greatness, swelling vanity; your sounds
of rejoicing are empty and heartless; your denunciations of tyrants, brass
fronted impudence; your shouts of liberty and equality, hollow mockery." But fewer commentators note that when, at the end of his speech,
Douglass predicted slavery's demise, he drew his "encouragement from
the Declaration of Independence, the great principles it contains, and
the genius of American Institutions," as well as from a spirit of enlightenment that he believed was growing on both sides of the Atlantic. After
emancipation, Douglass never stopped condemning the hypocrisy of
white Americans—or continuing to base his hopes for equality on traditions he and they held in common.

A self-critical conception of patriotism also led Americans on the left
to oppose their leaders' aggressive policies abroad. Anti-imperialists opposed the conquest of the Philippines after the war of 1898 by comparing President William McKinley to King George III. Foes of U.S. intervention in World War I demanded to know why Americans should die
to defend European monarchs and their colonies in Africa and Asia. In
1917, a mass movement led by socialists and pacifists called for a popular
referendum on the question of going to war. Neither group of resisters
succeeded at the time, but each gained a mass hearing and saw its
arguments incorporated into future policies. Congress promised independence to the Philippines sooner than colonial officials favored. And,
challenged by such antiwar voices as Debs, Robert LaFollette, and William Jennings Bryan, Woodrow Wilson proclaimed national self-
determination to be the core principle of a new world order.

A good deal that we cherish about contemporary America was thus accomplished by social movements of the left, speaking out for national ideals. It may be, as the idiosyncratic Trotskyist Leon Samson argued in 1935, that Americanism served as a substitute for socialism, an ideology of self-emancipation through equal opportunity that inoculated most citizens against the class-conscious alternative. But leftists made what progress they did by demanding that the nation live up to its stated principles, rather than dismissing them as fatally compromised by the racism of the founders or the abusiveness of flag-waving vigilantes. After all, hope is always more attractive than cynicism, and the gap between promise and fulfillment is narrower for Americanism than it is for other universalist creeds such as communism, Christianity, and Islam.

It's difficult to think of any radical or reformer who repudiated the national belief system and still had a major impact on U.S. politics and policy. The movement against the Vietnam War did include activists who preferred the Vietcong's flag to the American one. But the antiwar insurgency grew powerful only toward the end of the 1960s, when it drew in people who looked for leadership to liberal patriots such as King, Walter Reuther, and Eugene McCarthy rather than to Abbie Hoffman and the Weathermen.

Perhaps one exception to this rule was Malcolm X, who stated, in 1964, that he was a "victim of Americanism" who could see no "American dream," only "an American nightmare." But Malcolm was primarily a spokesman for black anger and pride, not a builder of movements or a catalyst of reforms to benefit his people.

He was, however, a prophetic figure. Soon after Malcolm's death, many on the left, of all races, began to scorn patriotic talk and, instead, to celebrate ethnic and sexual differences. In 1970, writer Julius Lester observed, "American radicals are perhaps the first radicals anywhere who have sought to make a revolution in a country which they hate." At the time, there were certainly ample reasons to consider Americanism a brutal sham. After World War II, the word itself became the property of the American Legion, the House Un-American Activities Committee, and the FBI. In the 1960s, liberal presidents bullied their way into Indochina in the name of what Lyndon Johnson called "the principle for which our ancestors fought in the valleys of Pennsylvania." Fierce love for one's identity group—whether black, Latino, Asian, Native

American, or gay or lesbian—seemed morally superior to the master narrative that had justified war abroad and racial exclusion at home.

Yet the history of the last thirty years has also exposed the outsized flaw in such thinking. Having abandoned patriotism, the left lost the ability to pose convincing alternatives for the nation as a whole. It could take credit for spearheading a multicultural, gender-aware revision of the humanities curriculum, but the right set the political agenda, and it did so in part because its partisans spoke forcefully in the name of American principles that knit together disparate groups—anti-union businesspeople, white evangelicals, Jewish neoconservatives—for mutual ends.

In the face of such evidence, many leftists would respond that civic idealism should not be confined within national borders. In a provocative 1994 essay, philosopher Martha Nussbaum argued that patriotism is "morally dangerous" because it encourages Americans to focus on their own concerns and minimize or disregard those of people in other lands. "We should regard our deliberations," she wrote, "as, first and foremost, deliberations about human problems of people in particular concrete situations, not problems growing out of a national identity that is altogether unlike that of others." Echoing her words, activists and intellectuals talk of challenging global exploitation with some form of global citizenship.

As an ethicist, Nussbaum is certainly on solid ground. Americans ought to take a massacre in Africa as seriously as one that takes place in lower Manhattan and demand that their government move rapidly to halt it. But she offers no guidance for how global leftists can get the power to achieve their laudable objectives. A planetary government is hardly on the horizon, and rich nations would no doubt hog its agenda if it were.

In the meantime, Americans who want to transform the world have to learn how to persuade the nation. At minimum, this means putting pressure on the national government, organizing coalitions of people from different regions and backgrounds, and debating citizens who think their tax money ought to be spent only at home. Disconnected as they are from any national or local constituency, global leftists now live at risk of being thrust to the margins—abstract sages of equity, operatives of nongovernmental organizations engaged in heroic but Sisyphean tasks, or demonstrators roving from continent to continent in search of bankers to heckle.

In the wake of September 11, the stakes have been raised for the American left. Even if the "war against terrorism" doesn't continue to overshadow all other issues, it will inevitably force activists of every stripe to make clear how they would achieve security for individual citizens and for the nation. How can one seriously engage in this conversation about protecting America if America holds no privileged place in one's heart? Most ordinary citizens understandably distrust a left that condemns military intervention abroad or a crackdown at home but expresses only a pro forma concern for the actual and potential victims of terrorism. Without empathy for one's neighbors, politics becomes a cold, censorious enterprise indeed.

There's no need to mouth the Pledge of Allegiance or affix a flag pin to your lapel or handbag. But to rail against patriotic symbols is to wage a losing battle—and one that demeans us and sets us against the overwhelming majority of Americans for no worthwhile moral or political purpose.

Instead, leftists should again claim, without pretense or apology, an honorable place in the long narrative of those who demanded that American ideals apply to all and opposed the efforts of those who tried to reserve them for favored groups. When John Ashcroft denies the right of counsel to a citizen accused of terrorism or a CEO cooks the books to impress Wall Street, they are soiling the flag and ought to be put on the patriotic defensive. Liberals and radicals are the only people in politics who can insist on closing the gap between America as the apotheosis of democratic strivings and the sordid realities of greed and arrogance that often betray it.

There is really no alternative. In daily life, cultural cosmopolitanism is mostly reserved to the rich and famous. Radical environmentalists and anti-IMF crusaders seek to revive the old dream of internationalism in a version indebted more to John Lennon's "Imagine" than to V. I. Lenin's Comintern. But three years after bursting into the headlines from the streets of Seattle, that project seems stalled indefinitely in the Sargasso Sea that lies between rhetorical desire and political exigency.

In hope of a revival, left patriots might draw inspiration from two voices from disparate points on the demographic and ideological spectrum. During the Great Depression, the white, conservative skeptic George Santayana observed that "America is the greatest of opportunities and the worst of influences. Our effort must be to resist the influence and improve the opportunity." At the same time, Langston Hughes—black, homosexual, and communist sympathizer—expressed a parallel vision:

> Let America be the dream the dreamers
> dreamed—
> Let it be that great strong land of love
> Where never kings connive nor tyrants scheme
> That any man be crushed by one above . . .
> O, yes,
> I say it plain,
> America never was America to me,
> And yet I swear this oath—
> America will be!

Throughout our history, and still today, the most effective way to love the country is to fight like hell to change it.

—2002

dissenting from the american empire
JAMES B. RULE

How long has it been since we heard that old catchphrase "late capital-ism"? The collapse of the Soviet Empire, and the rush of the leftovers of "real existing socialism" to find a place in the global market economy, give that expression a bizarre ring. For capitalism, we now realize, this may just be mid-morning. And such realization leaves us swimming in questions not just about the shape of domestic politics, but also about the new order of geopolitical affairs—now increasingly dominated by the kingpin of international capitalism, the United States of America.

Only command of the international market economy, it seems, can maintain the economic growth, the technological virtuosity, and the command of scarce resources necessary for world dominance today. Terrorists may threaten; rogue states may menace. These challengers may succeed in imposing much human suffering, but they will not change world boundaries or alter the global pre-eminence of the United States. For the immediate future, the United States has no rival in sustained ability to mobilize vast and sophisticated military forces, to capture and hold territory, and ultimately to make and unmake regimes in any corner of the world. Hence the question: what room do these facts leave those of us on the left for an alternative vision of world order?

It's hard to conceive of a political question bigger or more conse-quential than this. To get a grip on it, we need to think in terms of what Gunnar Myrdal termed "programs" and "prognoses." Programs are hy-pothetical scenarios, chains of events and processes through which the present might evolve into some desired future world. Programs in this sense, Myrdal holds, appeal for justification to prognoses—assessments of underlying social forces, of the constraints of entrenched conditions, or of the ripeness of untested situations for change. Programs without prognoses are apt to be nothing other than wishful dreams. Prognoses without programs are mere analytical speculation, holding little interest except to specialists.

Thus, more than sixty years ago, Myrdal and the co-authors of *An American Dilemma* posited programs for dismantling Jim Crow institu-tions—basing their arguments on prognoses of the openness of American society to change. Conservative critics loathed the program and derided the prognoses. As counterprognoses, they cited the supposed resistance of beliefs and attitudes underlying segregation, the blacks' and whites' alleged affection for segregated institutions, the purported unreadiness of black Americans to assume an equal role. Yet today their essential arguments are vindicated. Changes once held utopian or dangerous occurred more rapidly than many could have imagined; seemingly outlandish prospects of formal equality between the races became practical road maps for public action.

The American-dominated world order of the twenty-first century challenges the left to think as shrewdly, and as imaginatively, as the authors of *An American Dilemma* did about race in America. If I am right about essential elements of the prognosis—the indispensability of mastery over markets and technology in today's world, for example, and the supremacy of America in such mastery—what programs for the future can we entertain? What sort of world order consistent with the values of the democratic left could emerge from present-day realities of American world dominance? What must we on the left fear from this situation? Dare we identify possibilities for progressive change as bold as those named by Myrdal and his collaborators?

For the antithesis of a left vision on these matters, we need look no further than the platitudes of American officialdom. In this view, today's ascendance of American power represents the unanimous verdict of history on the superiority of American values. The superpower status of this country, however—and here come the programs—confers "global responsibilities." America's overweening military, economic and technological power make it "the indispensable country." In practice, this amounts to a mandate for this country to proclaim and enforce its writ throughout the world. Bush the Elder had it right, in this view, when he went to war in 1991; he was giving the world its first lesson that no country could get away with crossing the lines drawn by America for its new world order. Thus a program, in Myrdal's sense, of manifest destiny. Only a world where clear-cut rules of conduct are recognized by all players can support the peace and market-given abundance that all the world craves. And only the United States is in a position to dictate and enforce those rules.

This self-congratulatory emanation of American statecraft points to a vision of America's role that is not just unipolar but imperial, strictly speaking. Indeed, the language of empire is now gaining currency among this country's foreign-policy elites, who use it without apology. What this means in practice is that Washington will increasingly be taking key geopolitical decisions alone, consulting even close allies only after crucial directions have been set. It is a world whose big structures, and basic rules of conduct, radiate from a single national source.

Surprisingly, visions of Imperial America seem to be getting serious and not-altogether-unfavorable attention even among observers on the left. Empires are not always so bad, people point out. At least they ensure a modicum of order and peace. Why prejudge the American Empire, just because it *is* an empire?

Fair is fair. Let us not miss some signal accomplishments of American power on the geopolitical scene. One thinks of the defense of democracy in Europe fifty-five years ago; or the reversal of ethnic cleansing in Kosovo; or the quiet support for pluralism in Taiwan, even as the United States trims its sails to deal with Beijing; or the American willingness to broach human rights issues (however selectively and ambivalently) in world forums. Other empires would not have gone this far. But of course, if we credit such accomplishments, we are also obliged to take account of historic miscarriages of American power: support of some of the world's worst regimes, indifference to the sufferings of the poorest countries, plunder of scarce environmental resources and raw materials, and all the rest.

But we on the left ought to be devoting ourselves to something more than a balance sheet of pluses and minuses in American foreign policy. The question is not how we should rate the American Empire as empires go, but *whether we want to live in an imperial world.* Can't we expect something better than a regime where one country lays down the law for all others? Don't the values of the left incline us to a geopolitical system that is multilateral and collegial, rather than unilateral and peremptory? Shouldn't we be seeking a world order in which narrow national interest gives way to collective decision-making on joint problems? To the masters of realpolitik now calling the shots in Washington, such aspirations are utopian in the worst sense. I believe that they are utopian, much as Myrdal's program for undoing Jim Crow was utopian in the late 1930s.

In fact, the American Empire is hardly the only profound rearrangement of global affairs to arise in the last twelve years. In the eyes of history, it may not appear the most important. Running counter to the consolidation of global power in Washington are a collection of diametrically opposite tendencies—more diffuse and harder to read, but full of potential to yield a better world. These are trends toward multilateral decision-making among the world community of nations, an evolution toward collective definitions of global problems and away from maximization of national sovereignty and zero-sum definitions of national interest. These trends are manifest in the actions of states, but also in the expanded participation of non-state activists, from grassroots community groups to sophisticated global social movements.

These tendencies have borne some striking fruit over the last decade, in arrangements both heralded and obscure. These include efforts to limit emissions of greenhouse gases, to ban land mines, to protect privacy of personal data transmitted across international boundaries, to prosecute crimes against humanity, and to establish permanent UN forces available for peacekeeping. No one can say which of these efforts will ultimately matter the most, and any of them could yet fail completely. But what commands attention is not so much the ultimate outcome, but the quality of the underlying vision and the willingness of important elements of the global community to subscribe to it. Participating countries have been willing to identify supranational interests that could clearly run counter to specific national interests in future situations—and to build authoritative institutions to implement such larger interests. The underlying logic is diametrically opposed to that of a world governed by imperial *diktat*.

No doubt that is why Washington has gone to such lengths to oppose all these efforts. In case you hadn't noticed, the United States has carved out for itself the role of global naysayer to such multilateral developments. That opposition arises both from the executive branch and from Congress, but the Bush administration has orchestrated it to a fine pitch. In this view, no international engagements must be allowed in any way to diminish American sovereignty. America may mobilize its "allies"—read, clients—to support one worldwide initiative or another, after the crucial directions are set. But no one will get a hearing from this administration for the notion that the well-being of ordinary Americans might be better served by transferring decision-making power from the American state. One might as well propose steak tartare for the banquet of the next world congress of vegans.

For the prophets of empire, of course, aspirations for a more collegial organization of world power represent nothing more than self-deluding froth atop the deep currents of geopolitics. What matters in world affairs, they will remind us, is what has always mattered: the ability to "project" military power; the economic might to support and sustain such projection; and mastery of the technologies that generate national superiority, both military and economic, in the first place. If a few enlightened souls now have the luxury of concern for the environment, human rights, or the worldwide distribution of wealth, it is only because such high-minded thinking is protected by imperial power. No one should imagine, in other words, that yearnings for a more liberal or egalitarian geopolitical order have any weight of their own. How many divisions can Greenpeace put in the field? What disagreeable regime has Amnesty International ever ousted?

There is no reason to accept at face value the prognoses embodied in these statements—any more than one should accept the imperial programs they are intended to support. True, we must never imagine that ideas or ethical concerns alone, or the sheer desire for a better world, will automatically prevail over earthier forces. But it would be no less foolish to discount the weight of specific ideas and moral imperatives at specific historical moments. Joseph Nye, in *The Paradox of American Power*, speaks of "soft power," the knack of "getting others to want what you want." America, he holds, can muster a good deal of soft power, if it puts forward its most appealing face to the world. He might well have added that America swims against powerful currents when it seeks to impose its interests against worldwide consensus. Good ideas and shared impulses can generate "soft power" of their own, even when arrayed against the forces of empire.

To be sure, the potential power of particular ideas and values in any setting is a matter for subtle assessment. It was the genius of Myrdal and his collaborators to see that the intellectual and moral foundations of Jim Crow were vulnerable and that alternative understandings and practices might replace them relatively quickly. The prognoses so identified made it plausible to envisage a program of change that most at the time dismissed.

We ought to apply the same sort of hardheaded skepticism to the ideas underlying the program of American empire—notions that only overbearing and unilateral American power can provide for a decent geopolitical regime. Many straws in the wind support quite different prognoses. Among these is the simple force of example: multilateral measures, and the popular feelings giving rise to them, can be seen at least sometimes to work. Prosecutions of crimes against humanity are beginning to occur. The treaty against land mines was in fact signed, albeit without the crucial participation of the United States. When countries, the United States very much included, fly in the face of such broadly based multilateral arrangements, they pay a cost. As Myrdal pointed out, there comes a moment when information on alternatives to prevailing arrangements can no longer be ignored. World public opinion may well now be at such a point regarding the feasibility of multilateral institutions.

Note that many multilateral accomplishments registered thus far stem from the engagement of alert and assertive publics. Organized global citizens have been willing to challenge what were once sovereign prerogatives of states, on matters ranging from protection of whales to the exploitation of women and children in the international sex trade. Around the world, it appears, educated people are less and less willing to defer matters of grave ethical concern to the discretion of governments. And as such concerns are acknowledged, national elites are less willing, and less able to turn away such popular concerns. As Paul Wapner remarked in these pages eight years ago ("Environmental Activism and Global Civil Society," Summer 1994), the result is increasingly a "world civil society," in which organizations from Amnesty International to Greenpeace mobilize pressure and focus conscience across national boundaries. Globalization, obviously, is not just an economic affair.

I have never been much of an admirer of Hegel, with his notions of improvements in public life reflecting an ever-evolving world spirit. But it is hard to deny that public unwillingness to tolerate certain palpable, humanly engineered evils is growing, however incrementally. A growing slice of world opinion finds plunder of natural resources, destabilizing environmental conditions, torture of political opponents, government by armed bullies, suppression of indigenous cultures, debilitating international arms races, and a host of parallel developments unconscionable. Much as in the slow but relentless shift in world public opinion that ultimately undercut slavery—even as that peculiar institution produced great economic benefits for some—world opinion now seems capable of condemning certain atrocious actions that were long regarded as virtually inevitable, however unpleasant.

This is why it will not do for us on the left to restrict ourselves to providing a running "box score" on the successes and failures of imperial policies. That view simply takes for granted the most consequential issues now in the balance. If we miss this point, we remain helpless against the next gross abuse of imperial power—the next Vietnam, let us say—when it occurs. The left ought to choose a better role for itself than simple reacting to the workings of the American Empire after the fact. And the best way to do so is not just to support or criticize specific policies of the current regime, but to articulate a distinctive vision of a world community.

Inevitably, multilateralism brings its own costs and risks. Should world power indeed grow more collegial, America will experience new constraints. Meaningful limits on greenhouse gas emissions could limit economic growth. More egalitarian world economic relations could end some advantageous terms of trade for America. These are the fruits of empire, and Americans share in them, whether they intend to or not.

But such benefits will not outlast the heyday of the system that enforces them. The one thing that we know for sure about empires is that they do not last forever. In America's case, the magic formula combining economic might, technological mastery, and overwhelming military power will surely one day fail. Living through imperial decline is never pleasant for the parties concerned—witness, most recently, the collapse of the Soviet Empire. We ought to be asking what will be left, when America can no longer, at least single-handedly, enforce its will anywhere and everywhere around the world?

Americans—and thoughtful, politically active citizens of the entire world community—have a historic opportunity to help create arrangements that can endure, even as particular world power constellations come and go. This could mean institutions for environmental protection, for ready defense against aggressive war, for protection of rights of embattled minorities; for prosecution of crimes against humanity—the list of alluring possibilities goes on and on. In the long view, these opportunities surely warrant extraordinary efforts to attain.

By contrast, the imperial wisdom of the Bush administration betrays a shockingly short time perspective. As in its energy policies, the inner circle of the current regime insists on exploiting short-term advantage, disparaging any consideration of the world we will leave our children when the conditions of that advantage are exhausted. Like the world's reserves of fossil fuels, the conditions supporting American hegemony are finite. But for the imperial vision, what matters is supremacy in the here and now. It is a profoundly irresponsible approach to statecraft: the future it portends is desolate.

The worst of it is the chances that are being wasted. The world is arguably a less dangerous place now than it has been in many decades. With the end of the Manichean struggle between the Soviet system and the "free world," we ought to realize a "peace dividend" in terms of more than just money. The preeminence of the world's liberal democracies, in command of successful market economies, could well provide an incubator for the sort of multilateral global community entertained here. One has to wonder: if the shift to such an order is not possible now, at a moment of relative prosperity and stability, when will the moment come?

It is our role, on the left, to pose this question. We have no more crucial or distinctive contribution to make.

— 2002

acting alone

DAVID BROMWICH

Unilateralism is a weak name for the foreign policy sketched in "The National Security Strategy of the United States of America"—a document released by the White House in September 2002 and discussed inadequately in the press. The strong name for it is imperialism. We will be hearing more about that as Europeans come to assess the actions of the Bush administration in the light of this thirty-one-page manifesto. The document, prefaced by a signed three-page letter from George W. Bush, is in large measure a tissue of quotations and paraphrases of the president's speeches, and it has been clear for some time that the speeches are written by a clever and versatile team. The well-engineered bursts of pulpit eloquence are cemented by think-tank platitudes of a humbler workmanship, so that the total impression is at once bright and dull, commanding and crude. Even so, the National Security Strategy document bears looking into. This is the source that the Bush administration wants Americans to consult in order to understand the aims that guide our international actions. Each of its nine numbered sections is headed by a quotation from George W. Bush, and when you combine their effect with the world-definitive posture of the cover letter, you are aware of a deference to the personality of a leader that makes this production, by the standards of constitutional democracy, unusual. Practical wisdom in the face of terror comes to be identified with the always apposite words of a single man.

The first section gives an overview of the contents, the second a rhetorical portrait of the United States as the champion of human dignity. Four subsequent sections (3, 4, 5, and 8) are exclusively concerned with the attack part of defense. The football coach's apothegm, "The best defense is a good offense," is quoted. Defense proper, of the "homeland" in particular, turns out to be the subject of section 9, while two interpolated sections (6 and 7) deal with economic assistance, the imperative of the "free flow" of money and goods to build "the infrastructure of democracy" in the poorer countries of the world. As the document proceeds, it becomes clear that the National Security Strategy takes for its domain all of international relations and foreign policy.

Everything the United States could conceivably do in the world is now to be subsumed under the heading of a national defense that is itself an extension of homeland security.

The president's letter opens by pointing out the difference between the twentieth century and the twenty-first. The "great struggles of the twentieth century" were those "between liberty and totalitarianism." Liberty won; and this has become generally known. "People everywhere want to be able to speak freely; choose who will govern them; worship as they please; educate their children—male and female; own property; and enjoy the benefits of their labor." The simplicity of the thought is captured by the locution "people everywhere"—a phrase with roots in advertising. People everywhere want a good product. But the sense here slides perilously between two distinct facts. People everywhere may have a germ of the idea that they would like to see men and women treated equally and given the same educational opportunities. That does not mean that all people, in every part of the world, if asked whether they believe in the equality of women, would now answer yes. The underlying sense of the assertion is that the North Atlantic commercial democracies have discovered what people everywhere *will finally realize themselves to have wanted all along.* But this idealism is undercut by an equivocation. America will seek "to create a balance of power that favors human freedom." Slowly, then: as the balance of power favors freedom for more people, those people will discover how desirable freedom is. A moderate downturn weighing in late to balance the latest pounding directive is a recurrent rhythm of the document

In the twenty-first century, the enemies of freedom are secretly hostile or stateless persons who seek to obtain weapons of mass destruction. "As a matter of common sense and self-defense," the president's letter declares, "America will act against such emerging threats before they are fully formed." The last five words are crucial. We reserve the right to attack any country whose power is growing ominously, and the more so if it acts as a haven for such persons. Here is a central clue to the doctrine of "regime change" that now seems likely to extend beyond Iraq. But can such a policy be strictly military in its bearings? The president's letter admits the inadequacy of that approach when it says near the end: "Poverty does not make poor people into terrorists and murderers. Yet poverty, weak institutions, and corruption can make weak states

vulnerable to terrorist networks and drug cartels within their borders."
So we ought to do something to alleviate poverty, in line with our fight
against terror, provided the free flow of investment capital is permitted
in the countries we assist. "The United States will stand beside any
nation determined to build a better future by seeking the rewards of
liberty for its people. Free trade and free markets have proven their
ability to lift whole societies out of poverty." Readers with a short
memory may simply credit this. The truth is that free markets and
money-flows did no such thing for Indonesia or for Russia or for all of
sub-Saharan Africa in the 1980s and 1990s. Indeed, those methods had
the opposite effect: money departed faster than it came, and left behind
a gutted society.

Section 2, the real preamble of the document, recalls the American
commitment to universal values associated with human dignity. We
must defend liberty and justice "because these principles are right and
true for all people everywhere." That seems a vital point for American
civic education; and the authors might have added more without fear of
contradiction. We *trust* those who agree with us about these things more
than we trust those who do not. But there is a vast difference between
knowing that a principle is right and knowing that one has a right to
establish that principle by force. The sweep of the document assumes
that once we recognize the application of a principle to "all people
everywhere," we have a warrant to do whatever must be done to enforce
its acceptance. Such violent paternalism will always exist in tension with
the principle of liberty. The document goes on, by its very phrasing, to
give an illustration of the danger: "No nation owns these aspirations [to
liberty and justice], *no nation is exempt from them*" (emphasis added)—
as if acknowledgment of the aspiration were a burden lesser peoples
might well shirk. Combine this assurance with the stress on the flow of
money and goods from the more to the less powerful, and you gain a
sense of how the architects of American national security in the twenty-
first century are hoping to inherit the mantle of the architects of the
British Empire in the nineteenth. The conservatism of British imperial
policy held it wiser not to take on the tutelage of the whole world at
once. The abstention may have come from prudence and elitist arrogance—thin motives compared to the robustness of the National Strategy document—but just possibly that prudence added half a century to

the life of the empire. An acceptance of backward nations as backward, an agreement not to make them "progressive" and aggrandize the empire by money-flows and sudden fortunes, was one of the traits that distinguished British from, say, Belgian imperialism. If we Americans mean to give up that form of prudence or humility, the reason must be that we find ourselves so glutted with power that we have no further use for caution.

Section 3 quotes the president's speech of September 14, 2001, on the need "to answer these attacks and rid the world of evil." A seasoned former White House operative, Pat Buchanan, noticed several months ago what mainstream columnists have passed over in silence, namely that the Bush administration was committed to war against Iraq as soon as the president spoke his formula about the "axis of evil." That was an example of policy by speech-writing—a phenomenon peculiar to this administration, and yet common in it. Go back now to the phrase about our need "to rid the world of evil." There already, on September 14, 2001, was a signal example of policy by speech-writing, done with so small a touch as the omission of the definite article before *evil.* An alternative phrase must have offered itself and been rejected: "to rid the world of *this* evil." After all, the particular evil of a terrorist network such as al-Qaeda is large enough and dreadful enough to make its eradication a tremendous work of blended might and resolve. But omission of the definite article makes the evil of al-Qaeda identical with evil itself. Crush it, the grammar now asserts, and you will rid the world of all evil. Many of the president's followers are religious, with an apocalyptic tinge to their piety: a consideration that cannot have been far from view when the writer cut out a word and turned up the heat.

To rid the world of *evil itself.* If that is the task we are embarked on, it follows that we need only act well against the terrorists for evil to cease to be one of the conditions of life. This is not a contingent and political but an absolute and metaphysical statement, a promise of salvation such as only religions, until now, have dared to make and only the gods of religions have been supposed to keep. The present generation of terrorists in many ways resemble a kind of man the world has known for a long time. They seem to think about their crimes as Macbeth thought about his: "that but this blow / Might be the be-all and the end-all—here, / But here, upon this bank and shoal of time, / We'd jump the life to come." The inference from the president's "rid the world of evil" must be that such ambitious men will cease to exist—that once our battle is finished, no more such men will be born. But how can he know? Do we believe ourselves launched on a quest that when complete will have scoured human nature of its imperfections forever?

Section 3, the most substantive of the document, speaks of the necessity for "direct and continuous action using all the elements of our national and international power." This declaration is accompanied by an all-important phrase: "we will not hesitate to act alone." Why do individuals hesitate to act alone? They do so for the same reason that nations may hesitate: because the approval and sometimes the commitment of others may serve as a check against insanity. Whole communities may go mad as well as individuals—the twentieth century affords examples of that in Germany in the 1930s, and in China in the 1960s. People under the dominion of a passion that animates everyone, a fear that compels action and reaction in a single circuit, may collectively lose their grip on reason. Out of passion and zeal combined, they surrender the ability to do anything but temporarily quell the terror that holds them stunned and holds them together. It is for this reason, one wants to say, that a community that has the time to think ought to hesitate before acting alone. Yet before one can confront the document on this point, the argument shifts its ground. After the absolute assertion of a duty to act alone on behalf of all mankind, section 4 reverts to a moderate tone. We are informed that when "states falter" the United States will act to "restore stability."

Section 5 introduces the problem of *nations* that seek to obtain weapons of mass destruction. This was obviously written with Iraq in mind, and it repeats the Bush administration's recent charges. The leaders of such nations "brutalize their own people and squander their national resources for the personal gain of the rulers"; they "reject basic human values and hate the United States and everything for which it stands." There follows a justification of preemptive war: "The United States has long maintained the option of preemptive actions to counter a sufficient threat to our national security. The greater the threat, the greater is the risk of inaction—and the more compelling the case for taking anticipatory action to defend ourselves, even if uncertainty remains as to the time and place of the enemy's attack. To forestall or prevent such hostile acts by our adversaries, the United States will, if necessary, act preemptively." Given the depth of the uncertainty here described, what can be the meaning of "if necessary"? From every innocent person you kill, a new enemy may grow—a friend or relative of the victim or an appalled and angry witness. This irreducible axiom of moral psychology, which must never be forgotten, the document works very hard to make its readers forget.

With section 6, we find ourselves in the conventional domain of capitalist utopian thought. Free markets will "ignite a new era of economic growth." Those markets will put out their own fires, however, and bring—*stability*. For "improving stability in emerging markets is also a key to global economic growth." On this view of human nature and society, improving stability is synonymous with planting governments friendly to foreign investors. "International flows of investment capital are needed to expand the productive potential of these economics. These flows allow emerging markets and developing countries to make investments that raise living standards and reduce poverty." Again, the recent history of Indonesia would make a different point. Closer to home, so would Argentina. But the invocation of money flows is not a science touchable by facts: we are on hallowed ground, in the presence of Our Lady of the Market. Free trade is accordingly described as a "concept" that arose independently of financial practice, "a moral principle even before it became a pillar of economics." The truth is that the morality of free trade came with, not before, the practice of free trade in the nineteenth century, but an error of a hundred years cannot unsettle this trance of revelation where the good, the profitable, our self-interest, and our love of humankind all dovetail in a seamless artifice. The oddest detail of this section is an afterthought about "the environment," tucked in at the lower end of a column of journalist-bullets. "We will incorporate labor and environmental concerns into U.S. trade negotiations." The document goes on to summarize G. W. Bush's proposal for the redefinition of poisonous gasses. "America's greenhouse gas emissions," he declared in the course of defending his rejection of the Kyoto accord, would be reduced "*relative to the size of our economy*" (emphasis added). The economy comes before life and before breath. Eight drops of poison in an economy of two hundred is, relatively, an improvement on five drops of poison in an economy of one hundred.

There is a suspicion, now widely shared abroad, that the United States has become a dogmatic and intolerant nation in its understanding of happiness. The evidence normally cited is that we reject the possibility that any country could come to be happy, united, prosperous, and at peace by a method somehow different from our own. Section 7, on foreign economic assistance, will go far to confirm that impression. The document cannot bear to offer a strategy for nation-building without first attacking the very idea of nation-building. For that purpose, it adapts the language that the Reagan administration once deployed against welfare: "throwing money at programs," they called it, and to that derisive certitude of American politics the Bush doctrine adds an international dimension. "Decades of massive development assistance have failed to spur economic growth in the poorest countries. Worse, development aid has often served to prop up failed policies, relieving the pressure for reform and perpetuating misery." The document takes seriously, on the other hand, the idea of foreign shareholders buying stock in a developing nation. Something called the "Millennium Challenge Account" has been set up for countries whose governments "rule justly, invest in their people, and encourage economic freedom." Presumably, no such grants will be forthcoming to countries that favor cooperative local enterprise over private foreign enterprise. The intended analogy here is the "matching grants" offered by charitable foundations to people or institutions that have once proved their ability to raise money on their own. Be hospitable to American business, says the investment corollary of the National Security Strategy, and we will give you the money to allow you to welcome more of our investments.

In keeping with the same program, the Bush administration here announces that it will sponsor a "comprehensive reform agenda" for enlarging the activity of the World Bank. The instrument is to be increased contributions to the bank's International Development Association. Oversight of all these interlocking funds will enable the United States to monitor results more closely, and "we will also challenge universities, nonprofits, and the private sector to match government efforts by using grants to support development projects that show results." The free-flow of capital message could scarcely be more blunt. We mean to run the world the way you run a business. But the eager authors are not yet satisfied, and they make the case double-sure with italics: "*Open societies to commerce and investment.*" Most of the money for economic development, they explain, "must come from trade, domestic capital, and foreign investment. An effective strategy must try to expand these flows as well." The quasi-organic metaphor of "flows" is really a form of prayer—like the metaphor of growing the economy when nothing will grow on earth any more. And here is another afterthought: "*Emphasize education.*" Who will deny that "literacy and learning are the founda- tion of democracy and development"? This turn of section 7 might be taken to imply that people need to be educated before they can say exactly how much foreign capital they want to conduct into their native economies. But the logic of the section has gone the other way: first we make the poorer nations as much like us as possible by the inundation of money and goods; then we teach them what they have chosen and why they must go on choosing it.

A halfhearted penultimate section, "Agendas for Cooperative Action with the Other Main Centers of Global Power," concerns the need to leave ourselves some scope anyway for multilateral action. NATO is offered as the leading example of an alliance that ought to be preserved. Russia and India are mentioned in a tone that is confident, bracing, congratulatory if slightly superior. An attitude as paternal, but rather less warming, appears in a paragraph on China. Its leaders "have not yet made the next series of fundamental choices about the character of their state. In pursuing advanced military capabilities that can threaten its neighbors in the Asia-Pacific region, China is following an outdated path"—our path, admittedly, but the right path for no other country in the twenty-first century. The authors bring back the unilateralist mes- sage flatly, to round out the document, but the unscheduled yet hardly avoidable thought of China has left an after-chill. In dealing with so vast a political and geographic entity and so substantial a portion of the human race, can we actually imagine that we ought not to hesitate before acting alone?

Section 9 concludes the document with a pledge by the United States "to dissuade future military competition"—a canny misuse of *dissuade* as a simple transitive verb with an impersonal object. Dissuade here means in fact preclude by the show of force. And the show may matter more, the document suggests, as we move farther from our own borders. "The presence of American forces overseas is one of the most profound symbols of the U.S. commitments to allies and friends." The authors were well advised to cast that statement in a highly abstract form. It may require a mystical calculus to reckon how many troops are needed to perpetuate the symbolism in question on a cluster of bases like those the United States maintains in Okinawa. The forty-three thousand American soldiers now stationed on that island occupy the choicest one-fifth of the land, and school children pursue their studies under the roar of 26,000 flights of planes and helicopters a year: a landing or a takeoff about every ten minutes. Some unpleasant litigation in the 1990s, over incidents of rape, reckless driving and manslaughter, and the mass dumping of depleted uranium shells, suggests that gratitude is not the only common response to the symbol. But the idea that power could ever corrupt its possessor, or that it could be seen as corrupting, is not hinted at or properly to be inferred from a single detail of "The National Security Strategy of the United States of America." Defensive, ambitious, and self-contradictory as the document is, in the quality of its self-knowledge it is perhaps the most innocent statement of policy ever exhibited by a major power in the history of the world.

—2003

Contributors

Jervis Anderson   (1932–2000) was a *New Yorker* staff writer for thirty years. His books include *Bayard Rustin: Troubles I've Seen; A. Philip Randolph: A Biographical Portrait; This Was Harlem: A Cultural Portrait, 1900–1950;* and *Guns in American Life.*

Joanne Barkan   is author of *Visions of Emancipation: The Italian Workers' Movement Since 1945* as well as numerous works of fiction and nonfiction for young readers. A member of the *Dissent* editorial board, she lives in New York City and on Cape Cod.

Marshall Berman   is distinguished professor of political science at CCNY/City University of New York and a member of the *Dissent* editorial board. He is the author of *All That Is Solid Melts into the Air, The Politics of Authenticity,* and *Adventures in Marxism.*

Paul Berman   is the author of *Terror and Liberalism; A Tale of Two Utopias: The Political Journey of the Generation of 1968;* and *The Passion of Joschka Fischer.* A member of the *Dissent* editorial board, he is a freelance writer who has contributed to many magazines and newspapers.

David Bromwich   is Housum Professor of English at Yale University and a member of the *Dissent* editorial board. His books include *Hazlitt: The Mind of a Critic; A Choice of Inheritance: Self and Community from Edmund Burke to Robert Frost;* and *Politics by Other Means: Higher Education and Group Thinking.*

Mitchell Cohen   has been co-editor of *Dissent* since 1991 and began writing for the magazine in 1982. He is a professor of political theory at the City University of New York. He is the author of *The Wager of Lucien Goldmann* and *Zion and State* and editor of *Rebels and Reactionaries: An Anthology of Political Short Stories* and co-editor of *Princeton Readings in Political Thought.*

Theodore Draper   is the author of *A Struggle for Power: The American Revolution; The Roots of American Communism;* and *American Communism and Soviet Russia: The Formative Period.* A Fellow of the American Academy of Arts and Sciences, he is a recipient of the Herbert Feis Award from the American Historical Association.

Barbara Ehrenreich   is the author of *Nickel and Dimed: On (Not) Getting By in America; The Snarling Citizen;* and *Complaints and Disorders: The Sexual Politics of Sickness.* A frequent contributor to *Time, Atlantic Monthly,* and the *New York Times Magazine,* she is co-editor, with Arlie Russell Hochschild, of *Global Woman: Nannies, Maids, and Sex Workers in the New Economy.*

Cynthia Fuchs Epstein   is distinguished professor of sociology at the Graduate School and University Center of the City University of New York and a member of the *Dissent* editorial board. Her books include *Deceptive Distinctions: Sex, Gender, and the Social Order; Women in Law;* and *The Part Time Paradox: Time Norms, Professional Life, Family and Gender* (with Carroll Seron, Bonnie Oglensky, and Robert Sauté). She was a Guggenheim Fellow and winner of the 2003 Jessie Bernard Award of the American Sociological Association for lifetime achievement on gender research.

Todd Gitlin   is the author of *Letters to a Young Activist; The Sixties: Years of Hope, Days of Rage; The Twilight of Common Dreams;* and *Media Unlimited.* A member of the *Dissent* editorial board, he is a professor of journalism and sociology at Columbia University. He was the third president of Students for a Democratic Society and helped organize the first national demonstration against the Vietnam War.

Michael Harrington   (1928–1989) was a member of the *Dissent* editorial board and a founder of the Democratic Socialists of America. His 1962 book, *The Other America,* was crucial in inspiring the government's war on poverty during the 1960s. A professor of political science at Queens College, he was also the author of *The New American Poverty; The Long Distance Runner;* and *Socialism: Past and Future.*

Irving Howe (1920–1993) was *Dissent*'s principal editor and guiding spirit from the magazine's formation until his death thirty-nine years later. A National Book Award winner and a MacArthur Fellow, he was the author of *Politics and the Novel; World of Our Fathers; Socialism and America;* an autobiography, *A Margin of Hope;* and biographies of Sherwood Anderson, William Faulkner, and Thomas Hardy.

Michael Kazin is professor of history at Georgetown University and a member of the *Dissent* editorial board. A recipient of a National Endowment for the Humanities Fellowship and a John Simon Guggenheim Fellowship, he is the author of *The Populist Persuasion* and *The Barons of Labor,* and co-author with Maurice Isserman of *America Divided: The Civil War of the 1960s.*

Dwight Macdonald (1906–1982) was editor of the *Partisan Review* from 1939 to 1943 and the founder of the magazine *Politics.* He is a staff writer for the *New Yorker* and *Esquire* and a frequent contributor to *Dissent,* and his books include *Henry Wallace; The Root Is Man; Memoirs of a Revolutionist;* and *Against the American Grain.*

Norman Mailer was a frequent contributor to *Dissent* in the 1950s and a member of the editorial board until 1991. He is a Pulitzer Prize winner in fiction and nonfiction, and his books include *The Naked and the Dead; Advertisements for Myself; Armies of the Night;* and *The Executioner's Song.*

Deborah Meier has been involved in public schooling for nearly forty years as a teacher, principal, and writer. A longtime member of the *Dissent* editorial board, she founded a highly successful network of public elementary and secondary schools in East Harlem, the Central Park East schools, during the seventies and eighties. Her books include *The Power of Their Ideas; Will Standards Save Public Education?;* and *In Schools We Trust.*

C. Wright Mills (1916–1962) was a social scientist whose work inspired a generation of scholars and political activists. A professor of sociology at Columbia University, he was the author of *White Collar: The Ameri-*

can Middle Class; The Power Elite; The Causes of World War III; and *The Sociological Imagination.*

Nicolaus Mills   is a professor of American Studies at Sarah Lawrence College and a member of the *Dissent* editorial board. His books include *Their Last Battle: The Fight for the National World War II Memorial; The Triumph of Meanness: America's War Against Its Better Self;* and *Like a Holy Crusade: Mississippi 1964.* His writing has appeared in the *New York Times, Los Angeles Times,* and *Chicago Tribune.*

Maxine Phillips   was director of Public Information and Conferences at the Child Welfare League of America, then worked for Democratic Socialists of America as managing editor of *Democratic Left,* organization director, and finally executive director before coming to *Dissent,* where she is the executive editor.

Frances Fox Piven   is distinguished professor of political science and sociology at the Graduate School and University Center, City University of New York. Her work on voter registration was instrumental in formulating the "Motor-Voter" Act of 1994. Her books include *Regulating the Poor: The Functions of Public Welfare* (with Richard Cloward); *The Breaking of the American Social Compact* (with Richard Cloward); and *How the Rural Poor Got Power* (with Robert Coles and Paul Wellstone).

Samantha Power   is a lecturer in public policy at Harvard's John F. Kennedy School of Government. Her book *"A Problem from Hell": America and the Age of Genocide* was awarded the 2003 Pulitzer Prize and the 2003 National Book Critics Circle Award. She is the editor, with Graham Allison, of *Realizing Human Rights: Moving from Inspiration to Impact.*

James B. Rule   is professor of sociology at the State University of New York, Stony Brook, and a member of the *Dissent* editorial board. He is the author of books and articles on a variety of topics, including information and information technologies. Under a MacArthur Foundation grant, he is currently at work on a study of legislation and policy for the protection of privacy.

Bayard Rustin (1912–1987) was the first field secretary for the Congress of Racial Equality (CORE) and a civil rights organizer with Dr. Martin Luther King, Jr. He was chairman of the Executive Committee of Freedom House, an international human rights monitoring agency, and founder of Black Americans to Support Israel Committee (BASIC). Rustin contributed regularly to *Dissent* and sat on the editorial board from 1968 to 1975.

Michael Walzer is co-editor of *Dissent*. He began writing for *Dissent* while a student at Brandeis University, where he studied with Irving Howe and Lewis Coser. Since 1980 he has been a member of the faculty at the Institute for Advanced Study, Princeton. His books include *Just and Unjust Wars; Spheres of Justice;* and *Arguing About War.*

Sean Wilentz is Dayton-Stockton Professor of History at Princeton, and director of its Program in American Studies at Princeton. A member of the *Dissent* editorial board, he is author of *The Kingdom of Matthias: A Story of Sex and Salvation in Nineteenth-Century America* (with Paul E. Johnson); *The Key of Liberty: The Life and Democratic Writings of William Manning* (with Michael Merrill); and *Chants Democratic: New York City and the Rise of the Working Class,* which won the Frederick Jackson Turner Award and the Albert J. Beveridge Award.

Credits

Editor's Note: In order to meet space requirements, we have removed footnotes and in several cases shortened articles that were extremely long.

Index